D0765510

IN THE GREEN MORNING:
MEMORIES OF FEDERICO

BY FEDERICO GARCIA LORCA

The Cricket Sings: Poems and Songs for Children
Deep Song and Other Prose
Five Plays: Comedies and Tragicomedies
The Public and Play Without a Title
Selected Letters
Selected Poems
Three Tragedies

Francisco García Lorca

IN THE GREEN MORNING:

MEMORIES OF FEDERICO

Translated by Christopher Maurer

With a prologue by Mario Hernández

A NEW DIRECTIONS BOOK

HOUSTON PUBLIC LIBRARY

Copyright © by the Heirs of Francisco García Lorca 1980
Prologue and notes copyright © by Mario Hernández 1980
Translation copyright © 1986 by Christopher Maurer

All rights reserved. Except for brief passages quoted in a newspaper, magazine, radio, or television review, no part of this book may be reproduced in any form or by any means, electronic or mechanical, including photocopying and recording, or by any information storage and retrieval system, without permission in writing from the Publisher.

Photographs on pp. 1-2 and 133-134 used courtesy of the Lorca family.

Manufactured in the United States of America
This translation of *Federico y su mundo* first published clothbound and as New Directions Paperbook 610 in 1986.
Published simultaneously in Canada by Penguin Books Canada Limited

Library of Congress Cataloging-in-Publication Data

García Lorca, Francisco, 1902-1976
       In the green morning.
       (A New Directions Book)
       Translation of: Federico y su mundo.
       Includes index.
       1.   García Lorca, Federico, 1898-1936
2.   Authors, Spanish—20th century—Biography.   3.   García
Lorca, Federico, 1898-1936—Dramatic works—Addresses,
essays, lectures.   I.   Title.
PQ6613.A763Z63913   1986   868'.6209 [B]   85-28509
ISBN 0-8112-0969-5
ISBN 0-8112-0970-9 (pbk.)

R0155300081
HUM

New Directions Books are published for James Laughlin
by New Directions Publishing Corporation,
80 Eighth Avenue, New York 10011

CONTENTS

II.   FEDERICO'S   THEATRE

FRANCISCO AND FEDERICO GARCÍA LORCA

I

In the summer of 1925 Federico García Lorca wrote to a friend, "I am on a farm my father owns called Daimuz. It was here that Paquito, that imponderable gentleman, saw the light of day." Daimuz, which is close to Fuente Vaqueros (the poet's birthplace in the Vega of Granada) was filled with childhood memories for both brothers. And yet it was not there, at the confluence of the two rivers of Granada (the Darro and the Genil), that the "imponderable gentleman" Francisco García Lorca was born. As happened on so many other occasions, Federico was carried away by his imagination. Perhaps he was seduced by the rare beauty of the name Daimuz. In his letter Federico defines his brother with a touch of irony and replaces Francisco's true birthplace (Fuente Vaqueros, 1902) with a nobler-sounding one.

Federico's humorous definition of Francisco reveals the difference in their temperaments. Perhaps the poet was thinking of the separate paths opening before them. If Federico had no apparent vocation but his "emotion about things" (to borrow a phrase from one of his letters), Francisco's future seemed tangible and solid. In a second letter to the same friend (Pepín Bello), written that very summer, Federico adds:

Paquito is going to Oxford in October. . . . He sends his love. . . . I imagine Paquito turned into an Englishman—very serious, very elegant, and looking a bit like a wood duck, as do all those strange island people. You and I will stay in Spain: he-goat, rooster, bull, fiery dawns, patios bathed in white light, where the moisture brings lovely shades of green to the heartless old walls.

Federico reacts to his brother's trip (a trip never taken) with a string of vivid commonplaces: the light and loneliness of tragic Andalusia. Those incomprehensible "wood ducks" seemed very remote indeed.

The two brothers' temperamental and professional differences led to neither a lack of understanding nor a lack of affection. On the contrary. When Federico published his first *Book of Poems* (1921), rescuing part of his extremely abundant early production, he dedicated it "To my brother Paquito." This book would serve as his entrée into the literary world of Madrid. Its affectionate dedication reveals a sense of fraternal indebtedness. One of Federico's first compositions, which he later rejected, bore the epigraph, "To my brother (heart of steel)." No matter that Francisco was four years younger; he was already—would always be—a natural audience and a fine critic of Federico's writings, and would help him select and arrange his poems. We know that he played a part in the final arrangement of at least two books, *Book of Poems* and *Songs*, helping Federico to exclude poems which were less than perfect. On examining Federico's manuscripts, I have sometimes found comments in Francisco's hand. There is even a list of rhyme words for possible use in one of Federico's sonnets (a parody of Rafael Alberti). The two brothers were as closely united in their literary pursuits as they were in everyday life.

We might also evoke a fleeting scene from 1933, when Fernando de los Ríos was Minister of Education of the Second Republic. Don Fernando had taught both brothers at the University of Granada and continued to be their friend. The scene is described by the Spanish poet León Felipe, who inscribes the following message to Francisco in a copy of his touching book *Oh, este viejo y roto violín* (Mexico, 1965):

Paquito. Let me call you that. That was how Federico introduced you to me many years ago in Madrid, in the doorway of the Ministry of Education, when Don Fernando was minister. "This is my brother Paquito . . . he is a smarter and a better man than I." How Federico loved you! We have all loved you. . . . I have too. Allow me to dedicate this book to you with all my heart.

The text is dated March 1966. Many years earlier (New York, June 19, 1930) the same poet had dedicated another book* to Federico himself: "To the Phoenix, to the Spanish lyrical prodigy of the twentieth century." León Felipe had read fragments of *Poet in New York*, which Federico was then writing. His generous dedication recalls the epithet once given to Lope de Vega: "Phoenix of Wits, Prodigy of Nature."

To León Felipe's testimony we may add that of Federico himself. In 1927 the poet was preparing to launch a literary magazine called *gallo*. In the April 1928 issue—the second and final one—Francisco would publish, under the title "Encounter," fragments of a novel he had been writing. In February 1927 Federico writes enthusiastically to Jorge Guillén:

> I'm *crazy* with happiness. Don't say anything to anybody. But my brother Paquito is writing a *marvelous* novel. Just that: marvelous. And it's nothing like any of my things. It's delightful. Don't say anything yet. It will be a tremendous surprise. I'm not blinded by the infinite love I have for him. No. It's a reality. I'm telling you this because you're so much a part of *me*. It's a release for my happiness. My brother was inhibited by my personality (you understand). He couldn't blossom next to me, because my impulse and my art scared him a bit. He had to get away, travel, meet the world on its own terms. But there it is.**

"Don't say anything to anybody," the poet insists. And yet, ironically, Francisco, who was then in Madrid working on his doctoral dissertation, had to beg his brother to stop telling their friends about the novel: given the press of other obligations, he had no time to work on it.

Federico's enthusiasm was unrelenting. When *gallo* was about to appear he wrote to the art critic Sebastià Gasch, "In this issue my brother makes his debut as a writer, with a splendid prose piece that is totally Latin, totally Mediterranean."

The first-person narrator of "Encounter" is named Enrique, but no

Versos y oraciones del caminante (Libro II, New York, Instituto de las Españas, 1930). —*Tr.*

**David Gershator, tr., Federico García Lorca, *Selected Letters* (New York: New Directions, 1983), p. 102.—*Tr.*

doubt he is a double of the author. Like Francisco he has delicate eyesight and must wear tinted eyeglasses. Curiously, the woman of the "encounter" is named Matilde. In his "Ode to Salvador Dalí," Federico mentions the "thick curls of the heartless Matilde," and one of the characters in his play *When Five Years Have Passed*, the impetuous Friend of the protagonist, praises the figure of Matilde, one of his conquests. The same character says he prefers green fruit to ripe fruit, a trait he shares with the author of this book. These coincidences are only partial, for that is the way Federico deals with reality in his works. A thread of reality has been woven into the "fable." It is not even possible to ascertain which came first, the "heartless Matilde" of the poem or the one mentioned in the novel. But the name-play and the allusion to unripe fruit seem to hint at some sort of literary joke shared by the two brothers.

In 1947 Francisco wrote in the prologue to the American edition of *Three Tragedies*:

> I do not know to what extent I should have accepted the writing of an introduction to these three plays of my brother. Having accepted the charge, I carry it out, but only after having overcome an inner resistance. Because I owed him so much both in life and after his death, it seems to me that with the writing of this I contribute, even in small measure, toward the payment of a debt of fraternal love. Yet, perhaps that debt should be left undisturbed.*

The debt was repaid with generosity and intelligence, not only in the admirable pages of *In the Green Morning*, but in many other studies. And yet this book is no hagiography. The author inquires into his own spontaneous admiration for his brother's works, and he analyzes those works with extreme objectivity. It must have been difficult to deal with the emotional substratum of the poems and plays: hence the elegant scruple, dictated by love, which he mentions in the passage just quoted: perhaps the debt should be left undisturbed, and common experiences not be exposed to other eyes. But such misgivings crumbled before the public figure of Federico. Francisco wanted to contribute to his greatness. And he felt no resentment whatsoever about taking second place to him.

*Federico García Lorca, *Three Tragedies* (New York: New Directions, 1947), p. 1. —Tr.

When he wrote *In the Green Morning* (1959-1965), the author was in his final days as professor of Spanish literature at Columbia University. He had been commissioned to write the book by an American publisher. He began with the critical essays, undertaking them without reserve, with genuine enthusiasm. Not so with the biographical introduction; to write these "memoirs" he had to overcome an "inner resistance." From the ashes of the past arose unforgettable faces and anecdotes. He came close to finishing *In the Green Morning*, but the book was never really perfected. The return to Spain reopened old wounds. This, and the author's failing health, kept him from finishing.

Francisco García Lorca also wrote a number of poems. None was published during his life; he simply collected them in a little folder.* Perhaps he destroyed many of his poems, but everything seems to indicate that his output was very brief and was kept secret even from his family and closest friends. Although he wrote some very early poems about Granada (his "discovery" of the Albaicín and of the hidden corners of that noble, ancient city), most of the poems he left at his death belong to the first years of exile. They were probably written between 1940 and 1950, while he was teaching at Columbia University, New York. One of them, entitled "Ship," tells of the anguish of the voyage and of the exile just beginning:

> . . . If all were a never-ending dream.
> Never to arrive. Let them alone.
> Oh persecuted flesh.
> With your burden of misery
> go so slowly, that you will be
> a ship that has lost its course.

> . . . Si fuera todo un sueño que nunca se acabara.
> No llegar nunca. Dejadlos.
> Oh carnes perseguidas.
> Con tu pesado flete de miseria
> ve tan despacio
> que seas como un barco a la deriva.

---

*Many were published posthumously in *Poesía* (Madrid: Editora Nacional, 1984), with an introductory note by Mario Hernández.—*Tr.*

This is how Francisco evokes Federico—beloved memory—in a poem entitled "Nocturne":

At times a shadow . . .
You open your eyes even wider to see it
and the calm dusk
ignores you as it ignores the tree or the stone.
(Only your living shadow).

Or a murmur, so soft
that, in the yearning to hear it,
it suddenly dies
(Only your heart).

Or a scent,
so subtle that when one smells it,
it is your very memory that awakens.
(Only your memory).

Shadow, murmur, aroma,
Where does it carry you?
Where does it call you from?
At times a shadow . . .

A veces una sombra . . .
Abres aún más los ojos para verla
y la penumbra quieta
te ignora más que al árbol o la piedra.
(Sólo tu sombra viva.)

O un rumor, mas tan leve,
que en el ansia de oírlo
agoniza de pronto.
(Tu corazón tan sólo.)

O un perfume,
tan tenue, que al olerlo
es tu propio recuerdo el que despierta.
(Tan sólo tu recuerdo.)

Sombra, rumor, aroma.
¿Hacia dónde te lleva?

¿Te llama desde dónde?
A veces una sombra . . .

It is speech and the absence of speech, all of it—shadow, murmur, aroma—as tenuous as color, odor, sound. It is a circular poem, with the same verse at the beginning as at the end; an impossible yearning to recapture the living image of the brother, reduced to the pure shadow of memory. As in the works of Luis Cernuda, the poet addresses himself in the second person singular, as though he were trying to lend greater objectivity to his own shadowy perceptions. The tree and the stone of the first stanza recall a famous poem of Rubén Darío, entitled "Fate":

Blessed is the tree, for it can scarcely feel,
and more blessed still is the hard stone, for it no longer feels at all.

Dichoso el árbol que es apenas sensitivo
y más la piedra dura, porque esa ya no siente . . .

Curiously, Darío's poem had profoundly impressed Federico. He could recite it by memory.

Francisco García Lorca felt almost the same misgivings about his critical writings as he did about his poetry. In 1952 he published in Buenos Aires (Editorial Losada) a careful study of a nineteenth-century writer from Granada, *Angel Ganivet, Su idea del hombre*. The critic Gonzalo Sobejano has called this work "the best ever published on the thought of Ganivet, unimpeachable proof of interpretative intelligence, vivifying sensitivity, and love of Granada."* It was another twenty years before he published *De Fray Luis a San Juan. La escondida senda* (Madrid: Castalia, 1972), laying new foundations for the study of St. John of the Cross. He died suddenly in Madrid in 1976, leaving several other valuable studies. Besides *In the Green Morning*, he left an unfinished book on proper names in the works of Cervantes. This book, advance chapters of which were published in scholarly magazines, revealed a life-long devotion to Cervantes, shared from early childhood with Federico. Another book, this one completed, examined the *Fable of Polyphemus and Galatea* of Góngora, and still another, only half finished, dealt with

*G. Sobejano, "Con Francisco García Lorca," *Insula*, nos. 356-357 (1976), p. 10.—Tr.

his brother's *Gypsy Ballads*. A collection of critical essays, *De Garcilaso a García Lorca*, was published posthumously (Madrid: Istmo, 1984) with an introduction by Claudio Guillén, who calls Francisco García Lorca "one of the very greatest modern literary critics of the Spanish language."

But Francisco's modesty and reserve—a reserve that was never impolite—prevented him from attaching importance to his own work. In his smiling eyes there was something of the good-natured irony of Cervantes. He had some of the traits of the typical Granadan whom Federico describes in his lecture on the Baroque poet Soto de Rojas, "Granada (Paradise Closed to Many)": the unhurried man who savors the landscape around him, relishes good conversation, and yet "takes himself away," into the privacy of an inner garden. But the Granadan who is described in Federico's lecture straddles two time periods. The Andalusian sense of leisure, so greatly admired by Luis Cernuda, was accompanied among the young people of Granada in the 1920s, by an enthusiasm Federico once defined as "a burning faith, a white-hot faith in the dawning of a better day." Francisco himself would call it "a yearning for renewal." In diverse fields of endeavor, from criticism and literary creation to history, law, music, and painting, the two brothers and their circle of friends were struggling for a Spain that would cease to be provincial while retaining that which had made it unique and given it nourishment. In a little note written for the magazine *gallo,* Federico would say: "We give Granada our love, but place our thought on Europe. That is the only way we can discover the most subtle and best hidden of our native treasures."

II

In The Green Morning, memoirs and critical essays, seems to have been written almost without any previous note-taking. The manuscript shows barely any corrections, and the writing seems to have grown directly out of long, slow meditation. The few pages that *are* devoted to notes contain only bibliographical information and brief biographical data. These pages were simple reminders. Among the pages the author decided to omit are a few old anecdotes revealing the gift for story-telling which he inherited from his family:

To travel to Granada there was a stagecoach whose owner and driver, known for his enormous liking for wine, bore the English name Reeves. He used to stop the coach and slake his thirst at every inn along the way, and this made the travelers protest, not so much because of the delay as because Reeves' euphoria led to some rather erratic driving. I can remember how amused we all were at home by a slip of paper which Reeves had printed up and distributed among the travelers. It said something like this: "The passengers are hereby advised that this coach will make as many stops at the inns as the driver deems necessary. A. REEVES." Perhaps the most dangerous part of the trip during the rainy season was fording the Genil.

The stagecoach probably came from Fuente Vaqueros or Valderrubio. The latter village then had a much uglier name: Asquerosa.* The composer Manuel de Falla would change that name (whose Arabic origin alluded to water) long before the villagers decided to do so officially. In 1923 he and Federico had begun to work on a comic opera entitled *The Playactress*, and that summer, on August 18, Falla wrote to the poet, who was in Asquerosa with his family. After discussing certain aspects of the play he says that both he and his sister María del Carmen "often remember the wonderful times we had in Ask-el-Rosa, and we send our fondest wishes, hoping to see you here [in Granada] on your way to Málaga." Although the letter is addressed to the artist of the family, it was meant to be shared with everyone. For Falla knew that Federico's parents supported their son's total dedication to poetry. Besides, by then Federico had already finished his law degree (as had Francisco).

Of his parents' support there is abundant and early evidence, for example, the letter his mother sent him in Madrid in November, 1920, a few months before the fleeting première of *The Butterfly's Evil Spell* ("Don Gregorio's Evil Spell," some said unjustly, alluding to the impresario and playwright Gregorio Martínez Sierra). In her refined, undeniably English handwriting, which reveals clarity and intelligence, Doña Vicenta Lorca tells Federico:

You haven't said anything about coming, nor anything about your affairs with Martínez Sierra. You seem to have become a student—in appearance, at least—so we will stop bothering you. But, my child, I can't help it, so

*"Loathsome." Literally, "vomit-provoking." —*Tr.*

greatly do I long to read something of yours in print. In *your* handwriting, one cannot read your poetry without stopping all the time, and, frankly, one can't get any flavor out of it.

To this letter we can add another, written on March 29, 1921, before Federico has brought out his *Book of Poems*, the collection alluded to by Doña Vicenta:

> You don't say to whom you are going to give the book, and how long they will take to publish it. As you can well imagine, I feel more curiosity than anyone else, being a woman and, besides, your mother. We think it a fine idea that you pay for the book's publication yourself. As you know, your father is willing (as long as you both work) to do whatever is necessary. We are glad to hear you recognize that you have the talent and the ability to be a pure, exquisite artist, for that way you will undertake the struggle awaiting you with great courage, and not be discouraged by the criticism of ignorant people and the malevolence of those who envy you. There are always many such people in cases like yours. I shall ask the Virgin to help you and make everything turn out well, and grant you peace of mind, and not let you suffer on account of anything.

The letter suggests that *Book of Poems* was paid for by the poet's father, Don Federico, with the sympathy and approval of his mother. What is really interesting is that Federico has told his parents of his poetic ambition. It was one thing to ask them to pay for the publication of his book, and quite another to have told them of his most intimate hopes.

By now Federico was living at the Residencia de Estudiantes, Madrid, where he had enrolled in 1919, at the suggestion of Don Fernando de los Ríos. There is an important, undated letter signed by both brothers, telling of their arrival at the Residencia, probably in the Autumn of 1923. The first part of the letter is written by Francisco, who was about to begin studying for a doctorate in law.

> Dearest parents:
> Although I miss you more and more, I am perfectly well, and am just coming out of the daze that accompanies any radical change in surroundings. [In another ink:] (I have also made a radical change in pen, the other one was impossible.)

I am already finding my way around Madrid, although I haven't had many problems until now, because I always go everywhere with Federico, and that is why I have not studied very much, except for a few times at the Residencia; for there is much to see here, and sometimes curiosity gets the best of me. Besides, I am always meeting people whom Federico had told about me and who wanted to meet me.

Our accommodations at the Residencia are first-class. We live together in a sunny room and I feel very happy because, among other things, we have a splendid library, where I will settle down and study once I have gotten over these first few days of getting my bearings and seeing new things.

Much love to all. Kisses for Conchita and Isabelita, and for you a big hug from

PACO

It is the typical letter of a student to his parents, an affectionate rendering of accounts, a string of impressions after a change in surroundings. As will happen later with his brother's novel, Federico has built up everyone's expectations, praising his brother to his friends in the Residencia. Now Federico takes the pen, and shows off his endless optimism and telegraphic style:

Dearest parents:

We are perfectly fine, and very happy, for our friends have given us a splendid reception, and this shows how much they admire my work. Every day I feel happier to have followed my *own* path, for I believe I will reach the goal I have set for myself.

At the Residencia they received us very well indeed, and all my friends did everything [possible?], especially the wonderful Luis Buñuel, who has been unbelievably kind to both of us.

We will begin to study as soon as we unwind and Paquito sees what he has to see. Tomorrow I'm going to take him to the Prado, and on Monday we'll begin our normal schedule.

I'm enclosing a *side-long glance* at my work by [Adolfo] Salazar, which came out in today's *Sol*. The paper will reach Granada around the same time as this letter. It is a pretty little article, and it makes me look very good indeed.

I will write to Falla; meanwhile, give my very best to him and to his sister.

Good-bye. We will write often, for even though we don't write at length, it will be better for you to get our news every day.

Tell Isabelita I visited Ramón Gómez de la Serna and he asked for her and for all of you, and showed me a series of mechanical toys which are delightful, and did some sleight of hand for me. He is an extraordinarily original man!

Good-bye. Best to everyone, kisses to Isabel and Concha and a big hug and kiss from your son

FEDERICO

Remember me to Don Fernando [de los Ríos].
We will write him soon.
How are my cousins?
Tell Enriquito [cousin] we will write him.
Best to my aunts and friends.
Regards to Petra, Dolores, and Amor [the maids].
A kiss for Mama-yaya.

It is interesting to see how the poet associates the favorable reception given to him and his brother with the admiration his friends feel for "his" works. What seems to concern him is following his path as a creator, "my *own* path." The italicized word betrays his struggle to convince his parents that he is not cut out for a "profitable" profession, unless it be literature.

Two years later Francisco García Lorca would receive a government scholarship to study public law for a year (1925–1926) in Toulouse and Bordeaux. Shortly after he had arrived in Bordeaux, Federico sent him a postcard (undated, as are all his letters) showing the interior of the Cartuja.*

Dearest Paquito:
Tomorrow I will write at length about lots of interesting things. And what about you? Give me all the news. Your impressions of Bordeaux, the Surrealist youth, etc. I am sending you this postcard with this eastern Baroque, which says so much about Granada and all Andalusia. It is the *last* great thing left. Everyone is fine at home, and very happy you are having a good time and studying hard. Till later, a big big hug from your

FEDERICO

*The church of a former Carthusian monastery in Granada. The sacristy is an extreme example of the eighteenth-century style known as Churrigueresque. —*Tr.*

This brief text, with its surprising juxtaposition of Baroque and Surrealist styles, dates from 1925. Perhaps Federico had already read Breton's second manifesto.

The two brothers' quest, each for his own path, is reflected in a letter written to Francisco by Fernando de los Ríos (Granada, February 14, 1926):

> It makes me happy to see what enthusiasm and faith you put into your work. Yes, dear Paco, life has no meaning unless one searches for the inner voice, and listens for one's vocation, turning it into professional action. Do not abandon yourself, for only by remaining close to oneself may one become the complete man that is so badly needed—the man who builds an inner world for himself and thus finds inner peace, with an unshakable vision of life. Onward and upward, Paco!

The teacher and professor (the same man who would declare himself a "follower of Erasmus" when the U.S. Immigration Service asked him to identify his religion) feels remarkably close to the young student, and offers him his heart-felt advice.

Don Fernando, who was an ardent defender of the principles of the Instituto Libre de Enseñanza, was extremely respectful and tactful with others (nothing is more moving than his friendship with the Catholic Manuel de Falla, as shown by the letters they exchanged). And yet he was a real "terror" in prudish Granada. Sanctimonious women would make the sign of the cross and flee from his path. His daughter Laura, who at an early age became a close friend of the youngest Lorca child, Isabel, hardly found any playmates, so suspicious were their parents. When Don Fernando became Minister of Justice in the Republic and set up a Center for Arabic Studies, directed by Emilio García Gómez, it was stupidly rumored that "One Fernando conquered Granada* and another has lost it." But Don Fernando had his lighter side. A refined native of Ronda, he was a connoisseur of the bullfight and of *cante jondo* which he himself sang with thorough knowledge of that difficult genre. He was loathed, of course, by the political Right. Ian Gibson has shown that Federico's friendship with the Socialist leader was a contributing factor in Lorca's death and in those of others from Granada.**

---

*King Ferdinand, who expelled the Moors in 1492.—*Tr.*
**Ian Gibson, *The Death of Lorca* (Chicago: O'Hara, 1973), p. 132.—*Tr.*

A mentor to both brothers (neither of whom was involved in political groups), Don Fernando was probably closer to Francisco, for they shared some of the same professional concerns. But he could not help noticing the literary vocation of Federico. He was one of the first people to listen admiringly as the timid young man played Chopin and Beethoven on the piano at the Arts Center of Granada. In the letter to Francisco from which I have just quoted, he writes: "Last night Federico gave the first lecture in our friendly, brand new Atheneum. It was about Góngora and it had moments of great artistic beauty. If Federico studies hard and concentrates on his work he will become a great Spanish poet."

It was thanks to Fernando de los Ríos' help that the Barraca was founded, and the Lorca family was always welcome in this house. Federico would give a private reading of *Mariana Pineda* (1925) at Don Fernando's house in Granada, and a similar reading of *Yerma* in Madrid before its première in December, 1934. The brothers also felt admiration and affection for Don Fernando's wife, Gloria Giner de los Ríos, a schoolteacher, like Vicenta Lorca, who was totally devoted to her profession both inside and outside of class. The concern for education which we find in some of Federico's public statements and in his very conception of art is probably attributable to his mother and to the De los Ríos family. And thus, in his own way, he was following ideas rooted in the old Instituto Libre de Enseñanza.

But I have yet to quote the most important document recording the friendship between the two brothers: a long letter which Federico sent to Francisco when the latter was studying in Toulouse. This letter, too, is undated, but it was probably written in February, 1926.

The letter, which Francisco told me about when we were discussing the *Gypsy Ballads* (for it offers proof of how the "Ballad of the Spanish Civil Guard" is grounded in reality), begins with an allusion explained in the first part of this book: Federico's habit of leaving the light on at night in order to read in bed. This used to prevent his brother from falling asleep. The top of the first page is adorned with a drawing—the superimposed heads of two Pierrot figures, whose faces and single ruffled collar have been lightly colored.*

Dear Paquito:
Every day I have thought of writing you. I have missed you at night too,

*Reproduced on the dust jacket of David Gershator's translation of the *Selected Letters.*
—*Tr.*

when I look across at your empty bed, with the brocatelle curtain behind it . . . and guess what! I haven't once turned on the light!

I want to leave for Madrid in a few days. I have gotten my books ready, and they have turned out splendidly. They have a rare, surprising *unity*. I want to publish all three of them at the same time, for they complement each other and form a *first-rate* body of poetry. I"m convinced that their appearance can be an *intimate* happening—that's what my friends say, and they're all enthusiastic about the idea. I've made up my mind. I've worked hard on *polishing* things. The newly prepared *Suites* are delightful, they're deeply lyrical. Three books in all: a book of *Suites*, a book of short *Songs*— the best book of the three—and the *Poem of Deep Song* with the Andalusian songs. The gypsy balladbook I want to keep for later, and do a book of nothing but ballads. These past few days I've added several more, such as "Preciosa" and "The Arrest of Antoñito el Camborio." They are very interesting, and if you answer right away, I will send them to you. I have also finished the "Ode to Salvador Dalí," which is a very long poem—150 alexandrine verses.

This first fragment is extraordinarily important. The poet speaks with total confidence about his work, although only his closest friends are familiar with it. Once again Federico refutes the myth (fed, in part, by the poet himself) that he was unwilling to publish his works. Once the books have been finished and slowly revised, and once he has overcome his inhibitions about publishing something so pure and personal, he has no objection to sending them to the publisher. His brother would help him revise and select the poems of *Songs*, published a year later by *Litoral* in Málaga. What became of *Poem of Deep Song* and *Suites*? The first book did not appear until 1931 (Madrid: Editorial Ulises). The manuscript of *Suites* which Federico sent to Litoral was lost, and the book was not published until 1983, after André Belamich had reconstructed it from other manuscripts. Federico goes on to speak of *Mariana Pineda*, which he needed to have performed in order to convince his parents he could succeed as an author. Once his parents were satisfied, he would be able to study in Toulouse and Paris:

I want to go to Madrid to see what solution I can find for my Mariana—this will solve a lot of problems—and to arrange for [the publication of] my books.

And after I have done that, I would like to accompany you to Toulouse, and *devour* French and work there on the [poem] Diego Corrientes and create my lyric poetry which has its wings tied, although it is capable of taking flight.

I feel *capable* of creating a great, original *oeuvre*, and have *faith* I can do so. What I need is a secretary and a publisher, but these will turn up. I can *create*, but am virtually incapable of giving practical form to what I have created. Bowing to necessity, I have had to make a huge effort to do what I have just done. But you've no idea how much I've enjoyed myself. I have seen *completed* things I couldn't see before, and I've given balance to poems which <u>were</u> limping but which had heads of gold.

You ought to write me immediately and tell me what you are thinking about, and whether you think I should come with you to Toulouse. Don't you think such an immersion would be extremely useful before I go to Paris? In four months time I could put French under my belt.

Neither the playwright Eduardo Marquina nor the actress Margarita Xirgu (the first was acting as an intermediary) had answered Federico's insistent letters asking how soon *Mariana Pineda* would be staged. It would be another two years before the play was finally performed, in Barcelona. Perhaps these delays, borne with impatience, kept him from writing *Diego Corrientes.** Or perhaps it was the Andalusian element, reflected in the title, which kept the poem from being written. Federico had begun to grow tired of the confining atmosphere of Granada, and wanted to look for other airs and themes. And yet he finds Andalusia as wonderful as ever:

I made a splendid trip to the very heart of the Alpujarra. It took two days. Pepe Segura invited me. But when you come we'll have to go back. I have never seen such an exotic, mysterious place. It hardly seems part of Europe.

The people one sees there are incredibly beautiful. I shall never forget the village of Cáñar (the highest in Spain), full of singing washwomen and grave shepherds. Nothing could be newer, literarily speaking.

There are two well-defined races: the Nordic, Galician, Asturian, etc., and the Moorish, in all its purity. I saw a Queen of Sheba husking corn against a black and violet colored wall, and I saw the son of a king disguised as the son of a barber.

They are cut off from the rest of the world. They are refined and

*An eighteenth-century Andalusian horse rustler and bandit much admired by Romantic writers. —*Tr.*

hospitable and, except for the secretaries in the town halls, well aware of the beauty of the region. The local accent is dark and strange, and it falls on every syllable; they say *Búénos días*. Since there are no French or English travelers making "lyrical journeys"—thank God!—and Romanticism is a thing of the past, the Alpujarra will stay the way it is now. The region is governed by the Civil Guard. A sergeant in Carataunas, who was annoyed with the gypsies, tried to get them to leave. He called them to HQ, picked up some fire tongs, and pulled out a tooth from each one, saying, "If you are still here tomorrow, another one will *fall out*." Naturally, the poor gape-toothed gypsies had to leave. This Easter in Cáñar a little gypsy boy, fourteen years old, stole five hens from the mayor. The Civil Guard tied his arms to a piece of wood, paraded him through the whole village, whipping him with a strap and making him sing at the top of his lungs. I heard of this from a boy who had seen the parade go by as he sat in school. His story was movingly, bitterly real. All this has a surprising cruelty, and smacks of despotism in the style of Ferdinand VII.

The brief reference to the singing housewives and shepherds of the village of Cáñar suggests the landscape of *Yerma*. Thus did Federico remember scenes and atmosphere, extracting their dramatic or lyrical essences for later use in his works. His brother will tell us in this book of his prodigious memory and of the slow gestation of his works. The anecdote about the little gypsy boy takes us back to the "Dialogue of the Lieutenant Colonel of the Civil Guard" and to the song it ends with: "Song of the Beaten Gypsy Boy." But the dates do not coincide, for the dialogue was written on July 5, 1925, and besides, the lyrical-comical tone of the dialogue attenuates the cruelty of the incident, cruelty that is brutally evident in the letter. It is as though Federico were divining later events. Or perhaps he had already witnessed other such incidents. The point is that some of the *Gypsy Ballads* are based on a poignant reality, personally observed by the poet. But let us finish the letter, with its evocation of family and friends:

We are all fine. Mother and the girls are downstairs eating. Petra is bustling angrily about the kitchen, and father is in the garden. The sky is a dense blue, the color of lapis lazuli. Yesterday we went to La Calahorra in our Fiat. Falla came with us, and so did Valdecasas, Luna, Torres López and Segura. It was an unforgettable day. The Renaissance castle, with the Sierra Nevada in the background, is fantastic. The nobleman who built it, the Marquis of Zenete, once planned to marry Lucretia Borgia. On the way back we went through the melancholy cathedral town of Guadix. Falla reacted with enthusiasm. When we went down the street of Santa María de la Cabeza, in the purest Spanish style, we saw—almost intact—the House of the Zagal, with its Moorish design. Spain is endlessly fascinating, despite the North Americans who are carrying it away, bit by bit.

Good-bye. Hugs and kisses from your brother

FEDERICO

"A city of Andalusia," probably Guadix (the birthplace of Pedro Antonio de Alarcón) is the setting for *The Three-cornered Hat*, so it is easy to understand Falla's enthusiasm. Federico's letters seem to grow in importance the more he admires the person he is addressing. The variety of subject matter and liveliness of description make this one of the loveliest letters he ever wrote.

It is not the only letter showing how close the brothers felt to one another. Another newsy letter, written by Federico to his family, dates from 1929.

They have begun the rehearsals for my *Perlimplín*, which is going to be performed by the "Caracol" company. But the *Shoemaker's Wife* has been delayed. The *Shoemaker's Wife* will almost certainly be done like *Mariana Pineda*, first in the provinces and later, in October, Margarita [Xirgu] will put it on in the magnificent new Español theater.

Yesterday I had lunch with [Catalina] Bárcena, and she is willing to put on the play I gave her.

Most important of all, they have offered me a tour in America. This is still in the planning stage, but I can earn quite a lot of money there.

Needless to say, I'll keep you posted.

I would say yes. It would be a lecture tour to Cuba and some North American universities.

I would like to make this trip, which could bring me money and knowledge of other cultures.

My life is very simple. Paquito is studying hard, and he has a great future. Both of us have a great future, if God helps us.

Francisco was probably studying for his qualifying exams for the Spanish diplomatic corps, and Federico was working on the rehearsals for his exquisite chamber piece, *The Love Of Don Perlimplín with Belisa in Their Garden,* the première of which would be cancelled by the censors of Primo de Rivera. A few months later, he would make his trip to Cuba and New York, where he began *Poet in New York.* Even there he insisted on knowing the results of his brother's exams before anyone else. As though taking part in a family council, he writes:

> You must encourage Paquito whether he does well or does poorly. If he does poorly, it is not his fault, for he has worked hard, extremely hard, and in the next exams he will be one of the very best. But I know I needn't tell you this, for you're a wonderful family, like no other. But there's no harm, is there, in everyone expressing his own opinion? Anyway, if Paquito does well, send me a cable, right away. They get here the same day.

Francisco demanded much of himself, and withdrew from these examinations against the advice of a majority of the examiners. He entered the Diplomatic Corps of the Second Republic in 1931 and occupied the posts of vice-consul in Tunis and of secretary of the Spanish delegation in Cairo. In July 1936 Madrid heard of an assassination attempt against him. The news later proved false, but in hindsight it seems an omen of the tragedy about to befall the entire family. Francisco was in Cairo on the 18th of July at the beginning of Franco's military uprising against the Republic, and it was there he learned of the murders of his brother and brother-in-law in Granada (the latter, Manuel Fernández-Montesinos, was shot because he was the socialist mayor of the city). Francisco held out hope until the news was confirmed; communications with Granada had been cut off. In Madrid Isabel García Lorca, who was suffering the same anguish, moved in with the De los Ríos family. Federico had gone to Granada, as he often did in the summer, to relax with his family and to work on his poems and plays. Despite having expressed initial interest, he had recently turned down an invitation to give a series of lectures in Mexico. In his letter declining the invitation he said he was deeply involved with a new play, and wanted to see it through to completion.

One of the projects he was working on was *The Dreams of My Cousin Aurelia,* a work which belongs to the cycle of Granadan plays begun with *Doña Rosita.* All that remains of that play is a fragmentary draft, corresponding to an unfinished first act. During his first few days in Granada he also seems to have revised *The House of Bernarda Alba.* Federico, who probably never feared for his life, had his eyes on many other projects. He was thinking about future premières—*The Billy-Club*

Puppets in a new musical version and *When Five Years Have Passed*—
and spoke with enthusiasm of a great poem which he would entitle
Adam. He had also made progress towards the completion of a book of
sonnets. But death—such a familiar character and theme in his poetry
and theater—prevented him from ever reaching maturity as a creator.
Concha García Lorca, who was married to Manuel Fernández-Montesinos, has told about those bitter hours:

On the morning of August 22, I was in bed, in my house in Granada. I was
sick. How could I have not been sick? Two days before, they had killed my
husband. We were all sick during those desperate days. Federico had taken
the precaution of moving in with the Rosales family, who were friends of
ours. Wonderful people, although they were members of the Falange. But
what did that matter? Weren't many good people members of the Falange?
Federico used to say so himself. My brother was not a Communist. When
the Civil War broke out I asked him, "Look, Federico, you never talk about
politics, but people say you are a Communist. Is that true?" Federico broke
out laughing. "Concha, my Conchita, forget what people say! My party is the
party of the poor!" And he hugged me. But people said that Federico was a
Communist, so we thought he should hide in the Rosales house; that was
the safest place there was in Granada. On the morning of August 22 my
father came to my bedroom. He stood in the doorway and said nothing. He
was as white as a sheet. "Federico?" I asked him. And he answered,
"Federico." They had taken my brother away—even him!—and God knows
where. For the next three months my father refused to abandon hope. Not
me. I knew very well they had killed him, just as they had killed my
husband. Federico would never return.

The pathetic story requires no comment. Miguel de Unamuno, who
did not at first realize what was happening, would condemn the events of
those days in two terrible letters published by José Bergamín:

It is a stupid regime of terror. In this very city [Salamanca] there are
summary executions [. . .] For there is nothing worse than the marriage of
the barracks mentality with that of the sacristy. And then, the spiritual
leprosy of Spain: resentment, envy, hatred for intelligence.

It is moving to remember what Federico's mother had told him in
1921 of the ignorance and envy around him. Ignorance and envy had

slain a man "whose nature it was to love and be loved." Those are the words of his brother. León Felipe liked to remember how "one day they asked García Lorca 'for whom do you write?' and he answered, 'I write so that people will love me.' "

III

In 1936 Francisco García Lorca was appointed chief secretary to the Embassy of Spain in Brussels. The García Lorca family, with the exception of Isabel, was unable to leave Granada. In Brussels Francisco renewed his contact with Laura de los Ríos (the daughter of the Socialist leader), whom he would marry in 1942. In 1938 he was transferred to Barcelona, where he worked as chief of protocol in the Ministry of Foreign Affairs. He returned in 1939 to the embassy in Brussels, and when the Spanish Civil War ended he sought asylum in the United States. His sister Isabel was already living there, as was Fernando de los Ríos, who had been Spanish ambassador to the U.S. from 1936 to 1939.

In 1939 Francisco began to teach Spanish literature at Columbia University. The Spanish department there was directed by Federico de Onís, and Francisco would find a close friend in Angel del Río, who had been teaching at Columbia for many years. In 1940, with great difficulty, his parents and the rest of the family were reunited. His father died five years later in New York, having abandoned all hope of ever returning to Spain. Fernando de los Ríos, who had served to unite the Spanish exiles in New York, also died there in 1949.

These were difficult years. Francisco taught for awhile both at Queen's College and Columbia, and his unexpected change in career meant that he had to prepare a second doctoral dissertation (the book on Ganivet, mentioned earlier). As he followed the news reports of Allied advances in Europe, he hoped for an early return to Spain. This, of course, was not to be.

An important group of Spanish intellectuals was then living in exile in the United States. Two of them were the poet Juan Larrea and the filmmaker Luis Buñuel. Many of the exiles found teaching jobs at American universities, and some taught at the prestigious Middlebury Summer School. For nine years Francisco García Lorca directed Middlebury's Spanish courses. Among those who taught at Middlebury were Fernando de los Ríos (who also gave courses at the New School), the poets Pedro

Salinas, Jorge Guillén, Eugenio Florit, and Octavio Paz, the historians Américo Castro and Jorge Mañach, and the critics José Manuel Blecua and Enrique Díez-Canedo.

Besides Columbia University and Queen's College, Francisco García Lorca gave courses at Hunter College, Harvard University, and New York University. In 1947 he was named a counsellor of the arts and literature section of Unesco, and in 1955 he received a grant from the Bollingen Foundation. He was also director of the Casa Hispánica at Columbia University, a center of Hispanic studies created by Federico de Onís. Named *doctor honoris causa* by Middlebury College, he retired from Columbia in 1966 and returned to Spain.

In The Green Morning reveals an exceptional personal quality in Francisco García Lorca: his sense of literature as a way of life, rooted in popular tradition. His refined perceptions on literature are expressed with transparent simplicity. Some of his penetrating observations on his brother's theater could have been made by no other critic. They show the effortless familiarity with both the learned and popular traditions which his brother exemplified to such a high degree. In writing his memoirs of Federico, Francisco took a surprising path: we might almost say that he devotes more attention to the *world* of Federico than to the poet himself. This was the hardest path to follow, although it might seem the easiest. Francisco explores as only he himself could do, the elements of family, regional, and popular culture which help explain the "exceptional" nature of his brother's life and works.

As I said earlier, most of this book seems to have been written between 1959 and 1965. The manuscript is undated. The author conceived the book as a sort of "portico" to the critical edition of his brother's works, a project which had gotten underway in the early 1950s. After his death in 1976, his widow Laura de los Ríos decided to prepare the manuscript for publication and asked me to edit it. Not only did she want to carry her husband's work to completion, she also said she wanted to render homage to the two brothers. With the publication of this book a debt of fraternal love was repaid, and new light was cast upon the dreams and way of life of a forgotten world.

—Mario Hernández

TRANSLATOR'S NOTE

In the Spanish edition of this book, *Federico y su mundo*, Mario Hernández describes in detail how he and the late Laura de los Ríos prepared the manuscript for publication. Hernández divided the biographical material into chapters and supplied chapter headings; inserted illustrative texts from the works of Federico García Lorca; made stylistic changes; added dates and bibliographic footnotes; and corrected a few of the author's factual statements in the light of recent research by himself and others.

In The Green Morning is a translation of those parts of *Federico y su mundo* which I judged of greatest interest to English and American readers of Federico García Lorca. I have included all of the biographical memoirs except for a chapter presenting lengthy samples of Federico's earliest writings. I have also included all the essays regarding his theater. Don Francisco died before completing the section on his brother's poetry, and it has been omitted here.

With the patient, expert help of Peggy Fox, of New Directions, I have thoroughly edited the text established by Hernández and Laura de los Ríos. Repetitive passages have been omitted, as have two examples of "swinging" songs; a students' song alluding to Don Fernando de los Ríos (for this was a parody of a Spanish original unfamiliar to most American readers), and some of the less successful productions of Uncle Baldomero, Isidoro Capdepón, and the anonymous poet-geographer of Fuente Vaqueros.

The author is sometimes rather vague on chronological matters (for this book was not conceived as a biography), and, following Hernández' example, I have supplied still more dates in brackets and in footnotes. I have thus taken advantage of information not available to either the author or the editors. Much of this new material is found in Ian Gibson's recent biography, *Federico García Lorca. I. De Fuente Vaqueros a Nueva York (1898-1929)*, (Barcelona, Grijalbo, 1984).

The title of this translation is from a poem in *Songs*:

> In the green morning
> I wanted to be nothing but heart.

Cambridge, Massachusetts   —CHRISTOPHER MAURER
November, 1985

I. FEDERICO AND HIS WORLD

Federico (left) and Francisco García Lorca in 1918 at la Acera del Darro, their house in Granada.

The García Lorca children with their mother: (left to right), Federico, Concha, Francisco, and Isabel; (center), Doña Vicenta Lorca Romero.

Federico García Lorca (far left) and friends in the Andalusian countryside with Manuel de Falla (far right), 1926.

FUENTE VAQUEROS

From the heights, with the massive Sierra behind it, Granada gazes off into the musical remoteness of its Vega,* spotted with villages and hamlets. From the city's balconies, no one has ever failed to notice the marvelous chord formed by the Sierra, the city, and the plain. Like a note veiled in the distance and hidden on the plain by the poplars that line its rivers is the little town of Fuente Vaqueros, where Federico was born on June 5, 1898.

In the heart of the Vega lies the sprawling Real Soto de Roma, and in the center of the Soto, Fuente Vaqueros. The lands of the Soto once belonged to the Moorish kings of Granada, and when the city was conquered by Ferdinand and Isabella, the Soto became part of the patrimony of the Crown of Castile. Wastelands, then covered with trees and abounding in pheasants, were the King's rarely visited hunting preserve. In the eighteenth century a pleasure palace, called the Casa Real, was built on the foundations of an older building. As children we were fascinated by this palace and by its abandoned gardens, whose only remains were enormous centenary elms and spurge laurels.

We were born in the heart of the Soto, and when we were older we were puzzled by its name. Why *Roma*? We conjectured that the name had to

*Vega, a watered valley between hills.—Tr.

do with one of the little villages of the Soto, Romilla, or *Roma la chica* (little Rome), as it was sometimes called. The people of this village are called Romans, *romanos,* and this is why the unseen protagonist of Federico's play *The House of Bernarda Alba* is named Pepe el Romano. But Federico never learned of the poetic, probable origin of the name Soto de Roma: Romilla was once *Romiya,* in Arabic "Christian woman"—the *Soto,* or glade of the Christian woman.

To further enrich the poetry of the name, we can add that this Romiya or Romilla refers to Florinda, the unfortunate daughter of Count Julian, a character who is the subject of many beautiful ballads. It seems that there are Arabic traditions which attribute the founding of the Soto de Roma to the Count, who used it as a retreat to console his daughter.* We had no idea of the legend surrounding our birthplace. Had we known, the poetic figure of Florinda, lost in the mists of legend and the mists that rise from the nearby river, which almost laps the walls of the abandoned Casa Real, might well have become the subject of an "historical ballad" in the poet's *Gypsy Ballads.*

These lands of the Soto de Roma, vaguely tied to the beginnings of Muslim rule in Spain, were to be the scene of the extinction of that rule seven centuries later when Granada was conquered by the Catholic Monarchs. But the Soto's fields lay too close to Granada, the last redoubt taken by the Christians, to be able to figure in the traditional Spanish frontier ballads. Not so with Alhama, Álora, Antequera, and Lorca.

Our village is not far from Pinos Puente, and the unique Visigothic bridge that gives it its name, where, as legend would have it, a messenger of the Catholic Monarchs overtook Christopher Columbus after he had left the court and given up all hope of reaching agreement with the Crown. Closer still is the walled village of Santa Fe, founded during the siege of Granada. It was here that the Monarchs and Columbus finally signed the agreements which led to the discovery of America. How often, on our way to Granada, were we to enter its walls in our mule-drawn coach.

And yet I do not believe that as children in Fuente Vaqueros we were aware how close we lived to the sites of those historical deeds, which did not appear in our childhood folklore. Of the fighting with the Moors (no doubt those fields must have been the scene of forays and ambushes),

---

*According to legend, Don Rodrigo, the last of the Visigothic kings, saw Florinda bathing in the Tajo River and seduced her. Her father, Count Julian, took revenge by betraying Rodrigo and defecting to the Moors. As a result, the Moors invaded Spain.—*Tr.*

the only song that reached us (where did it come from?) was a six-syllable ballad of captives:

A la verde, verde,	At the green, at the green
a la verde oliva,	at the green olive tree
donde cautivaron	where they captured three girls,
a las tres cautivas.	where they captured all three.
La mayor, Constanza,	The oldest, Constanza,
la menor Lucía,	the youngest, Lucía;
y la más pequeña	and the smallest of them
llaman Rosalía . . .	is called Rosalía . . .

With its poignant, monotonous melody, the ballad tells how the youngest of the captives meets her father at the *Fuente Fría*, the "Cold Spring." Another poetical meeting by this fountain formed part, as we shall see later, of our family tradition.

The Soto de Roma would once again enter the history of Spain, during the Napoleonic Wars. When Napoleon had been defeated, the King and Queen gave the Soto to the Duke of Wellington along with smaller but choice neighboring properties like the Dehesa de Íllora and Molino del Rey. Wellington was also named Duke of Ciudad Rodrigo. At this point modern Fuente Vaqueros was founded. The name alludes to the generous fountain (*fuente*) which supplies the village with its excellent water. The mention of cattlemen (*vaqueros*) evokes a history of ranching. The town's moist grazing lands are now devoted entirely to farming and are among the most productive in Spain.

The royal gift was followed by total absenteeism. The extensive domain of the Soto, which included various villages and palaces, was administered by an Englishman, in our time a certain Mr. Mosting, who lived at times in the Molino del Rey, on the boundary of Íllora, an estate over which the Wellington family had kept full control. Only once, when we were very small and Mr. Mosting was away, did my father take us to Molino del Rey. Years later we would remember as the most exceptional part of the visit (today it is almost the *only* thing I can remember) the timid, agile movements of a stag kept in a pen.

The Duke's English administrator delegated his functions to a subordinate who lived in a house a little larger than any other in the village. People called it the Big House. When we were children, this foreman was a rustic-looking fellow by the name of Don Juan Bautista Sánchez, and he, too, lived (though this was difficult in a village as small and as friendly as Fuente Vaqueros) in an almost comic "splendid isolation" that everyone in the village resented.

The thousands of tenant farmers of the spacious Soto paid a small sum to the ducal administration. Over the years the use of the lands was handed down from fathers to sons, or the lands were sublet, so that, considering the smallness of that sum and the productivity of the fields, the tenant farmers were in effect owners of the land.

Almost everyone in Fuente Vaqueros had at least a small tract of land in the Soto, and this contributed to the village's open character. It was only very recently, and, I think, on very generous terms, that the House of Wellington entirely dispossessed itself of that rich farmland. Perhaps they were only bowing to the inevitable, to the march of time and of history. Perhaps the lands were too extensive not to have slipped out of their control.

The fact that they owned small, even tiny, parcels of extremely fertile land gave the villagers a certain well-being that doubtlessly influenced, without completely determining, their cheerful psychology. Something more profound, which we shall not try to explain, made the inhabitant of Fuente Vaqueros a more open, communicative, refined, wittier, and more graceful human being than his counterpart in neighboring villages. The village's physical appearance—its lay-out, its spacious promenade, the road bordered by enormous trees that led to the poplar groves along the river—revealed, in its rustic simplicity, noble, urban intentions. Fuente Vaqueros does not resemble villages in other countries, villages that sprout up by the side of roads whose straight or winding paths they meekly follow. Fuente Vaqueros was founded under the same conditions as the other villages in the Soto, and yet, unlike them, it gives the appearance of having been planned. Not even the military lay-out of Santa Fe de los Reyes is comparable. Fuente Vaqueros is an open village, bordering on its fields, meeting them more gently than is the case elsewhere, better suited for public gatherings, fairs, and other festivities.

Like a small rural replica of Granada, Fuente Vaqueros lies between two rivers, the Cubillas and the Genil. The Genil and the Darro are the two rivers of Granada, of which Federico would write:

| . . . los dos ríos de Granada | . . . the two rivers of Granada |
| bajan de la nieve al trigo. | come down from the snow to the wheat. |

I have always suspected that this scene, with the Sierra Nevada in the background, is viewed from the plain on which we were born, where the two rivers branch off into a number of murmuring irrigation canals. But Federico chose to give separate expression to these rivers, attributing to the Genil a rustic note and to the Darro a more lyrical one:

> ... el Genil duerme a sus bueyes,　　... The Genil lulls its oxen to sleep
> y el Dauro a sus mariposas.　　　　and the Dauro its butterflies.*

In his vision of the city's two rivers, whether separate or united, it is just possible that Federico was influenced by the fact that our first house in Granada, on Acera del Darro, No. 66, was close to the place, beyond the Puente de la Virgen, where the two rivers converge. Not far from our balconies, the Darro lost both its name and its waters, rosy with clay, in the more transparent and limpid Genil. What Federico thought of this, I do not know. When I was a child the imminent death of the river made me a bit sad. In fact, the image of the dead river appears in my brother's poetry.

The two rivers of Fuente Vaqueros also converge not far from the village, close to a farm our family owned that bore the lovely name of Daimuz Bajo.** We lived there when we were very young. My first memories are of Daimuz, and so is the first image I can remember of myself, of Federico, and of my parents, an image I have relived often and kept vivid and intact while so many other, later ones have completely disappeared. I was hardly old enough to walk, and my brother would have been about five. A wandering painter of windows and doors used to visit the farm, carrying a little box with paintbrushes of all sizes, with an accordion slung over his shoulder. He used to look for odd jobs in the villages and farms, and would sometimes play the accordion at parties and dances. Perhaps on this particular occasion he had been given some work to do at our farm. Our whole family had gathered just inside the door that led to our dining and living room, and Nicasio the painter-musician had begun to play. Perhaps it was my father who said, "Dance, Paco!" A little out of step with the music, I began to wobble to and fro, from one wall to another, the whole family laughing. I remember (or

*Dauro is the poetic name for the Darro. Federico uses both names in his poems.—Tr.
**Literally "Lower Daimuz."—Tr.

perhaps I have recreated the scene from later memories) that my brother was sitting beside Nicasio on the stairs that led to the rooms above. Federico was rolling with laughter.

Some think of water as the symbol of Granada. It could easily be the symbol of Fuente Vaqueros, for not only does water make the land fertile, but a fountain gives the village its very name. The people in the other villages of the Vega call ours *La Fuente*, "The Fountain." Every house has its own well, and to strike an abundant supply of water, one need drill down little more than a meter. Irrigation canals surround the village, and the most important one, the Atanor, passed by our house. Here the children liked best to gather. The dank green of grasses and sown fields, the "amphibious paths," the great poplars that flanked the rivers, the blackberries, reeds, and hawthornes, the willows on the sandbanks of the river, the hidden backwaters, the morning breezes that turned the poplars into "a thousand crystal tambourines," the moonlight that covered the ponds like a sheet of ice*—all of this permeated Federico's awakening to life and to poetry.

Because the village was of relatively recent origin, one will not find among its white houses a single prestigious old mansion with a shield or coat of arms. The only building that stood out at all, and not very much at that, was a very modest church. Back then there was also a tavern where more coffee than wine was drunk, and a casino for the more affluent farmers, including my father who, as the owner of Daimuz, was better off than anyone else. There was an extremely good physician, Don Salvador Pareja, who belonged to a distinguished line of physicians in Granada, and who attended my mother during the births of her children. Years later Don Salvador would talk to me about the vivacity and complex psychology of the village people. He had a fine sense of humor, and he made me notice that among the poorer classes one often found the psychosomatic disorders then thought to characterize only the wealthy classes. "These people need more than a country doctor to tend to broken bones, fevers, and childbirth," he used to say. "We now have carders with 'spleen' and blasé reapers." I believe that an intelligent doctor can discover the complexity of the human soul in any milieu, but Don Salvador believed that the psychological texture of Fuente Vaqueros was richer than that of any country village he had ever known.

*The author is quoting from the *Gypsy Ballads.—Tr.*

Among La Fuente's most important characters was an unforgettable pharmacist, Don Luis, a refined, courteous friend of the family who was terrified of thunderstorms. It was said that when a thunderstorm was coming up, Don Luis would withdraw into a dark room, light an oil lamp, and stare fixedly at the flame, so as not to see the lightning that penetrated the cracks in the blinds. It was probably my Aunt Frasquita who gave me this bit of confidential information. She was more terrified of storms than was Don Luis, though perhaps less so than her daughter, my cousin Aurelia.

On those summer days of complicated and fleeting thunderstorms, Federico used to make his way toward my Aunt Frasquita's house, as if he were going to a show. Federico used to tell me how our cousin Aurelia, who came close to fainting during thunderstorms, would lie back rather dramatically in her rocking chair and say, "Just *look* at me; I'm dying!" The last fragment of theater that Federico would write was titled *The Dreams of My Cousin Aurelia* [1936]. Federico took an ironic view of that candle-lit room and saw it as a theatrical situation. My mother told me that when these storms were beginning my aunt and cousins used to shout, "Federico is coming!" Once they had bolted the door against him, they could dramatize to their hearts' content.

While telling this, I remember that my father, who never had any fear of storms, took the precaution of equipping every house we lived in with lightning rods. I remember perfectly the installation of huge rods with three metal prongs each on our house in Valderrubio, and then on the two houses we successively rented in Granada, and on our Huerta de San Vicente. The man who did the work was always Emilio, a very tall fellow who spoke in a nasal voice and smelled of rubber electrical tape.

Federico did not inherit the fear of lightning, but I remember a certain thunderstorm when we were young. The two of us were walking from Valderrubio to Fuente Vaqueros, and all of a sudden, without our even noticing it, a storm came up. Halfway between the two villages, as we were going through the tall poplars that border the Cubillas, day turned to night. The fields were deserted and silent. A few heavy raindrops fell, and the wind began to rock the trees. Then, suddenly, there was a dry, formidable clap of thunder. An unsaddled runaway horse almost ran over us. Then came another more distant clap and the typical odor of ozone. Federico ran over to me, his face pallid, and told me that his cheek was burning. He said he had been touched by a spark of the lightning, which had, in fact, been blindingly bright. I drew near him, looked at his cheek, calmed him down, and we began our return in silence. I am unable to fix the date of this incident, but can still see the scene vividly. A certain confused image of a storm, in one of Federico's poems, is now made completely clear by the evocation of that episode:

Y el cielo daba portazos	The sky was slamming doors
al brusco rumor del bosque	to the rough murmur of the woods
mientras clamaban las luces . . .	and the lights were screaming . . .

As for the scar on the cheek, the scar left by the kiss of the lightning, it is borne by one of the characters in his theater.*

Among noteworthy people who lived in the village when we were children, I remember the parish priest, who bore the somewhat disrespectful nickname Father Pinch. His father had been a baker, and with the pinch of dough that he saved from each batch he paid for his son's education; at least this is what people said in the village. No wonder Fuente Vaqueros saw its priest in an ironic light: its people were very liberal in politics and had no time for formal religion. That priest must have saved very few souls in Fuente Vaqueros or anywhere else in the Vega. In some of Federico's creations there is a certain pagan note, a certain predominance of the earthly over the spiritual, a sense of justice rooted in a natural non-religious morality. All this originates, I think, in his observation of the countryfolk. Such interpretations emerged spontaneously as he tried to put himself in the place of his characters.

So that I can better convey the temperament of our village, let me skip ahead to the time when we were living in another town, known today as Valderrubio, where my father owned land. No two towns could be more different in character. Valderrubio was more concentrated, more cautious, less cheerful. The two towns are only a few kilometers apart, separated by the current of the Cubillas. Valderrubio borders on the Vega, but there the drylands have already begun: it is a village without a public fountain, a "village of wells." In a way *The Shoemaker's Prodigious Wife* could be the literary projection of the character of Fuente

---

*Victor, in *Yerma*. Near the end of Act I, Yerma says that Victor has "something like a burn" on his cheek. The same motif appears in Act II of *Doña Rosita the Spinster*; Rosita denies that her fiancé had a scar on his lip: "It was a burn, it was slightly pink. Scars are deeper."—*Ed.*

Vaqueros and *The House of Bernarda Alba* that of Valderrubio. In fact, some of the extravagant characters mentioned in *Bernarda Alba* actually come from Valderrubio. It was an extraordinarily sober village, and amusingly enough, in the taverns the men preferred tea to alcohol. But one thing that the two towns had in common was their indifference to religion, a trait even more pronounced in Valderrubio. And yet, the two towns were different even in this. I remember Valderrubio's proclivity for religious dissidence. Certain segments of its tiny population succumbed to the preaching of clandestine heretics. There was a small group, mostly women, discreetly known as "Protestants" or "Shepherdesses." The latter term came from the quack who converted them and who lived in Granada: he was known as the Father Shepherd.

In contrast, there is another village, equidistant from Fuente Vaqueros and Valderrubio, or perhaps a little closer to our village, on the other side of the Genil. This village tended more toward drinking and feuding, but zealously fulfilled its religious duties. It bore the cacaphonous name of Chauchina.* There, even miracles were possible. I remember the apparition of an image called the Virgin of Thorns, perhaps because it appeared amidst briars or hawthorns. The fame of this Virgin spread like wildfire through the neighboring villages, except for the *enlightened* Fuente Vaqueros. Somehow Federico, with his *joie de vivre,* apparent nonchalance, and uncomplicated charm, was a son of Fuente Vaqueros. Years later Federico would affirm, thinking of his country origins and his love of the earth, that "the psychoanalysts would say I have a rural complex."

In 1929, when Federico had been caressed by fame (*Mariana Pineda* had now been staged and the *Gypsy Ballads* published), Fuente Vaqueros wanted to honor the poet at a solemn gathering. Surely Federico, who fled from this sort of homage, accepted only because Fuente Vaqueros was his home town. Participating in the ceremony were people to whom he could not say no: Don Antonio Rodríguez, who was my brother's first schoolteacher, and Don Fernando de los Ríos, the socialist leader who was Federico's professor at the university, a mentor for whom Federico felt deep love and respect. The ceremony had been organized by the mayor of Fuente Vaqueros, Rafael Sánchez, a baker. This man exemplified the best people of the village, with his longing for self-improvement, his love of knowledge, and his desire for justice. An orphan, he

*Pronounced "Chow-CHEE-na."—*Tr.*

rose from apprentice baker to socialist congressman from Granada. Part of the homage to the poet consisted in the creation of a public library, to which Sánchez donated three hundred volumes.

When we were living in Granada, I remember visits from villagers, mostly from those who were grateful for past favors, or who simply felt friendship and affection. Rafael Sánchez' mother always visited us on her trips into the city from La Fuente. Tall and dignified and dressed in mourning, she might remind one of the mother in *Blood Wedding*. Her name was Felisa. All of this may or may not have influenced Federico in accepting the honors that his village was about to bestow on him. Telling about the ceremony will help me describe the atmosphere of Fuente Vaqueros and the nature of its relations with our family. Besides, it was on this occasion that Federico gave an educational speech about the cultural importance of books and the social function of libraries. Although the speech is less rich than the ones Federico usually gave, it reveals his vision of the village and its people. Because it has never before been published, perhaps I should give a small fragment:

I am deeply grateful, deeply indebted to this lovely village where I was born and spent a happy childhood, for the undeserved honor of your having given my name to the old church street. [The old name was later restored. But it is curious that in the neighboring village of Valderrubio where Federico wrote many of his works and where there is not the least external remembrance of my brother, there is still a street bearing the name of my father: Calle de Don Federico. If I may intrude for a moment, I will add that I do not resent the useless effort to remove my brother's name from a street in Fuente Vaqueros, and that it makes me proud that the name of my father transcended lowness and meanness.] You can be sure that I am thankful from the bottom of my heart and that when I am in Madrid or elsewhere and they ask me for my birthplace, I say that I was born in Fuente Vaqueros, so that whatever glory or fame I attain will also belong to this friendly, this modern, this liberal village, La Fuente. And you can be sure that I always praise it, both as poet and as its son, for in all the Vega of Granada—and I am speaking objectively—no town is as lovely nor as rich nor as emotionally endowed as this one. I do not wish to offend any of the beautiful villages of the Vega of Granada, but I have eyes to see and am intelligent enough to praise my home town!

It is built upon water. Everywhere the irrigation ditches sing and the poplars grow tall and the wind plays soft music in them in the summertime. At the heart of the village is a fountain that flows ceaselessly and above the rooftops are the blue mountains of the Vega, aloof and distant, as though they did not want their stones to reach this place, where the soft fertile earth makes every sort of fruit tree flower.

The character of its inhabitants singles it out among neighboring villages. A young man from Fuente Vaqueros stands out among a thousand. There he is, cutting a fine figure, his hat tossed back on his head, slapping backs, agile in conversation and in elegance. And in a group of outsiders, he will be the first to accept a modern idea or second a noble movement.

The young man from Fuente Vaqueros reveals himself in his sense of wit and grace, his liveliness, his longing for elegance and self-improvement. The fact is that the people of this village are born with a feeling for art—a feeling for art and for happiness, which is to say a feeling for life. I have often observed how upon entering this village there is a clamor, a trembling that wells forth from the deepest, most intimate part of it—a clamor, a rhythm that is social yearning and human understanding.

For the first time in its short history this village has begun to build a library. It is an important event that fills me with happiness, and I am honored to speak here at the moment of its inauguration, for my family has made an extraordinary contribution to the advancement of your culture. My mother, as all of you know, has taught many people in this village to read; she came here to teach, and I remember as a child hearing her read aloud to many people. My grandparents served this village with true spirit, and many of the songs that you sing were composed by an old poet from my own family.

This is a hurriedly-written sketch of the village, in which Federico's words are by no means charged with their usual poetry. But perhaps since these words were penned under special circumstances, they reveal more truthfully how Federico saw the village and its people, and his relation to them on a solemn, though surely (for him) bothersome occasion.

He read those words protected from the sun by an awning, surrounded by the swings and the shooting galleries of a fair, its music and its noises hushed for the ceremony. From the speakers' platform he could see the house in which he had been born. Numerous relatives and childhood friends were listening to him with the frank enthusiasm that was so typical of La Fuente, along with children who only knew that he was one of Don Federico's children and had been gone from the village for some years. How Federico must have longed to escape into lost corners of his childhood! But what a sense of duty and of loyalty kept him at his post as an orator!

FAMILY ORIGINS

Among my brother's papers there are several short autobiographical fragments which, judging from the large, clear, undefined handwriting, are probably among the first pages he ever wrote. Looking back from late adolescence—a period that lingered long in Federico—the budding writer recalls his childhood in Fuente Vaqueros. The first pages are a description of the village. Unlike the text which I have just quoted, these pages sound a, perhaps inevitable, sentimental note. Federico adopts a literary pose and produces a vision which, despite small falsifications, reveals some of the now distant sensations and feelings that touched his soul most deeply in childhood. One cannot help but notice the precocious awakening of a social awareness borne out by other childhood anecdotes.

The poet would surely have wished these pages to remain hidden. At the risk of betraying him, I shall publish them now, for in the clumsy strokes of his pen one can catch a glimpse of the poet he was to become. On the first page of these fragments, almost touching the top of the page, is the title "My Village":*

When I was a child I lived in a very quiet, very fragrant little village in the Vega of Granada. Everything that happened there and all its sentiment

*Probably written in 1917.—*Tr.*

come back to me now, veiled by a longing for childhood and by time. Through another temperament, I want to express all that passed through my mind, and describe the distant modulations of my other heart. All this is pure sentiment and the vague reminiscence of my crystalline soul. . . . In this village I first daydreamed about distant things. In this village I will be earth and flowers. . . . Its streets, its people, its customs, its poetry, and its iniquity are the scaffolding where my childhood ideas once took shape and then melted in the crucible of puberty.

This is no simple evocation of the past; it is the poet's attempt to recover his soul as a child, to describe, as he puts it, "the distant modulations of my other heart." Such an attempt in itself makes this early text a valuable one. In it we can hear the note of originality (in the literal sense of the word) that would later become a hallmark of one vein of Federico's art.

Here is how, in the first section, succumbing at times to literary mannerism, our writer describes Fuente Vaqueros. The fragment is entitled "The Peaceful Village":

The houses are small and white, and are kissed by moisture. The water of the rivers evaporates and covers the village in a cold, morning gauze, with so much silver and nickel that, when the sun comes out, the village looks, from a distance, like a great precious stone. Later, at noon, the mists are scattered and the village seems to slumber upon a blanket of green. The tower of the church is so low that it is barely visible above the houses, and when the bells ring, they seem to ring from the heart of the earth.

The village is surrounded by poplars that laugh and sing and are palaces for birds, and by elders and raspberry bushes that in summer give sweet fruit that is dangerous to pick.

When one draws nearer, there is the aroma of the fennel and wild celery that grow in the irrigation canals, kissing the water. In the summer, there is the smell of straw, and at night, with the moon and the stars and the roses in full bloom, all this blends into a divine perfume that makes us think of the spirit that formed it. On such nights the girls sigh and think of the eyes that will be the light of their lives. On such nights the men feel more deeply the bloody bass strings of a guitar. . . .

In the winter the poplars have no voice, and the village smells of pent-up water and of the straw that is burnt in the houses.

The village is formed by a huge square bordered by benches and poplar trees and dark, scary little alleyways which winter fills with phantoms and goblins. The square is a long one, and to one side is the church with its frieze of bird nests and wasp nests. At the door is a wooden cross with a lamp covered by cobwebs and overgrown with laurels and vines. Crowning the façade is the *Virgin of Childbirth*, her child in her arms, damaged by dampness and laden with medals and exvotos. . . .

Across from the church is the house where I was born. It is large and heavy and majestic in its old age. . . . Its windows have bars that can be rung like bells. When I was a boy my little friends and I used to strike them with a piece of metal, and the sound made us wildly happy. We used to pretend to sound the alarm for fire, or toll the bells for deaths and baptisms. . . . Inside, the house is cold and low. From its balconies the school girls used to recite poetry and sing songs when Our Lady of Beautiful Love passed by, and I was the king, with a flare in my hand. . . .

A sense of childish power awakens in Federico as he evokes his early youth. No doubt this was due to the economic well-being of my father, a farmer who had become rich (at least in comparison to the rest of the village) and also to the social prestige of the family, most of whose branches had succeeded in enlarging their modest patrimonies. Since its arrival in Fuente Vaqueros, our family had been a mixture of working-class people and small landowners. Their economic means were complemented by education, far superior to that of other country people, and by intelligence. For generations many of our relatives and ancestors had served as town clerks in the surrounding villages. Although it was badly paid, this was the one profession open to country people who could read and write but had no formal studies. We had but little knowledge of our ancestors. I believe that our family has always avoided speaking about the dead, despite the love which our parents' generation showed toward theirs in the allusions or comments made in the normal course of family conversations. Uneventful lives in a humdrum atmosphere somehow gave rise to strong personalities that are still proverbial in the village. If Federico himself had not written his plays and poems, he would simply be one of the more remarkable members of our generation, like his cousins Enrique, Clotilde or Aurelia, Elena or Salvador, all of whom possessed unusual wit or imagination or intelligence or individuality.

In discussing our family origins I can, with the help of my Aunt Isabel, go back as far as our great-grandparents, who were the first of our family to settle in Fuente Vaqueros. They came from Santa Fe, where my great-grandfather, Antonio García, was related to certain wealthy old families. In my father's day, we had not yet lost touch with them. I remember that they called my father "cousin," and that he used to refer to them as Cousin So-and-So Carrillo, or Rosales. We were then living in Granada, and these families no longer had a better social position than ours. My father had a deep sense of family loyalty, which extended even to distant relatives who were not very well-off or downright poor. He did what he could for them, and addressed them as relatives: Cousin Eduardo, Cousin Juan, etc. My father was entirely lacking in class prejudice, and perhaps this was only natural. He himself came from a rather humble economic background and had spent most of his life in a village, where he had both poor and rich relatives. He felt neither reverence for the powerful nor superiority toward the needy. I have never seen anyone so spontaneously and utterly devoid of social prejudice as he was. With his merry eyes, rustic countenance, and natural, straight-forward personality, there was something truly noble about him.

His father, Antonio, of whom we were speaking, went to Fuente Vaqueros as a town clerk. He was still a young man, but I believe he had already married Josefa Rodríguez [1831]. All we knew about Josefa was that she was beautiful and had blonde hair: our family still speaks of "the blonde grandmother," which is how my aunt and uncle used to refer to her. Music was an important part of my great-grandfather Antonio's home. He was a fine guitarist and taught his children to play that instrument. He liked to accompany them as they sang, especially his two oldest grandsons, Federico (my father) and Francisco (my uncle). Apparently, he loved to play *fiorituras* and ornaments making it nearly impossible for the children to sing, and my aunts remember my father's words of annoyance as a child: "Play it straight and don't get fancy."

My great-grandfather had two brothers, and one of them was Uncle Juan de Dios, who had also settled in Fuente Vaqueros, where he owned a small piece of land. My father used to refer to him, and to the rest of his household, with tender irony. Uncle Juan de Dios played the violin, which was much less common in those days than it is now, and, according to my father, his sense of pitch was so good that the village boys who were not very good guitarists, would stop under his window and serenade him with their instruments deliberately out of tune. He would storm out of the house (he had quite a temper) and shower them with insults. Then he would invite them in, tune their guitars, and offer them wine.

Considering how often this happened, perhaps there was some sort of tacit agreement between him and the young men. But they never seemed to discover the note of irony beneath his fits of anger. One of my older cousins, who has since died, told me the following story which seems scarcely credible: one day Juan de Dios went out walking, and the wind blew off his hat. The hat had a very stiff brim, and it went wheeling away on its own. More than once he failed to catch up with it, and he grew angrier and angrier. Finally the hat came to rest in one of the poplar trees along the promenade. He took out a revolver, fired twice at the hat, and turned away proudly. In the distance, people watched in amazement. I do not know what ever became of the members of his family. I was too young to know them personally. I do know that one of Juan de Dios' granddaughters, Luisa, was extraordinarily good at improvising verses. I am also told that, especially at lunchtime, Juan de Dios and his children used to argue heatedly over the strangest, most futile topics: the precise length of a "moment" in its minimum and maximum dimensions; and over tiny factual questions: whether or not the woodcock has feathers of a certain color on its neck. I remember things like this because they seemed so amusing to the rest of the family, but I lack important information regarding other family members. About my grandfather, for example, who was greatly loved by his children, I have hardly any information at all.

Grandfather Enrique* inherited the post of town clerk and to his own small ownings in the Soto de Roma he added the more abundant lands of his wife, grandmother Isabel. Enrique was the only one of my great-grandfather's four sons who could, and did, found a family, and it was a very happy one. Unlike his brothers, who were odd, non-conformist types, he either did not feel, or suppressed, any desire to leave Fuente Vaqueros or to live a more adventurous life. He was a family man, who had benefited from the interest taken by my great-grandfather Antonio in the education of his children. They had all been educated at home. None ever attended school, although grandfather Enrique, like his brothers, had read widely by village standards and had been tutored by his father in the law. My Aunt Isabel, who can be trusted on such matters, tells me that her father Enrique was such a good consultant that he was known even beyond the Vega of Granada. He also transmitted to his children a love of music.

According to his children, he was quite liberal in politics. He was a

*Enrique García Rodríguez, 1834-1892.—*Tr.*

fervent Catholic who went to Mass every Sunday and probably confessed at least once a year. He was president of the Brotherhood of the Souls in Purgatory, a cult that is widespread in Andalusia, perhaps the cult most deeply rooted in the people. Almost anyone who has entered a Spanish village church has seen roughly sculpted images or crudely executed paintings of naked bodies up to their waists in flames. Such vivid renderings of the suffering of the souls in Purgatory have always appealed to Spanish taste. The cult of the souls in Purgatory was the only one our nanny Dolores could really believe in. This tendency to give plastic, human form to religious sentiment is probably responsible for certain images in my brother's verse, as when he writes, in one of his most elaborate poems, "The Martyrdom of Saint Eulalia":

. . . Mil arbolillos de sangre	. . . A thousand little trees of blood
le cubren toda la espalda	cover her whole back,
y oponen húmedos troncos	and their wet trunks resist
al bisturí de las llamas.	the scalpel of the flames.

As president of the Brotherhood, grandfather Enrique used to organize and attend the parties and benefits at which money and food were collected for the poor. The parties used to end with dancing, and one girl, chosen from among the prettiest in the village, would give an embrace to the highest bidder. They say that some of these embraces fetched very high prices indeed, and that sometimes the lovely girls bestowed them distastefully on unwelcome suitors. The dance was held in a space closed off with benches brought from the church. As a permanent sign of his devotion, grandfather Enrique purchased a silver crown for the Christ of Victory—a crown still in use—to replace the old brass one.

My grandfather Enrique had three brothers, Federico, Baldomero and Narciso. I cannot imagine where those three names came from. Even the name "Federico," which was transmitted to my father and brother, was felt to be strange by my brother. In a certain poem of *Songs* he says:

Entre los juncos y la baja tarde,	Amid the reeds and the low afternoon,
¡qué raro que me llame Federico!	how strange that my name is Federico!

My great-uncle Federico was the oldest and most respected of the four brothers. He seems to have been a determined person, the most handsome and most gentlemanly of his siblings. The family's traditional love of music appeared in him with great strength. He earned a living playing and writing music for the bandurria in Málaga, where he finally settled down. He was such a skilled musician that when he was a soldier in Granada he was invited to play for Queen Isabel II. He gave bandurria concerts in the famous Café de Chinitas in Málaga, and his brothers came from the village to hear him. Aunt Isabel tells me that the Café de Chinitas, known throughout Andalusia as a flamenco café was not exclusively dedicated to flamenco, as is popularly believed, but offered many sorts of entertainment, including concerts by instrumentalists and even *bel canto*. The clientele was equally varied.

The presence of this musician, Federico, in suggestive, attractive, joyful Málaga, so different in character from melancholy Granada, was probably what made my father and his brothers feel so close to that city. On one of his trips to Málaga my uncle Francisco met a young woman from there and married her. In the following generation, Federico's and mine, we continued to feel great affection for Málaga, partly because of our lasting friendship with the poets Emilio Prados and Manuel Altolaguirre.*

Our love of Málaga and the new friends we made there had nothing to do with that forgotten family tradition. Perhaps our only link with the past was the fact that it had been my uncle Francisco who first taught Federico the song "El Café de Chinitas," which my brother and La Argentinita** later made so popular:

En el Café de Chinitas	In the Café de Chinitas
dijo Paquiro a su hermano:	Paquiro said to his brother,
soy más valiente que tú,	"I am braver than you,
más torero y más gitano.	more of a bullfighter, more of a Gypsy."
En el Café de Chinitas	In the Café de Chinitas
dijo Paquiro a Frascuelo:	Paquiro said to Frascuelo,
soy más valiente que tú,	"I am braver than you,
más gitano y más torero.	more of a Gypsy, more of a bullfighter."

*Prados (1899-1962) and Altolaguirre (1905-1959), both of whom were born in Málaga and died in exile, ran a small press and published the first edition of Federico's *Songs* (1927).—*Tr.*

**The professional name of the Spanish singer Encarnación López Júlvez, with whom García Lorca recorded "El Café de Chinitas" and other popular songs.—*Tr.*

Sacó Paquiro el reló	Paquiro took out his watch
y dijo de esta manera:	and spoke these words:
Este toro ha de morir	"This bull must die
antes de las cuatro y media.	by four-thirty."
Al dar las cuatro en la torre,	When it struck four in the tower
se salieron del Café,	they left the Café,
y era Paquiro en la calle	and in the street Paquiro
un torero de cartel.	was a first-class bullfighter.

Great-uncle Federico made one of his rare trips to Fuente Vaqueros in 1873, the year of the proclamation of the First Republic. These were restless times, and my uncle wanted to watch over the family. His brother Enrique, the town clerk, might easily have gotten involved in political problems. For one or two uneasy nights, my uncle did not leave his brother's side. Nothing happened and when all was calm, Federico left the village. My grandfather felt such affection for his brother that he named his first child (my father) Federico. My father gave that name to his oldest son, so at last it became customary in our family.

One of Federico's biographers writes (and perhaps it is true) that my great-uncle is buried in Paris in the Père Lachaise Cemetery, and that my father, on a trip he made from Fuente Vaqueros to Paris and Brussels to visit the Paris Exhibition of 1900, visited his grave. I think the story comes from my brother, though I cannot remember hearing about the cemetery. Around the house were some souvenirs from that trip: a multicolored fan which emerged from a huge key of reddish cardboard, with imitation rust spots, and some photographic reproductions, on brilliant sepia-colored paper, one of which, much to our delight, depicted the Manneken Pis of Brussels. From time to time my father would look at these mementos and tell us about the trip and the displays that he had found most interesting and exotic. He told us how much he had been interested in the exhibit of agricultural machinery. Years later [1934], Federico was to evoke that memory in a newspaper interview subtitled "Bravant Plows and His First Artistic Wonder"*:

It was around 1906. My homeland, a land of farmers, had always been tilled by those old wooden plows that could barely scratch the surface. That year, some of the plowmen had gotten brand-new Bravant plows (the name

---

*For the complete text see C. Maurer, tr., *Deep Song and Other Prose* (New York: New Directions, 1980), pp. 132-35.

22

sticks in my memory), which had won a prize at the Paris Exhibition of 1900. I was a curious little boy, and I followed that vigorous plow of ours all over the fields. I liked seeing how the huge steel plowshare could open incisions in the earth and draw forth roots instead of blood. On one occasion the plow hit something solid and stopped. The shiny steel blade had turned up a Roman mosaic on which was inscribed . . . I can't remember, but for some reason I think of the shepherds Daphnis and Chloë. So the first artistic wonder I ever felt was connected with earth.

The story of my father's visit to Paris and the introduction of the new farm implements form the basis of Federico's partially fantastical statement to the press. It was, in fact, a few years after the Paris Exhibition that the Bravant plows appeared in Spain. My brother was remembering their inauguration on our farm in Daimuz. But it is not true that our lands were once combed by wooden plows (with metal plowshares): these were only used on tiny parcels. What were used were the so-called turnplows. At any rate, the powerful Bravant plows, which were pulled by several pairs of mules (for tractors did not yet exist, at least not in the Vega), went deep enough to collide with the foundations of ancient buildings on our lands in Daimuz. That is what I deduce from what my father told me when I was a small child. Federico, who was four years older than I and had a remarkable memory, could very well have recalled all this more vividly.

Nevertheless, I do not believe what he says about the discovery of a Roman mosaic. If that really had happened, I would surely have heard about it. It is true, on the other hand, that on estates not very far from ours—Daragoleja, for example—they had found Roman ruins, including important mosaics which were studied at the time by scholars from Granada. I remember some small, unpainted vases, found in the fields at Daimuz, that we kept in our house in Granada, in the bedroom Federico and I shared. What matters in Federico's remarks is not the accuracy of the story, for it is half invented, but the historical tradition of those lands, and Federico's awareness of it. To this he added his own fanciful grain of salt, producing one of those half-truths or embroidered truths that have so often led his biographers astray.*

*Lorca's most recent biographer believes that the incident Federico tells about did, in fact, occur. Not only thousands of Roman coins, but also a large number of mosaics have been found beneath the fertile earth of Daimuz. (Ian Gibson, *Federico García Lorca. I. De Fuente Vaqueros a Nueva York (1898-1929)*, (Barcelona: Grijalbo, 1984), p. 51.) —*Tr.*

UNCLE BALDOMERO: MINSTREL AND POET

Another of Enrique's remarkable brothers was Baldomero. The family did not like to talk about him, but he was difficult to ignore. Federico and I knew him personally. And though our parents never objected to Federico's literary career (a subject about which much nonsense has been written), I have always thought that when Federico showed signs of unusual musical talent and, later, an inclination for poetry, my parents always remembered the somewhat unattractive figure of Baldomero García.

According to my Aunt Isabel, Baldomero had been stricken by paralysis as a child, and, as a result, one of his legs (the right one, I think) was shorter and half crippled. He wore an orthopedic boot with a very thick sole, and it is with vague feelings of strangeness, tenderness, and anguish that I remember that boot, his clumsy gait, the delicate voice he had as a man, and the cleanly poverty of his dress.

He was an exceptionally gifted musician, who played many different instruments, especially the bandurria and the guitar, and he was famous for his fine musical taste and the perfect pitch of his singing. His repertory included several sorts of *cante jondo*, especially *javeras*.* One of the few times my mother spoke to me of him, she said, "He sang like a

*The *javera* or *jabera* is a variety of flamenco sung in ⅜ time with an instrumental introduction.—*Tr.*

seraph." He was something like a village minstrel, and his love of music was matched by a talent for making up songs (both words and music) which circulated among the people. This is what Federico refers to in his speech to the people of Fuente Vaqueros when he says, "Many of the songs that you have sung were composed by an old poet from my own family."

Baldomero—a Bohemian with a biting, sarcastic wit and a nasty temper—composed much light verse, including an imaginary trial before a judge of Fuente Vaqueros, in which the minstrel demands that one of the village women pay him what she owes him for having sung at a family party. The song is written in the free, easy style of the ballad, and has some of the bantering humor we find so often in the age-old genre of court trials set to verse in colloquial Spanish. Using a false name, the poet describes himself as a professional minstrel. Bringing out his physical defects, he has a laugh at his own expense:

> . . . Bernardo Gómez Rueda
> está de los dos pies zambo,
> pero en cambio tiene buenas
> la cabeza y ambas manos,
> porque, como dice el vulgo,
> no tiene pelo de ganso.
> Es su carácter festivo,
> pero el pobre vive aislado,
> con motivos para estar
> más triste que un camposanto.

> . . . Sabe tocar y cantar
> por lo fino y por lo basto:
> y en los bailes y reuniones
> donde con gusto es llamado
> —porque su gusto es dar gusto
> con sus toques y sus cantos,
> a todos los concurrentes
> muy satisfechos dejando—,
> va siempre, y con eso ayuda
> a su sustento diario.*

* . . . Bernardo Gómez Rueda / stands on two crooked feet, / but there is nothing

The defendant in the trial is a one-eyed woman, and the poet cannot help but laugh at a lawsuit between a lame plaintiff and a one-eyed defendant. There are stretches of lively dialogue. This is how his opponent is portrayed:

> El actor guardó silencio,
> y Juana, sin detenerse,
> pero con voz no muy clara,
> como el que en sus dichos miente,
> contestó abriendo y cerrando
> su ojo tuerto, sucio y verde.*

It seems to me that, for a popular ballad, the fragments which I have quoted show wit, skill, attention to detail, and even, despite the tone of crude realism, a certain feeling for nuance.

Baldomero García also attempted serious, elevated poetry, striking the religious and moral note that was common in the nineteenth century. In fact, near the close of the century he published a little book whose title page reads: *Everlastings. A Little Collection of Religious and Moral Poems*, by Baldomero García Rodríguez, Granada, published by the Loyalty Press, 1892. The title, subtitle, name of the printshop, and year of publication demand that we not judge too harshly. It would be easy to criticize this modest little book, published, like so many others of the same style, in an obscure, provincial printshop. More than the book, what interests us is the historical fact, the strange existence of this minstrel-poet of Fuente Vaqueros, Federico's great-uncle.

Poetry in the village had its highs and its lows. Baldomero was not the only poet, although he was the only native one. There was a school-teacher in Fuente Vaqueros who had written a *Geographical Description*

---

*The actor fell silent, / and Juana, without delay, / in a voice that was not very clear, / like the voice of one who lies, / answered, opening and closing / her crooked, dirty green eye.

---

wrong / with his head or his hands, / for, as the expression goes, / he hasn't a silly hair on his head. / He has a merry disposition, / but the poor man lives all alone, / with good reason to be / sadder than a cemetery.

. . . He knows how to play and sing / in style both vulgar and refined, / and he goes to dances and parties, / where people are pleased to invite him / —for his pleasure is to give pleasure / with his playing and his songs, / leaving everyone present / very satisfied— / and this helps him / earn his daily bread.

of Granada and Its Province, wholly in verse. But Public Opinion, in the figure of Frasquito, the most eloquent and expressive of our uncles, decided that the book was not poetry. He would often recite entire stanzas from that interminable geographical-poetical composition, bringing out all their humor:

> Al lado está Sierra Elvira
> escarpada al que la mira,
> con baño termal al pie.
> Muchos aseguran que
> su suelo es volcanizado,
> y que una vez inflamado
> produce sacudimientos
> y terremotos violentos
> que amenazan al poblado.*

When my uncle recited these lines, he would ignore the enjambment of line four (*"muchos aseguran que"*), in order to rhyme it grotesquely with the preceding one (*"con baño termal al pie"*).

We were too young to know the poet-geographer. My uncle told us of him when we were children. The only reason I mention him is to point out that, although my cousins and I were much amused, and were capable of "literary appreciation," this sort of humor left Federico completely cold. Federico would have been interested in the author as a man (he was, apparently, a pompous, empty person who was hard on his pupils), but my brother was quite incapable of appreciating such intellectual play, for which he was little gifted.

On the other hand, Federico liked to repeat, over and over, expressions he had happened to hear which symbolized a situation, a state of mind, or a personal way of speaking. Once, when the family was at a spa in Lanjarón, in the province of Granada, Federico and I were sharing a room that opened onto a courtyard. From there we could hear the voice of the owner's wife, who was always scolding the maids. After one angry outburst we peeked out our window just as the owner's wife was indignantly leaving the courtyard. The maid, who was hanging out clothes,

---

*Beside her is the Sierra Elvira, / which slopes down to the beholder, / a thermal spa at her foot. / Many people say that / it is on volcanic soil, / and that, when active, / it produces tremors / and violent earthquakes / which threaten the populace.

lifted her eyes to the window and carefully said, with a long suffering air, *"Nus tiene jarticas"* ("She has us all a bit fed up"). Never did anyone so greatly appreciate the implied solidarity of a plural and the emotional charge of a diminutive: a lesson in style that Federico learned for his theater. Of course, the best examples of such popular locutions cannot be reproduced. In them we find the most successful adverbial phrases and futures of probability in the Spanish tongue.

I know from family tradition that Uncle Baldomero was a man who fell in love very easily and that, given his physical appearance, this often led to disappointments, recorded in his music and poetry. It is said in the village that, when not so young, the poet was jilted by one of his fiancées, who left him for a handsome young man. In a burst of indiscretion Baldomero wrote verses alluding to what had happened, and, though no grave accusations were made, the girl's reputation was slightly blemished. I can still remember the joyous tone of the melody and the first lines of the lyrics. I also remember singing the song without realizing it was a true story, and this shows that it had become popular and went on being sung after the historical facts had been forgotten.

Uncle Baldomero had a singular gift for disdain. It is said that on a certain memorable occasion Fuente Vaqueros received a visit from the famous *cantaor* Juan Breva, then an idol. He sang in the casino. Baldomero, who probably thought himself a much better singer than Breva, did not deign to attend. He was probably the only villager of note who was absent. Apropos of this, one of our uncles—I am not sure whether it was Francisco or Enrique—told Federico and me of a conversation with Breva. The singer (who had been elaborating on the false and fleeting nature of success) said that for him everything came to an end with an oil lamp and a blanket on the floor. Tidy vision of death! Those who know Federico's poetry will remember the "Flamenco Vignette" in his book *Poem of Deep Song*, where he glosses Breva's words:

. . . Quise llegar a donde	. . . I tried to arrive
llegaron los buenos,	where the best people did.
¡Y he llegado, Dios mío! . . .	And I have arrived, o Lord! . . .
Pero luego,	But then,
un velón y una manta	an oil lamp and blanket
en el suelo.	on the floor.
Limoncito amarillo,	Little yellow lemon,
limonero.	lemon tree.

Echad los limoncitos	Throw the little lemons
al viento.	to the wind.
Ya lo sabéis! . . . Porque luego,	Now you know! . . . But then,
luego,	then,
un velón y una manta	an oil lamp and a blanket
en el suelo.	on the floor.

It is curious that in his *Poem of Deep Song* Federico devotes special attention to only two great old singers whom he did not know: Silverio Franconetti and Juan Breva, each of whom is evoked in a "vignette." He may have read a description of Juan Breva, but one can see that he must also have had direct information about him from my uncles. The poems clearly show the different ways he learned of the two singers. When he speaks of the more remote Silverio, he says:

Entre italiano	Between the Italian
y flamenco,	and the Gypsy style,
¿cómo cantaría	how must he have sung,
aquel Silverio?	that Silverio?
La densa miel de Italia	The dense honey of Italy
con el limón nuestro,	and our own lemon
iba en el hondo llanto	were in the deep wail
del siguiriyero.	of the chanter of *siguiriyas*.
Su grito fue terrible . . .	His cry was terrible . . .

When he speaks of Juan Breva, the poet shows he has firmer information:

Juan Breva tenía	Juan Breva had
cuerpo de gigante	the body of a giant,
y voz de niña.	and the voice of a girl.
Nada como su trino . . .	Nothing like his trill . . .

That line, "and the voice of a girl," is too precise, too graphic not to be the echo of something Federico had heard by word of mouth. Among the *cantaores* one finds the husky, torn, dramatic voice that seems to be required for chants where pathos predominates. But one also finds those pure, transparent, more subtle voices that make Federico say, referring to Juan Breva,

. . . Era la misma	. . . It was pain
pena cantando	itself singing
detrás de una sonrisa.	behind a smile.

Don Antonio Chacón (the one *cantaor* known as "Don") also sang in a delicate voice, and this was probably the school to which Baldomero, "the seraph," belonged. These two schools would correspond, in bullfighting, to those of Seville and Ronda, as represented by Joselito and Belmonte.* Forced to choose, Federico would have preferred the more heart-rending and dramatic style. Rather than the chant of his great-uncle Baldomero, he would have been attracted to the terrible cry of Silverio, which, our poet said, "used to open up the mercury of the mirrors."

I remember Baldomero's delicate voice from the only encounter I ever had with him. Sometimes, when summer was over and the harvest was done, we would return to Granada in a mule-drawn cart. I would always ride in the front with the driver and, if the two mules were not too restless, I was allowed to take the reins. It was daybreak and we were near the poplar grove along the Cubillas. I shall never forget the murmur of the trees and birds in the morning cool, and the harmonious jingle of the mules' collars. The animals had been going along at a lively trot, but now came to a halt before the figure of a man who was coming toward us on a neatly bridled burro. My father got down to shake the old man's hand. He was none other than Uncle Baldomero, who had graying, nearly white hair and (so I remember) a finely sculpted head, like that of my father's sister, Aunt Matilde, who had a delicate cameo-like profile. The thick sole of the orthopedic boot made Baldomero's twisted leg very noticeable. In that delicate voice of his he was arguing with my father. My father asked him, at a distance from the carriage, "Why did you come without telling us first? You can see we're on our way back to Granada." I have the feeling, now, that my father's first words were the ones that carried the meaning. Baldomero had wanted to say good-bye forever. He was very old and he was sick. Now he was feeling a little better, and he had not wanted to postpone the visit. The words were ringing in my ears: "Why did you come?" There was both affection and reproach in my father's voice. Baldomero's was thankful ("What would become of me without all

---

*For Federico's thoughts on the style of Juan Belmonte (1892-1962), see *Deep Song*, p. 58. Belmonte's manner was more innovative and emotional than that of his rival Joselito (José Gómez Ortega, 1895-1920).—*Tr.*

of you?") and apologetic. I have the feeling that both spoke like wounded men, my father more so than Baldomero. I have since learned that Baldomero died in Santa Fe among strangers, surrounded, by his own choosing, by very poor people, with whom he shared what my father sent him.*

I cannot say how this encounter affected Federico, what he remembered of it, what value he attached to any of these early events, which, rarely spoken of, turned up later in his works. It is possible that something of Baldomero filtered, perhaps only vaguely, into some of the characters in his theater. The figure of the failed poet appears in one of Federico's plays: in *Doña Rosita* there is a schoolteacher (Baldomero too taught school at times) who writes poems in a learned, rhetorical style, and whom I can identify, without any doubt at all, with a real person. But the character in the play stirs the embers of a certain old social rebelliousness. He is the only character in *Doña Rosita*, except for the maid, who voices any direct social criticism, a feature which had nothing to do with the real person on whom he was modelled. Also, the character is lame, unlike the real Don Martín. This is the way Federico describes him: "He carries a crutch, to relieve his shrivelled leg. A noble type with great dignity and an air of definitive sadness."

*Gibson (*Federico García Lorca*, p. 58) has discovered that "Baldomero did not die in Santa Fe but in Granada . . . on November 4, 1911, two years after the García Lorca family moved to the city. He was 71 years old. . . ." He adds that the family was probably unaware that Baldomero was living in Granada.—*Tr.*

GRANDMOTHER ISABEL RODRÍGUEZ

Let us skip from the branch of our paternal grandfather to that of our grandmother. Here the outstanding personality is grandmother herself, Isabel Rodríguez [1834-1898], of whom her children (my father and his brothers and sisters) always spoke with affection and admiration. She was the daughter of well-to-do farmers who owned enough land in the Soto to live very comfortably. One of her daughters was named Isabel (principal informant for these biographical notes). In fact, of her nine children, five named their daughters Isabel. The name might have been used even more, had its proliferation not become so inconvenient: several of those Isabels were living in the same village. I remember that to distinguish between them one had to add the second family name: Isabel Ríos, Isabel Palacios, Isabel Roldán, Isabel Lorca, etc. Because it was never the custom in Fuente Vaqueros to pass on first names, the continued use of "Isabel" shows what affection the family felt for my grandmother.

Grandmother Isabel embodied the liberal spirit which she transmitted to all her children. Federico has remarked that one of his grandfathers—in fact it was a great-grandfather—had been a volunteer in the Carlist wars. This was the father of our grandmother Isabel. His name was Francisco Rodríguez, and while very young he had embraced the cause of Queen Cristina.

The young man enlisted, was taken prisoner by the Carlists and held for seven years. Fourteen years after enlisting, he returned to Fuente Vaqueros. I am not sure what he had been doing during the seven years since he had left prison, but he seems not to have been in touch with the family. A little after he went away, his mother gave birth to a daughter, and this he did not know. On his return to Fuente Vaqueros he entered the village by the Santa Fe road, the most important access road, which passes close to the fountain. Francisco walked down the steps that lead to the fountain, not to slake his thirst, I imagine, but to sample the crystalline coolness remembered by all who are away from the village. It was a way of proving to himself that he had really returned. Around the fountain was a group of girls, and Francisco asked them, not without fear, if So-and-So Rodríguez and his wife were still living in the village, for he had come to see them. A wide-eyed girl answered that they were. "And if you want, I will show you where, for I am their daughter." "Then you are my sister," Francisco answered, and, arm in arm, they left the fountain.

I cannot say whether Federico ever heard this story, which really occurred and is the sort of thing about which ballads were written. I heard it from the old people in the family, after Federico's death. When the Child in *The Shoemaker's Prodigious Wife* (in whom we find so many of the author's childhood memories) offers the Wife "the great sword of my grandfather, the one who went off to war," perhaps Federico did not know that his own great-grandfather, returning from war and imprisonment, had resembled a hero in a ballad, with a recognition scene by the fountain.

The young man settled down, married a woman from the village, and, was by turns a farmer and a schoolteacher. It is said that he did such a fine job of educating his daughter Isabel that an inspector of schools on his way through Fuente Vaqueros offered her a job as a teacher, which she refused.

I have a bit of information that speaks very well for Francisco Rodríguez. In my Aunt Matilde's house was an enormous black notebook that looked like a ledger in which he had written little studies analyzing the character of his pupils. These studies formed a precious gallery of children's portraits, revealing a notable gift for observation and a sharp, penetrating mind. I read the portraits when I was old enough to judge them well, and I remember feeling deep admiration. I found sketches of people still known in the village, and even family portraits, written with objectivity and understanding. In one room of the house, amid abandoned objects like leather sieves, strings of onions, and an old shotgun or two, was my great-grandfather's "huge sword" and a pair of epaulets, the only things left, beside his legend and his portraits, of this Francisco Rodríguez, the namesake of all the other Franciscos in the family, myself included.

Grandmother Isabel had inherited her father's liberal views. She married my grandfather Enrique, and there was probably no one else in Fuente Vaqueros who could have shared so completely his love of literature. She was always the first in her house to read new books, which had to be brought from Granada. In fact, she sometimes made special trips to buy them. No doubt her favorite Spanish poets were the Romantics Zorrilla and Espronceda, especially Zorrilla. Grandmother seems to have preferred *The Rose of Alexandria*, the *Orientals*, and especially *For a Good Judge, a Better Witness*. The latter was an attractive work, ideal for reading aloud. Grandmother Isabel had a gift for reading aloud, one that was rather common in our family: Federico would be the prime example. She liked to read to her children, and they were often joined by neighbors who enjoyed being read to. Not only did she read them the poetry of Zorrilla, the octaves of Espronceda's "Poem to Teresa," the *Rimes* of Bécquer, and the poems of Lamartine (another of her favorite authors), she also read them novels: Dumas and especially Victor Hugo, for whom she felt great enthusiasm. In her room was a life-size plaster bust of him.

I should add that my grandmother was not the only woman in the village who gave readings. There was another woman, not a member of our family, who, I think, used to imitate my grandmother, and gave readings of novels in installments. My mother used to tell Federico and me, with an ironic smile, how this woman would bring the dialogues to life, pronouncing the characters' names emphatically, just as they sounded in Spanish. Whenever the plot was interrupted by descriptions or moral or psychological reflections, she would skip ahead, saying, "This is rubbish. Just rubbish." I mention this because Federico liked to imitate the scene, embroidering on what my mother had told us.

The household tradition of reading aloud, which increasing literacy (not to mention various mechanical devices) has almost eliminated, was hardly peculiar to Fuente Vaqueros. But the truth is that in my village it survived until quite recently. As late as the 1920s, Don Fernando de los Ríos, whose campaigning took him to every village in the province, was surprised at the villagers' wide knowledge, not only of political authors but also of literature. The custom of readings and group discussions, alive now only among the laborers, was still in existence. I wonder if the memory of my grandmother Isabel, which was not yet completely extinguished, helped prolong that tradition in Fuente Vaqueros. Her admiration for Victor Hugo, who was known as a liberal, was passed on to her children and, I should add, to her grandchildren, myself included. When Hugo died, my father purchased an edition of his complete works. They had a red binding, with gold-tipped pages and numerous color illustrations, some of which I could reproduce even today, so vividly do I remember them. This was one of the books which, along with a deluxe edition of *Don Quijote*, illustrated by Moreno Carbonero, accompanied us whenever we moved from one house to another.

The works of Victor Hugo were among the first books I read, and I believe the same was true of Federico. I am not quite sure how one could trace the impression left on him by Hugo, whom he read as a child and as an adolescent. Hugo's influence may be detected in Federico's first literary compositions and also, perhaps, in a few ambitious early poems. His echo reaches as far as *Book of Poems*.

Federico's familiarity with the characters of Hugo is reflected in the following anecdote. When we were living on the Acera del Darro (the date of our move is easy to remember, for [two years later in 1910] we were able to see Halley's comet from our balcony), we shared the same room. Federico was never able to fall asleep without reading, sometimes for a very long time. But I couldn't fall asleep with the light on, and have never liked to read in bed. This was a daily problem. Finally we agreed that Federico would read on every other night. But Federico made me promise that, before turning out the light, we would recite the following dialogue:

FEDERICO   Pécopin, Pécopin.
ME: Baldour, Baldour.
FEDERICO: Turn off, turn off
ME: the light, the light.

Only then would he put out the light without reading. But even when he was reading, if he saw that I was not completely asleep, he would softly say, "Pécopin, Pécopin," before turning off the light. Sometimes I took this with a grain of salt, and sometimes I answered with an expletive.

I believe that the names of Pecopin and Baldour come from *La*

Légende des siècles. The little anecdote reveals my brother's whimsical character and the way he used to tease people, especially me. But it also shows how spontaneously those two names occurred to him when he wanted to reach a somewhat arbitrary agreement. Perhaps the two characters were illustrated in the pages of that unwieldy edition of Hugo, which was our initiation into literature.

I remember that on the flyleaf of the first volume, on rich paper with a flowery border, there was a sonnet in longhand, written by some member of our family. After a stupendous eulogy of Hugo, who is pictured as a titan, the author complains that his inspiration has been betrayed by the clumsy Spanish of a mediocre translator, whose name, I think, was Labaila.* I cannot identify the author of that sonnet. I had always believed it was my grandfather Enrique, but my Aunt Isabel now tells me that this would have been impossible, given the date the book was purchased.

I can add a few more details regarding my grandmother Isabel. She was less devout than her husband, less of a churchgoer. In fact, she had a certain anticlerical streak, and was decidedly liberal in politics. She was "liberal" in another sense of that very Spanish word: she was generous. If she was as generous as they say, as generous as her grandson Federico, her liberality must have bordered on excess.

Her religiousness, of which she gave so few outward signs, was tinged with fantasy and an attraction for the supernatural. She seems to have had a poetic soul. A skeptic in other matters, she did believe in miracles. My Aunt Isabel tells me that her older sister Enriqueta (one of the nicest, most communicative people I have ever met, a sort of female version of Federico, though more down to earth, almost a mother to my sister Concha) had been paralyzed as a child in one hand, which she had worn for a long time in a bandage. Great-grandmother made a novena (to St. Anthony, I think). She prayed devoutly and on the way home from church she removed the bandages. The girl moved her hand and was cured. I heard the story from the most skeptical of Isabel's children, whose only comment was to raise her eyebrows.

---

*The book has been identified as *Victor Hugo. Obras completas vertidas al castellano por don Jacinto Labaila.* (Valencia: Teraza, Aheria y Compañía editores, 1888). See Eutimio Martín, *Federico García Lorca, heterodoxo y mártir* (Université de Montpellier Paul Valéry: Thèse pour le Doctorat d'Etat, 1984), p. 134. The dialogue recited by Federico and his brother alludes to the "Légende du beau Pécopin et de la belle Bauldour," letter XXI in Hugo's *Le Rhin (Ibid.,* p. 152).—*Tr.*

Another of grandmother's traits, one which Federico inherited, was her extraordinary ability to communicate with others. She seems to have had that certain spark that made people forget themselves and trust in her friendship after only a few moments in her presence. And yet, Federico did not have the physical features of his grandmother, but those of his grandfather Enrique. One special thing about Grandmother Isabel is that she refused to have her picture taken. The source of this physiognomical digression is my aunt Isabel, who tells me that in her parents' family there were two markedly different branches. The same is true, and is easy to observe, in our own house.

These two different groups go back to the two distinct physical types of our grandparents. My grandfather Enrique left his resemblance more forcefully than did his wife on his eldest children. Those who took after Enrique were my father, my uncle Francisco and my aunt Enriqueta: they are all cast from exactly the same mold as Federico and my sister Concha, whom a certain distinguished relative from the city used to call "Doña Enriqueta" as a child. This branch of the family has a more open, more popular, cheerful, instinctive and spontaneous air, and probably a nicer one. The other branch is more refined, reserved, and intellectual and perhaps, in certain cases, more intelligent, for example, my uncle Enrique whom my father probably preferred to any of his other brothers. The physical features of my grandmother Isabel were inherited by my younger sister, according to my aunt Isabel, who cried when she saw her for the first time, and exclaimed, "She has her grandmother's eyes!"

FROM VALDERRUBIO TO FUENTE VAQUEROS:

MY PARENTS' GENERATION

From the marriage of Enrique and Isabel were born nine children,* the eldest of which was my father. All of them married, had children, and lived simultaneously in Fuente Vaqueros. After my parents moved to Granada [1908], we used to return in the summertime, not to Fuente Vaqueros but to the neighboring village of Valderrubio, where my father had bought land. Trips from one village to the other were easy and frequent, and the entire family used to gather at our house on the feast of San Federico. We had more than forty first cousins of all ages, and the family crowd was joined by their spouses, the nannies of the newborn children, and the drivers of carriages and carts. In later years my mother always remembered the celebration with a certain horror, for she also had to reckon with our neighbors in the village, who came en masse to greet my father on his saint's day, not without having sent ahead a couple of roosters—some of them quite gigantic—bottles of anisette or biscuits, and baskets of candied fruits. One of the village tavern owners used to make huge buckets of ice cream and iced drinks from hazelnuts and almonds. Federico and I used to lick our lips as we watched the process. I can remember vividly how Cervera, the tavern owner, a small, very thin

*Federico, Francisco, Matilde, Luis, Francisca, Enrique, Eloisa, Enriqueta, and Isabel.— *Tr.*

man with a huge mustache, used to uncover the bucket and scrape the frozen liquid off its sides with a clean, well-worn wooden paddle. Federico used to eye the sweets greedily. As a child he was extraordinarily fond of them, a trait he lost in later years. My mother used to keep the preserves under lock and key or hide them in strange places, as she did with the pounds of chocolate to be used at breakfast and the quince jelly that we prepared in enormous batches. The tremulous red jelly, made from the heart of the quince, was usually eaten by Federico, with the servants' connivance, before it reached the table. One had to be especially careful about the sour cherries, preserved in liquor, which Federico pounced on at the homes of all our uncles, aunts, and acquaintances. It was fun to watch him getting the cherries, or the enormous dark grapes, out of their glass jars with a long knitting needle from my mother's sewing kit.

Even in this we were very different. What I liked best was fruit that came straight from the tree, even green fruit. At those family celebrations I ate the candied fruits only after carefully removing their sticky, glazed skins. I liked fruits with stones: plums, peaches, apricots. I cannot remember Federico ever climbing a cherry tree, for example, and filling his pockets and shirt with fresh cherries. The ones I preferred were the least sweet, firmest, and least red, called "kid's-hearts." Federico never once ate a quince or a handful of haws, but he was fond of the sweet melons we used to grow. Speaking of melons, I remember a scene in the house at Valderrubio: Federico was cutting a very ripe, speckled melon, which he distributed like this: a slice (*cala*) for Concha, a little slice (*caleta*) for Isabel, a tiny slice (*calilla*) for me, and a nice hefty one (*calona*) for himself. This was the sort of teasing he often indulged in, and I bore it with patience, though as a child I was known as a hothead.

The stables and corrals were close to the village houses, and this meant flies. One chased them away with a fly whisk made from a long reed, with ribbons of curly tissue paper, dyed red or green. The whisk made a swooshing sound when it was waved, and the sound scared away the flies. We used to shut the windows and doors of the living room until it was quite dark, leaving one of them open a crack, and the flies, attracted to the light and frightened by the whisk, would fly out. When performed properly, this little operation did not leave a single fly. There in the half-light, in wicker or canvas rocking chairs, we would talk or doze away the siesta. The sun would enter through some tiny slit and project on the ceiling the figures that passed by outside: the mule cart that was going down the street, the deformed silhouettes of pedestrians. Federico would get up and move about with the whisk in his hand, entoning a barely audible word. Then the voice would trail off and the whisk would go on "repeating" the word indefinitely. Sometimes the word was the comical diminutive of my first name.* This irritated me, but because the offense was never really articulated, I could hardly get very angry or tattle to our mother.

At the family gatherings I was describing, the young men would often go out riding together. As we were leaving the village, the children in the streets would shout, "A race! A race!" Federico never rode a horse. We already owned the two that did the longest service at our house, a white mare, the tamest animal I can remember, named Jardinera [Gardener], and another more spirited, black one named Sanguijuela [Leech]. More than once, Federico has evoked the figure of my father on a white horse: it was Jardinera.

My father did his best to curb my love of riding and keep me from getting hurt. He tried to make Federico ride, but to no avail. Once in the corral, while my mother stood by smiling and Concha and I laughing, he managed to get Federico seated on Jardinera. The animal stood completely motionless. I should explain that Federico inherited, to an exaggerated degree, the sedentary tendency of my father. In my father's case it was compensated for by his vocation and profession as a farmer.

My family's enthusiasm for music was passed on to my parents' generation. My grandfather taught all his children to play the guitar. But without a doubt it was the youngest, Luis, who showed the greatest gift for music. Even as a child of seven or eight he could play difficult compositions on a fife with glass keys which his father had bought him. This prompted one of our rich relatives in Santa Fe, Teresa Rosales, to give little Luis one of her three pianos. Every week a music teacher would come to Fuente Vaqueros from Santa Fe to give him lessons. Uncle Luis enjoyed music until his death, and not only did he play, like Federico, with extraordinary charm, he also had rapid, well-trained fingers. I remember a neighbor going by the window of the room where my uncle was playing some of his improvisations. "How well Don Luis plays!" she said, "And how fast he can go!"

Many years later, when we were living in Granada, my father bought a piano for Federico from Matilde Rosales, the sister of Teresa. It was an

*"Paquiteta," the author writes in an earlier draft.—Tr.

40

upright, and Uncle Luis tried it out. This was the first piano Federico ever had. Several years later, my father bought him the best piano available in Granada, an excellent baby grand which we still have, and for which Federico felt great affection. It bears the trademark of López and Griffo, Barcelona, a company long extinct. We noticed later that the piano had been built in Germany; perhaps only the case had been made in Spain.

Following the family tradition, which my mother seconded even more enthusiastically than my father (he was content to supply the wherewithal), my father got all of us to study the piano. Our first music teacher was Don Eduardo Orense, organist at the cathedral and pianist at the Casino, a pious man who looked like a priest. I remember the first day our mother took us to his house to arrange the lessons. Don Eduardo used to test his pupils' pitch by asking them to sing something for him. I sang a rather spicy song from the *zarzuela,** The Little White Cat,* drawing a benevolent smile from the teacher and a blush from my mother. I stopped taking lessons when I grew bored with solfeggio, and so, later, did Isabel. But Federico and Concha, the two who were most alike, went on with their piano playing. Despite his clumsiness at other things, Federico's fingerwork was extremely good. But all of this occurred later, when we were living in Granada and our country childhood had become citified.

I do not know how the family hierarchy was organized at our grand-parents' house. I can say, from what I myself have observed, that my father was a sort of *pater familias* whom all eight siblings and their spouses implicitly recognized as their indisputable leader—not in a servile way, but with great brotherly affection. My father was their advisor, and there is probably not one of his siblings who did not receive protection and help—in some cases vitally needed help—from the pater-nalistic eldest brother. In praise of my father, I could recount numerous cases of self-sacrifice in times of difficulty. My father had a Roman idea of authority, which he never abused, and which grew out of his love for them. Such family togetherness was not all that rare in Spain in those days, nor is it now. What was, and is, remarkable is that such a large family recognized one visible head. And this was true not only of those who had an angelical disposition, like Uncle Luis, but also of those who had independent, willful, strong personalities, like Uncle Francisco.

*A form of Spanish operetta developed in the seventeenth century and revived in the nineteenth.—*Tr.*

Federico was probably conscious from a very early age of belonging to the most respected and most prosperous branch of the family. So, probably, was I, though I hardly gave it a thought. But Federico, from the time he was a little boy, felt the weight of his socially privileged position. Of this there is written proof.

The eldest son of Don Federico, or Uncle Federico, was undoubtedly the object of a thousand attentions in the neighborhood, the school, and the family. Federico was the first to break free of this situation, and though he never really clashed with my father, he did not understand this family solidarity, one of whose external signs I have already mentioned: the summer celebration of my father's saint's day. My father would have liked our cousins to be our best friends. Federico was very fond of them, it is true, for almost all of them were charming. But his affections went beyond the family. My father, who applied the word "cousin" to people we did not even know, and, when they were not close enough to be considered cousins, used to call them relatives ("our relative Ricardo," "our relative Leiva . . ."), would lecture Federico about family togetherness, to no avail. This would be easy to misunderstand: by nature Federico was a very affectionate person.

My grandparents Enrique and Isabel lived on the income from his work and from the lands she inherited. My Uncle Luis, who was physically and spiritually delicate, and was capable of religious emotion, studied for a career in the church, but abandoned it after a few years because of ill health. My Uncle Francisco, or Frasquito, as we used to call him, helped my father with the farmwork. My Uncle Enrique was a town clerk in neighboring villages, and I think that he also made a living as a tenant farmer. My father's first wife was a lady from a nearby town. She brought land with her when she married into our family, and upon her death it was bequeathed to my father. He used to keep a portrait of Doña Matilde Palacios* (for that was her name) in our house, and Federico has described the curiosity, tinged with anguish, he felt whenever he looked at the picture of that kind-looking woman, who could have been his mother.

---

*Federico García Rodríguez married Matilde Palacios Ríos in 1880. She died in 1894. Asked in 1928 about his childhood, Federico remarked, "My father was a widower when he married my mother. My childhood is an obsession with certain silver place settings and with portraits of the woman 'who might have been my mother,' Matilde de Palacios. My childhood is learning to read and learning music from my mother, and being the richest and bossiest kid in the village." Arturo del Hoyo, ed., F. Garcia Lorca, *Obras completas* (Madrid: Aguilar, 1980), vol. II, p. 969.—*Tr.*

It was then (my mother was probably already a schoolteacher in the village) that my father, who was known as a good man and an excellent farmer, undertook the purchase of a farm. I am referring to Daimuz, which I have already mentioned. It had abundant irrigated land, excellent drylands, and spacious poplar groves along the Cubillas River. It was a family operation. Even today those lands provide the principal income of our extensive family. My father, who had the most money, kept the largest part of the farm for himself, and also some magnificent irrigated lands a bit further away on the Zujaira plain. This tract was smaller, and we still own it. It was at Zujaira that Federico wrote and signed the compositions that went into his *Book of Poems* and other early works, not all of which have been published.

Before he bought Daimuz, my father had a farm manager named Pastor. My father had been godfather to one of Pastor's sons, so he used to call him Compadre Pastor. My father felt deep affection for him and often praised his honesty, loyalty, and intelligence. My mother always spoke of him with as much love as did my father. And my father liked to tell how, when he bought the farm, Compadre Pastor had advised him: "Let your brothers choose whatever lands they want. You must insist on one thing: even if your lands are the worst, they should all border on each other." And this is what happened, so that the land was worth much more when my father tilled the arid spots and began irrigating them with canals that Pastor himself laid out. He did so with excellent results, ignoring the advice of all the experts my father brought from the city. I never knew Pastor, but Federico did, as is proven by the following anecdote (which also shows what a remarkable memory my brother had).

We were living in Granada on the Acera del Casino, No. 33, and my mother happened to mention Compadre Pastor. Federico asserted that he remembered him perfectly and recalled his death very vividly. My mother smiled and told him that this was impossible: "You were so little that I was still carrying you around in my arms." But Federico described the room in full detail, where the coffin had been placed, the people present, and even their remarks. My mother interrupted him. She was amazed and also, I think, a bit frightened. "Quiet, child! What a memory God has given you!" Perhaps Federico was a little older than my mother had thought,* but now, while going through his papers, I have found,

*Federico was seven years old at the death of this family friend, whose real name was Salvador Cobos Rueda (Gibson, *Federico García Lorca*, pp. 55-57). The prose piece was probably written in 1917.—*Tr.*

among the earliest ones, a few pages of childhood memories, with a little sketch of Compadre Pastor. Federico seems older. The poet is remembering his friendship with Pastor, and Pastor's final illness and death.

The kitchen was full of wood smoke and cigaret smoke, and because of the flames the figures cast fearful shadows. . . . I was dozing, caressed by my Compadre Pastor, and half asleep I heard a voice saying "All of you, keep quiet!" and then one of his sons took me in his arms to where my mother was and she pressed me against her bosom and covered me with kisses. Every night the same thing happened, and often my mother did not let me go into the kitchen. But when she was not looking, or had fallen asleep, I used to run to the kitchen and go to sleep in the arms of my Compadre Pastor. . . . And then one day, it was not to be. He was very old and had a high fever. . . . My parents were alarmed, and I feared for his life. . . . The doctor said he was very sick, and would not get over that illness. . . . And then my father sent for all the doctors in the surrounding villages, but all said the same thing. I went to visit him because he asked for me. . . . He looked as though he were dead, with his mouth half-open and his eyes closed. When I entered, he opened them, and when he saw me he smiled sweetly, the way he used to. My mother took me in her arms and sat me down on the bed. He sat up in bed, helped by a niece, and passing his hands over my face he caressed me for a while. And then he kissed my hand and, with a heavy sigh, fell back on the pillows.

In the fragments that follow Federico describes the death of this character. Compadre Pastor became a sort of family legend, for he had helped to make my father's fortune. It was he who had urged him to buy Daimuz, the farm which is such an important part of my earliest childhood memories. This farm had belonged to an aristocratic family of Granada, and no doubt it had been in their hands since the time of the conquest of Granada [1492]. I say this because the property deeds went back without interruption to a remote epoch. They were an archive in themselves. Federico and I often passed the hours looking at these documents, written in a very difficult script, to see how the first names of the title holders had changed over the years. Sometimes they sounded like characters in an old play: Doña Sol, Doña Elvira, Don Lope. There were even more archaic ones, like Doña Mencía. The oldest documents, if they were in fact deeds, were in Arabic. At any rate, though I suppose it hardly matters, those lands did not come to our family through the disentailment of the nineteenth century, when the reactionary Spanish bourgeoisie bought for pennies the choice lands taken away from the Church by liberal governments.

Federico spent the first years of his life in Fuente Vaqueros on the street where we were both born. Later we moved to Church Street, slightly closer to the center of the town. The only heat we had in that simple village house came from the fireplace and from the charcoal brasiers, no match for the harsh winters. I remember the cold and dampness of my clothes, due to the nearness of the water. I can still remember the temporary "ponds" formed when the lands were flooded to drown the weeds and the larvae of insects. I can see the seasonal passage of the wood ducks, the flight of the little snow birds, and remember the pleasure of breaking the film of ice that covered the puddles, pools, and carriage ruts. When I was older and could ride a horse, I remember the pleasant sound of the hooves breaking through the ice. The same sensation of cold and of playing with the ice was in Federico's mind when he wrote about his childhood games.

Given our difference in age [four years], I can barely remember Federico back then, but I have been able to collect lore about his earliest childhood. He must already have had something of that rare charisma that so many people witnessed in him when he was older. My mother told me that Federico was so popular as a child that she often had to let him eat at the houses of relatives and neighbors. And this seems an early indication of his independence from family norms.

Although he learned to speak at a very early age, in him music came before words. He could carry a tune unusually well even before he could speak. And this does not surprise me in the least, for the same was true of my daughter Isabel: she could repeat whatever was sung to her long before she could speak.

People have often spoken with great exaggeration of the physical clumsiness of Federico's movements. Certain biographical sketches depict him as slightly lame. The truth is that when he was older he had a very personal way of getting around, best described in his own words: *"¡Oh, mis torpes andares!"* ("Oh, my clumsy gait!")* But when he was young one did not even notice that clumsiness: one could only detect it in his reluctance to participate in games that required great physical agility.

*Don Francisco is quoting from "Madrigal de verano" ("Summer Madrigal"), dated "August, 1920 (Vega de Zujaira)" and published in *Book of Poems*, 1921.—*Ed.*

Federico has written of his memories of childhood games, and he does so with no consciousness of any sort of limitation. It came as a surprise to the entire family when, at military age, an examination (performed, we might say, for the purpose of finding physical defects) revealed that one of his legs was several millimeters shorter than the other.

Federico could hardly be called agile, but he never had any difficulty in making trips to the Veleta,* where one had to ride part of the way on a mule and walk for long stretches. When the going got rough, he would simply shout, "Death to mountain climbing!" to the amusement of his fellow hikers. But I believe that these were the only times he ever participated in sports, and I am not surprised that he himself helped to spread the utterly false legend of a necessarily sedentary childhood. On one occasion [1929], when sports had become a sort of literary cult, he declared that he was a good tennis player. The truth is, he never touched a racket in his life. Federico is more of an "author" when he writes autobiography or talks directly about himself than when he is revealing himself in some literary work. And this is why one must correct, or entirely redo, certain profiles of the poet, including some of those drawn by people who knew him well.

A few years ago, an American writer sent me the manuscript of a book about Federico, in which she studied his work through the interpretation of the subconscious meaning of his poetic symbols. She gave great importance, as is usual, to his childhood, and she imagined Federico as a tormented child in a wheelchair, who was unable to speak until he was four years old. The book was ingeniously structured around this supposition. When the woman in question came to see me, I spoke kindly of her work, but felt obliged to tell her that Federico had been a rather precocious child with a happy boyhood, as could be abundantly proven from the testimony of family and friends and even from the poet's own statements. The woman had followed the written account of one of Federico's closest friends and confidants, and she had supposed, with good reason, that the friend could not have invented such things. "It is very possible," I told her, "that the one who invented them, embroidering on a grain of truth, was Federico himself." The woman, who saw her book collapsing, said to me bitterly, "So then, your brother was not a serious person. He was a totally unreliable man." "Totally unreliable," I answered, and that was the end of the conversation.

*At 3,392 meters, the Veleta is the second highest peak in the Sierra Nevada and the third highest in Spain.—Tr.

This might be the right moment to clear up some false ideas about Federico's pronunciation, for his voice was never recorded, and here too the truth has been slightly distorted. The poet Jorge Guillén once asked me if Federico pronounced the Spanish *"c"* as a *"th."* Juan Ramón Jiménez has imitated Federico's speech in writing, transcribing it as though he wanted to reproduce the speech of an ignorant gypsy.* Federico might well have spoken that way without ceasing to be the poet he was. But in fact he did *not*. My brother's Spanish was that of the Vega, as spoken by my father, softened by the city Spanish of Granada. I have already mentioned the two branches of the family present in our house, and I suspect that this was also the case in my grandfather's. My Uncle Francisco and my father had a more rural pronunciation than my Uncle Enrique, my Aunt Matilde, or my Aunt Isabel, who is still alive, in case anyone wants to listen to her.** It is a refined sort of speech, without any extreme deformities, and yet very characteristic of Granada.

Federico believed that the forms of popular speech possessed their own legitimacy, and he often employed them in writing. For example, in his poetry he uses the present participle *sonriyendo* (for *sonriendo*), spelled the same way he pronounced it. (I too sometimes pronounce it that way.) He would also write *yerba* instead of *hierba*, and to this, at least, Juan Ramón cannot have objected. It is also true that certain apparent misprints in *Impressions and Landscapes* and *Book of Poems* are really attributable to his Andalusian pronunciation. For example, the diminutive *delantaritos* ("little aprons") is used in Granada: *delantar* instead of *delantal*, a pronunciation one might hear from servants. Federico also tended not to pronounce the diphthongs in words like *gorrión, avión,* etc., considered to have three syllables (Juan Ramón had the same habit, as may be seen from his verse). The same thing occurred with the noun *chirrión* (meaning, in the Vega, a small carriage pulled by a small draft animal), which turned into *chirreón*, which is as markedly trisyllabic as *torreón*. And no doubt Federico gave a more open sound to the vowels in certain words, as is common in Granada, and this is one thing Juan Ramón found strange.

But my brother was perfectly aware of the peculiarities of the Granadan dialect. He would sometimes imitate the speech of Granada, describ-

*The author is referring to a passage in Jiménez' *Olvidos de Granada* (Granada: Biblioteca de Escritores y Temas Granadinos, 1969), p. 48—*Tr.*
**Isabel García Rodríguez died in 1973.—*Tr.*

ing a scene he had witnessed and dwelling on some particularly expressive phrase, drawing it out with all its peculiar sounds and intonations. He never transcribed, never used any dialectic language in his writings, as did Juan Ramón on occasion. And yet he gave literary expressiveness to the tonality of local speech, the timbre and ring of the voices of Granada. His own voice was a middle-sized one, tending towards bass, with less than excellent tonal quality. He was expressive in his speech, with the marked hand movements that are ordinary in Spanish. Ramón Gómez de la Serna used to tell me that the secret of Federico's expressivity was in his hands. When the word came out of his mouth (Ramón said), Federico would take it in his hands, stretch it, modulate it, give it new sounds. He played with the word as though it were an accordion.

Unlike those of so many other writers, his voice was never recorded in the *Archivo de la Palabra*.* Its founder, the philologist Don Tomás Navarro, used to tell me in New York that he could never get Federico to come to a recording session. He added, without resentment, that Federico had made several dates but had not kept them.

---

*An oral archive founded in Madrid, before the Civil War, by the Spanish philologian Tomás Navarro Tomás.—*Tr.*

FEDERICO IN ALMERIA
AND OUR FIRST HOUSE IN GRANADA

Federico was taught to read and write by an excellent public school teacher, Don Antonio Rodríguez Espinosa, of humble social extraction but with reasonably advanced ideas. He was an ardent Republican, a man of integrity, and a champion of progress and the intelligence. He was a liberal, with the anticlerical vein which was then common in such people. He was also proud and physically imposing. In the village he quickly made friends with my father and his brothers, especially with my father, and their friendship was never interrupted. In Don Antonio's final years, after he had retired to a modest little house in Madrid and my father had already died, I remember how the old schoolteacher dwelt with an almost painful gratitude on the small favors that my father had done for him—favors which came easily in a house as well-off as ours. They made several trips together to Madrid, some of them occasioned by Don Antonio's professional problems. Don Antonio used to tell of the tactful way my father had stayed with him in cheap lodgings. To make their meals palatable, they sprinkled them abundantly with vinegar: "Even the stew!" Don Antonio would say, laughing. He had a love of letters, especially oratory, and occasionally lifted his pen to praise the beauty of Granada in resonant, well-measured stanzas that sounded much like Zorrilla and somewhat like the Modernist sentimentality of Villaespesa.

I do not believe that any of this had any influence on the later poetic vocation of Federico.

Don Antonio was married to an extremely kind lady of equally proud bearing. She must have been a great beauty when she was young. The couple had admired Federico as a child. When my brother was older and famous, Don Antonio liked to tell, lovingly and enthusiastically, of little things that he had said and done. Federico was very talented at certain subjects, but at others—mathematics for example—he was much worse than the average student. Although he had an excellent memory, my brother was never, not even as a child, a conscientious student. He was quite undisciplined and showed little taste for work. It always surprises me that Don Antonio, who was so careful, such a rationalist with a serious, academic bent and a penchant for useful knowledge and mechanical progress, felt such affection for Federico. But he did.

Later, he was promoted to a teaching post in the city of Almería, and a group of children from Fuente Vaqueros went to that city under Don Antonio's tutelage to prepare for the exams leading to admission to secondary school [1908]. Among them were Salvador, the son of my Uncle Francisco, an accomplished blond-haired child; Enrique, my Uncle Enrique's son, whom Federico would meet many years later in Argentina; and a boy from Valderrubio, Enrique Baena, whom my father called a "relative" and who was probably both the envy and the consolation of my brother. This Enrique had an underdeveloped intelligence and was very dull, without interests of any sort, but he was extremely good at mathematics. He could do the most complicated problems in his head, and he was an antidote to Federico. I believe they got along very well. I remember my brother speaking of him with admiration.

Everyone who was with him during that stay in Almería remembers that Federico received preferential treatment from Doña Mercedes, Don Antonio's wife, who kept him supplied with clandestine sweets. Some remember that, in the midst of those comrades and cousins, some of them older than he, Federico revealed himself to be a nuisance and a practical joker. Cousin Salvador, a sentimental boy who was always falling in love, had conceived a precocious Platonic attachment to a good-looking girl who used to pass regularly in front of the teacher's house. It seems that the girl, who was rather short, wore very high heels. Federico nicknamed her "The High Heeler," and this is how she was referred to by the entire group. The prudent Salvador did what he could to hide his irritation.

Federico's stay in Almería was not a long one. He developed a gum infection with very high fevers. Notified by Don Antonio, my father went to bring him home. I remember Federico, his face still swollen, sitting pensively at the window of the house in Valderrubio or practicing some easy chords on my Aunt Isabel's guitar.

It would be difficult to say, in the absence of any indication by Federico himself, how he was influenced by the memory of Almería. In fact, the city is named only once in his poetic geography, in the *Gypsy Ballads*. There the word Almería evokes the "rigid distances" so characteristic of its landscape. But in the same book, in the ballad of "Tamar and Amnon," the arid, calcined landscape, the light that falls on the earth like a cautery, the moonlit terraces, the walls and watchtowers, the Alcazaba in the background, the dawn warm with the murmurs of grapeleaves and fish, sea, and vines, seem to bear the imprint of that city. Because I am convinced that the poet's creations always start out from a reality he himself had experienced, we can suppose that the ballad's background is Almería. That setting is associated, on his lyrical map, with memories of violence, such as the event which gives rise to *Blood Wedding*.

The purpose of the trip to Almería was for Don Antonio to prepare Federico for his secondary school entrance exam. Federico took the exam later in Granada when we had moved from Valderrubio to the house my father rented in the city, at Acera del Darro, No. 66. It was a very large house with three stories, a colonnaded courtyard, and a garden. We lived there for several years, perhaps for the whole time that Federico was in secondary school. My sister Isabel was born there. The rest of us were born in Fuente Vaqueros.

My Aunt Isabel, my father's only unmarried sibling, came to live with us. She was a model companion for my mother, and they felt like sisters. She was tall and slender, very much a García. She played the guitar and sang extraordinarily well in a delicate voice. I shall never forget the melancholy *habaneras* she sang. We would hear them again in Fuente Vaqueros, sung by our older cousins, especially Aurelia, who had enormous dreamy eyes and accompanied herself on the guitar. These songs probably impressed Federico too. Much later they reappear in his theater, where their languid sentimentalism is blent with an ironic lyricism. I remember a certain stanza of the *habanera* "*Tú*" ("You"):

La palma,	The noble palm
que en el bosque se mece gentil,	that sways in the grove

tu sueño arrulló,	lulled you to sleep,
y un beso de la brisa	and the kiss of the breeze
al morir la tarde	when the afternoon was dying
te despertó.	awakened you.
Dulce es la caña,	Sugar cane is sweet,
pero más lo es tu voz,	but sweeter still is your voice,
que la amargura	which rids the heart
quita del corazón.	of bitterness.
Y al contemplarte	And when I behold you,
suspira mi laúd,	my lyre sighs
bendiciéndote, hermosa sin par,	and blesses you, peerless beauty,
porque Cuba eres tú.	for Cuba . . . is you.

When Federico made his trip to La Habana [1930], he was to meet the author of this *habanera*, which he had heard as a child. It is by the Cuban composer Eduardo Sánchez de Fuentes, the uncle of the poet Eugenio Florit. We still have a copy, effusively dedicated to Federico by the composer. Langorous world of moonlit balconies, this world of the *habanera*:

Yo le pregunté a la luna	I asked the moon
qué era lo que tú pensabas	what you were thinking about
cuando de noche, tan triste,	at night, when sadly
a tu balcón te asomabas.	you came out on the balcony.

Florid visions, where one sometimes hears the cooing of a dove:

Un camino te haré;	I will make you a path
de azucenas y nardos,	and adorn it with
jazmines y rosas,	lilies and spikenards,
te lo adornaré . . .	jasmine and roses . . .

Federico raises all this to real poetic tension in the ten-lined strophes at the end of the first act of *Doña Rosita the Spinster*. Here are a few lines reminiscent of the *habaneras* I have been quoting:

. . . rompes con tu cruel ausencia	You break, with your cruel absence,
las cuerdas de mi laúd . . .	the strings of my lyre . . .

| Una noche adormilada | A night which slumbered |
| en mi balcón de jazmines . . . | on my balcony of jasmine . . . |

. . . jazminero desangrado,	A bloodless jasmine vine
por las piedras enredado,	twined among the stones
impedirá tu camino,	will block your path,
y nardos en remolino	and my roof will be wild
pondrán loco mi tejado.	with swirling spikenards.

There may very well be other such reminiscences in *Doña Rosita*; these are enough to prove the musical presence of America.

Among those we occupied in Granada, the house on the Acera del Darro is the one Federico remembered best, perhaps because those adolescent years left such a deep impression on his work. But there was no break with country life. It was kept alive through the continual visits of relatives who came to Granada to shop or to visit and stayed at our house. It was a form of living contact with Fuente Vaqueros, enhanced by frequent visits from the farmers who came to ask for my father's advice, and sometimes his help or influence, in their business matters.

I kept a garden, and raised pigeons on the topmost floor in a room that opened onto the flat rooftop and also in a corner of the little stable at the back of the garden. One of the garden walls was completely covered by an enormous lemon tree. Sheltered from the wind, it flowered and gave fruit. It was a shady garden, with a grapevine covering a finely paved area where there was a little water jet. In the center of the garden was a splendid magnolia tree. On the back wall geraniums grew, and in the flowerbeds there were blue and white violets and everlastings. On another wall was a red rambler rose and an enormous honeysuckle vine. In the cool lower rooms and spacious pantry were the fruits friends and relatives used to bring us from the country: big round watermelons from the Soto, quinces, and apples. My father was very fond of fruit trees, and used to plant them everywhere, even along the sides of the roads, where they often fell prey to the village children, much to the frustration of Federico, their self-appointed guardian. My father contented himself with the fruit they brought us.

The memory of the syringas and other flowers in the garden reminds me of the altars that Federico used to set up on the top floor in a room next to our bedroom which had a wall of glass panes overlooking the garden. The image on the altar was a small, relatively modern but delicate Virgin which my mother always kept in her bedroom. There were roses from the garden, and small white flowers called *varicas de San José*.* But the dominant whiteness and fragrance came from the syringas. Old bedspreads or white lace curtains covered the altar, flanked by high wooden pedestals with flower pots, which my mother always loved. I have told on another occasion of the ceremonies and prayers which Federico directed, with our sisters, the maids, and myself for an audience.** He gave fire-and-brimstone sermons and others about the Passion of Christ. Federico demanded an instant emotional response from his listeners, and this was generously granted him, especially by the maids and by a distant cousin of my mother who practically lived at our house and did the sewing. My mother used to say that Eduarda Miranda Lorca (for that was her name) had once been extraordinarily beautiful. Then a widow, with a rather unfortunate life, she had an only daughter who went mad and died young. Eduarda was a woman of distinction and humility. She had a great heart but was not very intelligent. I doubt she left much of a trace in Federico's memory, unless it was to contribute to his compassionate understanding of the well-kempt and well-hidden poverty that, together with suffering and patience, fills people's eyes with shadows of melancholy and resignation. I am thinking of a certain female character in *Doña Rosita the Spinster*.

For the eight or nine years that we lived on the Acera del Darro, we had maids from all parts of the Vega, and to them my brother was greatly indebted (he has said so in his writings).† It was from them that he learned the songs and ballads of Spanish folklore. None meant as much to him as Dolores, nicknamed "The Goldfinch" in her native village, Láchar.

Dolores came to our house as my wet nurse when my parents were still living in Fuente Vaqueros. Her husband had died shortly before she gave

---

*"Rods of St. Joseph" (*varica* being the popular Andalusian diminutive of *vara*).—*Tr.*
**In the prologue to *Three Tragedies*, p. 3.—*Tr.*
†In his lecture "On Lullabies," García Lorca writes: "For a long time now these wet nurses, maids, and other domestic servants have been doing the important job of carrying the ballad, the song, and the story into the houses of aristocrats and the bourgeoisie. Rich children know of Gerineldo, Don Bernardo, Tamar, and the Lovers of Teruel [characters in ballads] thanks to the admirable wet nurses and domestics who descend from the mountains or from far up the river to give us our first lesson in Spanish history and brand our flesh with the harsh Iberian motto: 'Alone you are; alone you will live.'" See *Deep Song*, p. 11.—*Ed.*

birth to a stillborn child. She remained part of the household until, after many years, when we were already grown up, she went to live with a married daughter. Even then, Dolores had one foot in our house and the other in that of her daughter. She remained agile until she was very old, always helping in whatever way she could.

I always remember Dolores dressed in black, a color which was hardly suited to her cheerful character. Her language was very picturesque, and some of her expressions reappeared in Federico's work. All the maids in his theater bear a vague resemblance to this real character, and the maid in *Doña Rosita* is almost identical to her. Dolores' devotion to the four of us was extreme. She was ready to obey our every wish. There was no fair, parade, circus, procession, or other spectacle to which she was unwilling to take us, and she would conspire with us to obtain parental permission. Dolores often referred to us, especially to me, with the possessive pronoun usually used only by mothers: "My Paco," she would say, and often this would annoy my mother. Without really wanting to, Dolores created a certain rivalry with our parents for our affection. I am sure that, if she had had the economic means, she would have tried to satisfy our every whim.

Generous with her affection, which she bestowed on anyone in need of it, she was also very emotional. She had an innate yearning for social justice, which derived from an elemental Christian feeling. This trait appears in the maid in *Doña Rosita*, who is the character that, as I have said, best recreates the sort of person Dolores was. I wonder whether her kindness was not hereditary: her father used to be called "The Blessed Padre" in his village. And yet her goodness was not meek and religious; it was outspoken and independent. A spry, cheerful, chatty figure, the nickname they had given her fit her perfectly: the Goldfinch. We hardly ever called her that, but when we did she rather liked it. She had a certain natural morality, and was far from severe when it came to sexual transgressions. This is another trait Federico reproduces in his theater: exaggeratedly so in the Old Pagan Woman of *Yerma*, and more discreetly in the maid of *Doña Rosita the Spinster*.

Dolores was totally illiterate. My mother had made several attempts to teach her to read, without the slightest success. She believed herself quite incapable of it. Therefore, Dolores meant fresh contact with the spontaneous, popular values my brother enjoyed. When Federico spoke of the educational role of maids, and how they put city children in touch with the poetry, songs, stories, ballads, sayings, and other living expressions of the countryside, he was thinking principally of Dolores. She taught me many riddles, including a few spicy ones, and lots of tongue twisters, some of them equally indelicate. Federico puts a riddle and a tongue twister in the mouth of the maid in *Doña Rosita.*

Dolores was a resolute woman who did not let herself be "enslaved" (that was how she always put it). In Granada my sister Concha used to attend a lycée for girls which was run by nuns, most of them French. I think the directress was called by her last name: Sister Garnier, a disciplinarian with a sour face. I knew her because in the same school I used to take private French lessons, from a timid and very kind-hearted little nun. Federico was never interested in these extracurricular activities, though my mother tried very hard to make us learn French, a subject taught inadequately in our regular classes. Perhaps this is the place to say (for whatever literary importance it may hold) that although Federico was able to read French, he could not even say "good afternoon" in that language, nor in any other foreign tongue.

To return to our story, one day Dolores went to pick up my sister and found her shut up in a cubbyhole under the stairway. She was being punished for some supposed infraction during recess. When the child came out into the presence of Dolores and Sister Garnier, she was nearly hysterical. The nun demanded that before she went home Concha should kneel down and beg her pardon. Dolores' reaction was predictable. She threatened to cut off Sister Garnier's head if the girl so much as tried to kneel down. I doubt that the directress understood all that Dolores then said to her (at least I *hope* she didn't): "*I'll* show you how we deal with French principals!" My mother must have deplored the whole situation, though she seems to have approved of Dolores' intentions (the child had not done anything wrong). But it was a long time before my sister went back to that school, which my mother herself had attended as a girl, and where she had made some beautiful pieces of embroidery. We still have one framed specimen (I think the framing was Federico's idea): a little needlepoint sampler of Saint Vincent, lettered "Made by Vicenta Lorca." My brother has revealed his tender love of embroidery in different ways.

Federico liked to dress the maids in disguise and have them perform little shows. I remember the theatrical "happening" surrounding the Granada premiere of a play by Villaespesa entitled *The Palace of Pearls.* I can remember one of our maids, Julia la de Gabia, reciting, half in earnest and half inventing the lines, the Modernist verses of Villaespesa. She had learned a few popular passages, including the one dedicated to the fountains of Granada and the monologue "Does anyone know love?" The maid recited them in a very strong accent (from the Vega) and imitated the gestures of the great actress María Guerrero. Federico had decked her out in "oriental" splendor. She was very dark, and he had whitened her face with rice powder. The poor woman was too simple to know how funny she looked as an actress, but, with a cruelty that is sometimes typical of children, we relished every detail.

Perhaps that was the night that Federico dressed up Dolores in another costume. Adding the finishing touch—an old, broken, open umbrella—my brother told her, "I dare you to go like that to the door of the theater." Dolores was not to be dared. Her only reply was to walk all the way to the door of the Cervantes Theater, where, to prove it, she bought a paper cone of peanuts from a woman who kept a little stand that was open on the nights of performances. Dolores just missed arriving at the hour when the theater let out. Even so, it was the most brightly lit, crowded place one could imagine, and this is why Federico had dared her to go. My mother reprimanded Dolores for having accepted the dare. The man at the theater door might easily have taken her for an escaped lunatic.

Dolores was rather forgetful, and sometimes made my mother very angry. Once, when my mother was away, she forgot (and we children forgot) to give food and water to a canary of which my mother was extremely fond. For a while the bird sang despairingly. The silence of the tiny animal is what led us to discover it had died from starvation. I remember what an impression this made on Federico and on everyone else. We could not reproach Dolores: all of us had forgotten the bird.

THE ACADEMY OF THE SACRED HEART
AND THE INSTITUTE

When we arrived in Granada, my parents began to think about sending Federico and me to school. The one with the most distinguished student clientele was that of the Brothers of Charity, which was conveniently located on the outskirts of the city not far from our house. But we never went there, no doubt because my father disliked the idea of having his children attend a religious school. We were sent instead to the Academy of the Sacred Heart of Jesus, where, despite the name, the director and all the teachers were laymen. And the director, Don Joaquín Alemán, was a relative of my mother.

There were three groups of students: the youngest, which was the group I entered; the secondary school students, who attended the Institute in the morning and the Academy in the afternoon, where the teachers reviewed their lessons and prepped them for their exams (this was the group that Federico entered); and, lastly, the university students, who were called boarders, for they only lived at the Academy, and did not take any classes there. These were the oldest, and there were always a few wayward ones who gave the director problems. It was said that some of them used to drop from the front windows of the Academy to sneak out on their nightly escapades.

The Sacred Heart was on San Jerónimo Street, near the Institute and the University, but far from our house, so that we had to cross the city every day. Federico was more sensitive to the cold than I was, and I remember that sometimes in the winter he would begin to develop chilblains, which were then quite common. I can remember him on his way to school in his corduroy-lined boots, which I myself never bothered to wear. We did not always go together, for our class hours were sometimes different. Federico went to the Institute on his own, but at first I went with Dolores. After dropping me off, she usually went to the market, which was near the Academy. If it was early we used to go to the market first, and I remember watching her with admiration as she bargained over meat, fish, or even minor purchases like garlic and parsley. Federico and I completed our whole secondary school education at the Academy. My brother was four years older than I, a considerable difference at that age, but we were together for much of the time at the Institute and at the Academy of the Sacred Heart (for the program lasted six years). In fact, we studied under some of the same professors, sometimes simultaneously, and had many of the same experiences. Neither of us felt much enthusiasm for school, Federico even less than I.

The Academy was located in one of those big rambling Granada houses that might almost be called manorial. In the hall was an old, toothless janitor who was nearly always in a bad mood and always eating bread. We did not know his name, and when we called him we simply said "Janitor!"

The entrance hall led to a courtyard with granite columns, paved with great slabs of stone. I can still feel the dampness, especially in the lower rooms where my group had its classes. In the courtyard was a splendid basin made of different kinds of marble. It was built into the wall, a typical feature of the architecture of Granada. We had a similar fountain with two water spouts in the courtyard of our house on the Acera del Darro. The theme of the mask with water flowing from its mouth appears in Federico's works.

The city's plumbing system, which was ancient and full of defects, made the water of Granada dangerously unhealthy. Typhoid was endemic. The guidebooks warned tourists, in red letters, not to drink the water of Granada, a city full of the water jets, fountains, basins, and cisterns that appear so often in my brother's works.

Those of us who lived in Granada were practically immune to disease, but not the people who were passing through or living there temporarily. Once or twice each autumn semester classes would be suspended so that we could attend the funeral services of students from provincial villages who had been stricken with typhoid.

Because of this problem, there were stands selling water and itinerant water vendors, as there are in some cities of Africa. These waters came from uncontaminated springs, then still abundant, and they gave rise to the connoisseur who could distinguish one water from another: the "water tasters," Federico once called them.* My father, who was extremely careful about hygiene and who dreaded disease despite his robust health, used to fill a cistern at our house with water from the Avellano, the most famous fountain of Granada, one with a great literary tradition. It was there that Angel Ganivet had founded the so-called Confraternity of the Avellano.**

In the courtyard of the Academy of the Sacred Heart was a four-legged wooden tank lined with brass, into which water was slowly filtered. One drank it from a little porcelain vessel, used by everyone, secured by the handle with a little iron chain. Federico and I each had a collapsible aluminum cup, but never used them. We drank by pressing our mouths against the spigot and, when the filter slowed the passage of the water, sucking as hard as we could. Sometimes there was a line.

Federico was not spared from typhoid. He was about fourteen years old when the disease hit him with a terrible virulence and brought him to the verge of death. The treatment included hot baths, and they installed a huge zinc tub in our bedroom, which I had to leave. I remember the buckets of water coming up from the kitchen, and how my parents tried to hide their anguish, and the get-well present Federico received: a very pretty gold and silver pocket watch. I began to use it and lost it a little later. Federico did not wear a watch, and my own, which was made of two tones of silver, had begun to show its age.

It was typical of my father to give us these gifts when we were recuperating from some illness, however minor. The doctor was at our door every time someone had the slightest ache or pain. When we went to the country, my father was always careful to pack whatever medicines he thought might come in handy. There was no pharmacy in Valderru-

---

*In his short story "History of this Rooster," in which he explains the mythical founding of the literary magazine *gallo* (rooster), the poet writes of his protagonist, Don Alhambro: "Furthermore, he became an excellent water taster; the finest, best-documented water taster in this city of a thousand waters" (*Obras completas*, Vol. I, p. 1152).—*Ed.*

**See p. 104.—*Tr.*

bio, and he never forgot to bring diphtheria vaccine. More than once my father's precautions saved the life of a local child. Perhaps he was especially cautious because one of his sons, Luis, died of an infection when he was only two years old. Luis had been born between Federico and me.

My mother, who was so delicate, confronted sicknesses, especially her own, with incredible fortitude, bordering on stoicism. After giving birth to my sister Isabel she was ill for a long time. The best clinic in Andalusia was in Málaga. It had been founded by a famous local doctor, Don José Gálvez. Private hospitals were then very rare; the word hospital applied exclusively to public institutions that were run through charity and served the poor and thus, Doctor Gálvez's clinic was called the Noble Hospital. And that was where my mother was taken.

We visited her on several occasions. Those train trips (Concha, Federico, and I) were happy ones, for in our desire to see our mother we hardly remembered her illness. We had to pass through the unforgettably picturesque surroundings of Loja, where an incredible number of women with lovely flutelike voices sold their wares: water of incomparable coolness and transparency, and sweet rolls that were locally famous, and with good reason. My father used to get off the train to buy two pretty little jugs of water and a supply of sweet rolls. They were so delicate that, wrapped in white paper, they made a huge bundle but hardly weighed anything at all. They seemed made of air. The operation was repeated in Loja on the trip back. Entering the region of Málaga, the train went through even more beautiful places: the lands of the border ballads—Antequera, Cártama, Alora "the strong-walled"*—amid orange groves. At some stations we would buy limes, which were disappointingly tasteless but fun to eat. They would sell them right on the branch, and there was sometimes a fragrant blossom. When we went through the incredibly beautiful canyon of the Chorro we would press our faces against the train windows. Between one tunnel and another—as though in a lightning flash—we could see the vertical gashes of bluish rock, dissected by the green, cold, motionless water of the river.

On one of these trips, at a station where the train had made a useless stop, a freight train pulled up beside us, carrying baskets of fat, shiny brown acorns that made our mouths water. My father got off the car and

*"Alora, la bien cercada" is the first line of a traditional Spanish ballad. For a translation see Edwin Honig, García Lorca (New York: New Directions, 1963), pp. 25-26.—Tr.

went to look for someone who might sell him some. The whistle blew: our train was about to leave. My father reached up and scooped two big handfuls of acorns from a basket, climbing back onto our train when it was already in motion. He had to pass us the acorns through the window. I have always remembered the incident with distaste, admitting to myself that it was a little act of thievery on my father's part, and it is now time for me to pardon him with a smile.

During my mother's long absence, maternal authority was shared by Aunt Isabel and Dolores. In *Doña Rosita* there is a similar struggle for supremacy between the maid and the mistress of the house, who is Rosita's aunt.

It is probably after she came home from the Noble Hospital that my father bought my mother a pair of exquisite diamond earrings. He used to make such purchases from a local watchmaker with bulging eyes. I can still remember this man in his shop on Mesones Street, designing the setting for a gold coin that hung from my father's watch chain. Federico was always after my father to buy him, from the same store, a gentleman's ring. These were gold rings with dark, smooth stones. My father made a joke of it, and kept putting off the purchase. My parents finally bought him the ring on a trip they made to Madrid. It had a blue stone, and Federico wore it for a long time as a young man. They bought me an excellent camera, and I took a whole battery of photographs, almost all of which, unfortunately, have been lost. But in fact this camera was the source of most of the family photographs that have been published in different books about Federico.

I have digressed from what I was saying about my parents' attitude towards illness. Once she had returned from the hospital, my father was more solicitous than ever of my mother, whom he used to call both by her name Vicenta and, more affectionately, "Niña." The only way he could convince himself that she had fully recuperated was by getting her to go out at night. I can remember the ritual dialogue:

"Are you all right?"

"Yes. I'm all right."

"You mean really? Really really all right?"

My mother would nod, and off they went to the theater, though she often had a fever.

While we were still living on the Acera del Darro, my mother had a mouth infection and had to have her teeth removed. She passed the trial admirably. In order to get it over with, she urged the dentist to do all the extractions at one sitting, but to this he said no. Her first dentures fit her perfectly. My father, on the other hand, had excellent teeth that lasted until he was quite old. When he did need dentures, he went to every dentist in Granada, but none of their dentures ever fit him properly, and they used to turn up in every drawer of the house. He even went to the jail where a famous dentist was imprisoned, and asked him to make him a new set, and these he liked somewhat better. He made one more attempt with a young dentist who later became famous in Granada. Federico accompanied him one day, and while they were in the waiting room my brother began looking at the photographs dedicated to the young dentist by some of the local luminaries. Among them was the pompous effigy of the then archbishop, with the following dedication: "To the imminent odontologist don J.G." No one had ever noticed the spelling mistake, and when word of it began to spread, the portrait was discreetly removed from the waiting room. But this happened much later.

I want to add a few more recollections of the Academy of the Sacred Heart. The huge shady house on San Jerónimo Street was not an attractive place. Federico was both docile and undisciplined, and sometimes a little willful. He never liked the idea of studying subjects which did not interest him, and did not feel the same sort of schoolboy pride that I did. I must admit that neither of us was ever afraid of being reprimanded by our father for getting less than excellent grades. I was more conscientious than Federico, but when the school year was nearly over, and exams were drawing near, and my father saw me busier than usual, he used to call me aside and say, "Listen, I don't care *what* grades you get. If they fail you, too bad for the teacher! So now you know!" My mother was much more concerned than he was about our studies, and would gently draw us from play to our books. How often I heard that refined voice saying, "Federico, study!" The years in high school and grade school were no doubt unhappy ones for Federico, for the subject matter did not interest him, and it was made even less palatable by his teachers. And yet, this experience took permanent hold in his memory and is reflected in his work.

The teachers at the Academy reviewed with us the schoolwork we were doing at the Institute. Their salaries were always very low, and even as a student Federico sensed the drama of these lives, full of economic hardship, capturing them later in his work. These assistants at the Academy usually got along well with the students, who were not very numerous.

The mathematics teacher was a very strange fellow named Benito Campoy, who was always rubbing his bloodshot eyes with a handkerchief. The students spread the rumor that his eyelashes grew inward. He had a job on the city police force: perhaps he was an administrator or helped with the payroll. The fact is that he was a skilled hypnotist, and we used to say, without knowing whether or not it was really true, that the police used him to hypnotize those who had been arrested for minor offenses—pickpockets, for instance—to make them confess. He was an excellent teacher, who treated the students with understanding, and he knew how to hold their attention with anecdotes, pointed allusions, and spicy epigrams. That myopic little man had a true sense of humor, and he was one of the teachers that Federico always remembered with affection. He would often speak in class about gastronomy and about the succulent dishes that his family could afford to eat only once a year. He did a perfect imitation of the noises that different foods make when they are fried, and I can still remember how he reproduced the sounds of a broiling ham. He once told the class how at Christmas they had given him one of the famous Trevélez hams, which, he said, he had hung in the dining room. He, his wife, and his two children stood, one in each corner of the room, gently pushing the ham to and fro. The swaying ham perfumed the room. "You rich boys," he said, "will never understand that."

When the director was loudly reprimanding a student or group of students, his voice carried into the classroom, and Don Benito crossed his hands on his chest and said, with a bow, "What a beautiful voice the director of this accredited amusement arcade has!" When some student did a math problem on the blackboard, Don Benito would call for an ovation of collars, and we would tap our fingers against our starched collars. On one occasion, another teacher was absent, and his class had been combined with Don Benito's. Believing the director to be away, Don Benito suggested we imitate with groans, shouts, and cries the torments of the damned. Imagine the uproar when Don Benito asked, "How do the condemned shout in hell?"! Hearing the noise, the other children poured in, even the smallest, who looked tearful and frightened, along with the director, who used the occasion to try out every register of his well-timbred voice. A few days later Don Joaquín could not keep from smiling as he told about what the mathematics teacher had done.

Another teacher—one who appears under his own name in *Doña Rosita*—was Don Manuel Consuegra, the Latin teacher, who had once studied for the priesthood. A great bullfight enthusiast, he used to applaud students' translations with bullfighting terms like "Ole!, that was a real *pase de pecho*," or an *espantá*, or a *goyetazo*, depending on whether it had been a hit or a miss.

This teacher was a personal friend of the director, more so than the others. He was the only one I ever saw in Don Joaquín's roomy apartment, which was in a house next door to the Academy and communicated with it. Don Joaquín was fond of animals. He had a well-kept dovecote in the tower of the Academy and kept canaries in a sunny little upstairs room. Don Manuel Consuegra was extraordinarily superstitious. One fine winter day Don Manuel, Federico, and I were sitting around a table in that cage-filled room, our feet resting on the charcoal brazier. Knowing Don Manuel's weak point, Federico uttered the dreadful word "snake." At that very moment, one of Don Joaquín's best specimens gave a few agonizing, pitiable shrieks and fell to the floor of its cage, as if struck by lightning. Indignant and frightened, Don Manuel kept repeating to the speechless Federico, "You see, boy? You see?" I have never been able to explain that strange coincidence, but I think it was the source of Federico's peculiar attitude towards superstitions. He said he did not believe in them, but, ironically, he insisted that one ought to respect them. When salt was spilled, Federico picked up a pinch of it and tossed it pompously over his left shoulder. And when somebody spilled wine, he would dab his ear comically with what had been slopped on the tablecloth. Though he did not want to believe it, perhaps the canary incident remained in the back of my brother's mind.

For awhile there was an assistant at the Academy who did not give classes, but was supposed to keep order during recess periods and study hours. His last name was Canito, but they turned it into a first name and called him Don Canito. He was a very young man, well-mannered and good-looking. I think he lived at the Academy. It is said that one afternoon, when the director was out and classes were over, the boarders decided to find out if it was really true that this assistant wore a corset. They bound him to a column in the courtyard, under the bell that signalled the beginning and end of recesses and classes. The story goes that once they had tied him up, they poured water on him from an upstairs window, and rang the bells to lend solemnity to their actions. We heard rumors about all this, and I cannot swear to its truth. It is certain that Canito did not last long at the Academy. The incident is recounted, in less detail, in *Doña Rosita,* where Federico gives theatrical expression to a struggle between students and professors which I, less attentive or less observant, never noticed.

The teacher who made the deepest impression on Federico was the one who was in charge of the literature classes, including one entitled "Literature and Literary Theory." This was Don Martín Sheroff y Aví. We had more contact with Don Martín than with other teachers, and knew him more intimately. He appears in *Doña Rosita* under his own name, although I believe he had many more facets and was a much richer personality than the character in the play. He was lacking the tired, resigned melancholy of his literary counterpart, as well as the consciousness that his life had been a failure. If Don Martín was aware of this, he never complained. The real Don Martín played out his role with a good-natured touch of the grotesque.

He was neat and trim, though his suit was shiny with wear, and he always dressed in navy blue, with a spotless, very high, celluloid collar and a black silk cravat. There was a certain elegance in his bearing. He had a wide nose and small, lively eyes, was rather tall, and not in the least stooped with age. He dyed his hair, and it acquired a dubious reddish color that went rather well with his facial features. The red was most noticeable in his abundant mustache. I remember seeing him once in front of the Guevara bookstore, where textbooks were sold. He was on the sidewalk and I was standing in the street. As I looked up at him, the sunlight was bringing out the different colors in his mustache. I couldn't help smiling, and Don Martín, smiling even more broadly, almost laughing asked, "What are you snickering at?" He knew perfectly well what I had seen. I did not answer him.

Don Martín had wanted to be a writer. He was the author of a number of unperformed plays, and sometimes—very rarely, I think—he published poems in the local periodicals. He would write theater reviews whenever an important company came to town. He gave admirable recitations from the literary texts we were studying in class, and he was the professor who best knew how to establish friendly relations with his students. He had no family and lived by himself in a very modest boarding house. Apart from his contributions to the newspapers, he had published a collection of short stories. "Matilde's Birthday" was the title of one of them and the title of the book. He felt true devotion to literature and especially to poetry. All of these features are depicted by

Federico. It is strange that Federico portrays him as being lame. I do not remember any teacher with that defect, and perhaps my brother was influenced, as I said earlier, by the memory of Uncle Baldomero. Don Martín had never studied letters formally. He had a diploma in pharmacy. We found this out when our studies were over and, after the death of its owner, they made him manager of a pharmacy near the University. This sort of arrangement, which paid very well, was often sought after by the widows and orphans of pharmacy owners, who wanted to carry on the business. I think that his name was even painted on a large sign: "Farmacia del Licenciado Don Martín Sheroff." In these situations, the substitute merely lent his name, not his services, to the owners. It surprised us that Don Martín was a pharmacist—it was the last thing we expected of him. But his economic position would improve. And then, as if fate were playing a trick on him by bringing to light what the poet had so incessantly hidden, Don Martín died only a few days after his change in status. I do not know that he ever saw his first payday. In *Doña Rosita* Federico mentions the detail of his being a pharmacist.

One day, walking down the street, perhaps at the door of the theater, Don Martín stopped to greet three young lady friends, shaking hands with each: Amor, Caridad, Clemencia (Love, Charity, Clemency). Even in Andalusia, where women's names are often abstract nouns, the accumulation and simultaneity seemed excessive and truly theatrical. If I had not seen this myself, I would have believed it an invention of Federico, who liked to tell about the incident.

Despite its name, the only religious instruction which the Academy of the Sacred Heart offered its pupils was preparation for First Holy Communion. I know personally how little preparation we were given, and at the Institute the situation was no different, despite the classes in religion given by an old priest. He had only a few students, all of them voluntary. Federico had more religious training than I, for all I remembered was the basic catechism of Father Ripalda, which I studied when I was very young at the school in Valderrubio. Federico had a thorough knowledge of Church ceremonies, knew ritual phrases in Latin, and attended various ceremonies, at least the solemn ones: High Masses at the cathedral, offices for the dead, etc. On one occasion he spoke with emotion about the churches of Granada in Holy Week, when the altars were covered with violet cloths,* and I can still hear him pronouncing

*See "Holy Week in Granada," in *Deep Song and Other Prose*, pp. 54–56.—*Tr.*

the word *tenebrario* with great relish. Literary fragments which he wrote in late adolescence* reveal religious feelings which cannot easily be described: there is mystic longing, immersion in a vague, musical world, pathos, despair, wounded sensibility, pantheism, and poetry. All these are fused into one lofty chord which is still audible in *Book of Poems*.

Federico's studies never gave him the slightest satisfaction that I can record. Despite his talent for drawing, he had to make a huge effort just to train his hand to make regular letters in calligraphy, then a required subject. I remember him complaining, irritatedly, on only one occasion— he had received a mediocre grade in literature. The grades he received were never very good, a humble "Pass" at best. I have said that our father demanded little of us, but on that occasion Federico felt humiliated and claimed to have done very well on his exam.

Because I heard about it from Federico's own lips, I can describe an incident in chemistry class at the Institute. When the teacher asked for the daily lesson, the student would go up to a platform where the teacher's desk and a big blackboard stood. On this occasion, my brother knew nothing of the lesson. The teacher was dictating certain formulas, and Federico was supposed to write them on the board. I am sure that Federico, who had his timid side, must not have liked the idea of exhibiting his ignorance to the class. His mind went blank. The teacher, Don Juan Mir y Peña, was from the Canary Islands, and he had a strange way of pronouncing certain letters. "Write on the board $B_h + B_1$," that is, B sub h plus B sub 1. But Don Juan pronounced "b" as "p." And Federico, who had surely never even opened the textbook, heard only strange meaningless sounds: "peesupaich plus peesup one." Don Juan Mir, irritated by his inaction, shouted, "Write it! Come on, write it! Peesupaich plus peesup one! I am not speaking Chinese!" But it *was* Chinese to poor Federico, who stared, paralyzed, as peesupaiches tumbled from the teacher's angry lips.

Such experiences must have been very unpleasant for my brother, who had to undergo the torment of taking exams on materials he had not studied. He compensated for all this with escapes to the highest parts of the city: the Bola de Oro, the Alhambra, the Albaicín. Our parents were aware of his absences from the Academy, but not of those from the

---

*The author is probably referring to a series of prose pieces entitled *Místicas*, written in 1917 and 1918.—*Tr.*

Institute, for roll was usually taken there by an assistant who was easily outwitted.

At the University he even had the vexation of being expelled from a class. This happened in the economics course taught by Don Ramón Guixé y Mexía, who was the model for the pedantic professor in *Doña Rosita*. He was a tiny little man with a long black beard and a solemn way of speaking. But his voice was high and songlike. As was inevitable, this combination of elements struck my brother as funny on the first day of class. He told me later that he had sat down in the first row and suddenly, with no advance warning, Don Ramón stuck up his hand, formed a circle with his index finger and thumb, and began to shout, "The Polis! The Polis! The Polis!"* Federico had an attack of laughter so violent that the professor invited him to leave the room. That was the end of economics for my brother. He never returned to class, and he suffered the usual academic consequences. But this happened at the Law School.

---

*"The state" in ancient Greek.—*Tr.*

THE UNIVERSITY AND ITS PROFESSORS

After passing a year of preparatory courses common to both Letters and Law [1915-1916], Federico enrolled in the program in Letters. In this school he made the acquaintance of a remarkable professor of art history, Don Martín Domínguez Berrueta, who was to exercise great influence on his life and work. This relationship ended with a break that could not be mended. I do not know how well qualified Don Martín was academically, for I never attended his lectures, and I do not believe that he ever published any scholarly work. It was on this ground that he was attacked by those who were not his friends. Perhaps in those days one would have had to do original research in order to be a good teacher of art history, for there were only scattered studies and no coherent history of art. No one in Spain had ever formed an organic vision of Spanish art comparable to Menéndez y Pelayo's overview of Spanish literature. Only Don Manuel Bartolomé Cossío, the discoverer of El Greco, could have written such a book, but he did not. I do know that Don Martín established a personal, almost familial relationship with his students, whom he entertained at his house (a continuation of his university teaching) with the assistance of his wife, a woman of singular beauty and distinction.

Don Martín used to make art trips with his students, who were then very few. Some of these trips were short, like those he made to the lovely cities of Úbeda and Baeza [1916]. In Baeza, Antonio Machado was teaching French at the Institute, and Federico had his first contact with the great poet. My brother told me they had visited Machado at his home, and when Don Martín, after introducing the students and chatting for awhile, decided to read, in the presence of the author, the "Ballad of Alvargonzález," Machado gently took the book from his hands and read the poem himself. Federico described the scene to us, imitating the great poet's grave, measured voice.

Federico derived such pleasure from these trips (his first contact with the art of cities beyond Granada) that he himself organized new expeditions to Baeza and Úbeda with some of his friends. The object of these non-academic trips was to savor life in those small cities by strolling through their streets, gazing at the landscapes, visiting the casinos, talking with the local friends Federico had already made, and having an occasional brandy. In Baeza the pharmacist had a lovely daughter, and we passed repeatedly under her window to see if she would appear. Federico had described her to us, and later we met her. This girl's vivacious beauty, and that of many others, seemed out of place in Baeza, which we imagined to be entombed in its past. Such a contrast struck a note of feminine frustration that appears later in my brother's theater.

I shall never forget one particular night when we sat by the fountain in the Square of the Cathedral. There was a full moon and a strong wind was playing with the clouds, alternately darkening and illuminating the scene, and hiding or giving a spectral glow to the Cathedral and the Palace of Javalquinto. Someone evoked the figure of San Juan de la Cruz.* Despite the greater beauty and artistic density of Úbeda, we felt an inexplicable preference for the more reserved atmosphere of Baeza.

Don Martín's class made another, more important trip through Castilian lands. Federico's first book, *Impressions and Landscapes* (1918) grew out of these excursions. I seem to recall that some of his "impressions" were published in the local newspapers of the cities visited by the group, as were some of the writings of Federico's brilliant companion Luis Mariscal, who was studying two careers at once, both Law and Letters. I remember this because my brother said, with a certain ironical benevolence, that Mariscal was always using the expression "crepuscular orange," believing it to be a real literary discovery.

I think that Don Martín, a man of fine sensibility, had an accurate idea of Federico's worth, and, overlooking his academic defects, was extremely

*St. John of the Cross was prior of the Carmelite monastery in Baeza, and died in the monastery of Úbeda in 1591.—*Tr.*

fond of him. Federico's artistic personality had already begun to appear, and his communicative vitality and frank, generous enthusiasm were beginning to ripen. Perhaps Don Martín sensed Federico's future possibilities, and he felt a just satisfaction—pride, even—in having contributed to the awakening of his powerful poetic instinct.

A few minor attacks on Don Martín had come from our tertulia* in one of the cafés of Granada. Quite possibly, the journalist in our group, José Mora Guarnido, who has since written a biography of Federico (in which he successfully evokes the poet's youth, though not without a good many small inaccuracies)** wrote an article referring unfavorably to the professor while eulogizing his student. This would have been when Federico published *Impressions and Landscapes*.

Mora was learning the trade of journalism. He was better educated and a better, more ingenious writer than his colleagues in the city. He was ambitious and wanted to draw rapid attention to himself by means of articles (some of them excellent) on national and local politics. In some, he resorted to direct personal attack. Once, with notable injustice, he called a priest who was very active in social groups, was high in the hierarchy of the cathedral, and was a nephew of the archbishop, "a provincial abortion of Caesar Borgia." Later on, this man would become a deputy in the Cortes. He was one of the only priests who remained loyal to the Republic during the Civil War, and I have no doubt that, had he been in Granada at the outbreak of the war, he would have suffered the same fate as my brother.

The publication of Federico's book resulted in his definitive break with Don Martín [1918]. Federico had dedicated it "to my old music teacher" and not, as would have seemed natural, to the art professor to whom a large part of the book was indebted. The essays in *Impressions* show us only the author himself, describing the landscapes, gardens, and monuments, without giving any details about the trip, his professor, or his travelling companions. This greatly displeased Don Martín. The whole family regretted the breaking up of this friendship, for through Federico my family had become friends of the Berruetas. I do not know if my brother, who was always essentially timid, could have done anything to soothe his teacher. I have thought it proper to clarify the episode, for I

*A gathering of friends who meet regularly, usually in a café, to discuss literature, sports, politics, etc.—*Tr.*

**José Mora Guarnido, *Federico García Lorca y su mundo* (Buenos Aires, Losada, 1958). Mora immigrated to South America in the Fall of 1923. His memories of Federico cover the years 1915-1923.—*Tr.*

have been asked about it more than once, and it has never been interpreted correctly.

As long as my brother could study subjects like the history of art or literature or elementary concepts of philosophy, he did fairly well. But failure was inevitable in subjects requiring greater effort and discipline. When he was confronted with Arabic or Hebrew, Federico fled, as was to be expected, without even attempting to study them. He got as far as the final examination in historical grammar, but went down in failure. Mora then published an article in the *Noticiero Granadino* insisting that, failure and all, Federico would bring more days of glory to the Spanish language than all the students who had passed the subject without hardship or distinction, and probably without preparation. Though Mora may have been right, his thesis was academically unsound. The professor in question, Don Eloy Señán, was a respectable, competent, and well-meaning old man who had done his duty in failing Federico. It would not be inaccurate to say that my brother had hardly even glanced at the material—very dry material, to be sure.

Federico's increasing difficulties in the School of Letters and the lack of any serious pressure from his family, resulted in his being a "nominal" student for a few years, and then trying his fortune in the School of Law, where he passed a few easy subjects.* This was a moment of crisis in both the University and the Institute. The subjects were taught either by ancient professors or by their sluggish assistants. I myself, four years younger than Federico, witnessed the almost total renewal of the teaching staff and a general improvement in academic standards, thanks to efficient and conscientious professors. Federico had to confront an almost totally new School of Law when my father demanded that he work towards an academic degree, in return for which my father would continue to pay for his trips to Madrid and his long stays at the Residencia de Estudiantes, where he came into contact with new generations of artists and writers.

To be sure, my brother never had to discontinue these trips, and my father paid for the publication of his first books without ceasing to pressure his son to get a diploma—a diploma "in anything." My father's belief in the importance of a university title was probably shared by all

---

*Gibson (*Federico García Lorca*, p. 302) writes that between 1916 and 1920, Federico passed only one subject, history of law. For the story of both brothers' academic careers, see Jacinto Martín Martín, *Los años de aprendizaje de Federico y Francisco García Lorca* (Ayuntamiento de Granada, 1984).—*Tr.*

fathers back then. Perhaps also, in his case, one can detect the attitude of the well-to-do farmer who wanted his children (and Federico was the eldest) to have the academic degree which neither he nor his brothers had received, though some of them showed more mental ability and were far better educated than are hundreds of university graduates. In a society much more closed than ours, the degree was a means of access to future positions. We were expected to be "career men." My father's insistence had nothing to do with class prejudice, for my sister Isabel also studied, and in the provincial atmosphere of Granada it was rare for a girl "of her class" to attend and graduate from the Institute. She was probably the only daughter of a property owner then attending the Institute. This helps explain my father's attitude towards Federico.

But my father, who was anything but a dreamer, never really expected his son to earn his degree and enter a profession. If he ever *was* laboring under that illusion, Federico rapidly disillusioned him. I have a bad memory and am sorry I cannot recall the date of a conversation I once had with my father. He put such force into what he was saying that the episode made a lasting impression. It was a little before one of Federico's trips to Madrid. My father and I were alone in the study of our house on the Acera del Casino. He said to me, "Look, Paco, your brother insists on going to Madrid, with no other intention than to *be* there. I am allowing him to do so, because I know he is not going to do what I want. He will do whatever *he* wants [my father's way of putting it was somewhat stronger], which is what he has done since the day he was born. He is determined to be a writer. I don't know whether he is talented along those lines, but since that is the only thing he wants to do, I have no choice but to help him. So now you know."

Federico had already taken his first steps in the theater and in poetry and was beginning to be known beyond Granada when he decided to finish his studies in Law [1920]. I have already pointed out that the University was in the process of renewal. The students who were "intellectually-minded" had become good friends with the new professors, some of whom were quite young. The first of these professors, chronologically and otherwise, was Don Fernando de los Ríos. He had always been quite close, for family reasons, to the founders of the Institución Libre de Enseñanza, one of whom was the distinguished Francisco Giner de los Ríos, whose personal influence, direct or indirect, helped to shape

Spanish liberal thought during the last third of the nineteenth century and made an important contribution to the awakening of a new sensibility. Anyone who even begins to study the history of contemporary Spain rapidly encounters the name of Don Francisco. And without going beyond the field of literature, we can mention that the educative influence of Don Francisco contributed to the formation of poets like Juan Ramón Jiménez and Antonio Machado. Unamuno himself was not unaffected by the genius of Don Francisco Giner.

It was Don Fernando who epitomized this new attitude and these new ways of life—including academic life—in Granada. Both inside and outside the University his pedagogic importance was considerable. He established friendly contacts with the students, a new phenomenon in Granada, at least for our generation. His excellent library was open to all of us, and he encouraged us to use it. He made his influence felt in the city's cultural groups. He founded the Granada branch of the Socialist Party, and always represented it in the Cortes. It cannot have been an easy job, but he tried hard to break up the system of bossism that prevailed in the traditional parties then vying arbitrarily for power. Many qualities were needed, including courage, and Fernando possessed them. An exemplary character, if ever there was one, an excellent speaker both in prepared lectures and off the cuff, he gave generously of his rich personality. And yet there was no trace of proselytism in the way he treated us, much less in his university teaching. Don Fernando was an extremely courteous man, which made people want to reciprocate. Even the rank and file of the Socialist Party addressed him as "Don." The workers greeted him by doffing their caps, and he answered them in the same ceremonious manner. Federico always enjoyed seeing (and recounting with his own peculiar sense of humor) how sometimes the driver of an elegant landau, a vehicle becoming quite rare, would lift his braid-trimmed top hat when the professor passed. Don Fernando would lift his own hat in reply, and the passengers inside the carriage, believing they had been greeted, courteously responded. And thus the coachman provided a sort of link, a fleeting one to be sure, between the upper middle class and the reprobate "labor leader."

One need not suppose that Don Fernando had any direct influence on Federico's unarticulated political ideology. Our group was markedly apolitical, for the most part, and spontaneously rejected the discipline of any one party. What all of us favored was a generous, open-minded Left with a social conscience, keenly critical of Spanish society, above all of provincial society. And this was resented in the little world of Granada, which thought of us as "intellectuals," a vaguely poisonous plant.

There is likewise no need, when we seek Federico's inspiration for one of the *Gypsy Ballads*,* to remember the Civil Guard's violent reprisals against Don Fernando's followers in the villages of Granada.** These incidents, which Don Fernando denounced in the Cortes, may have had some role in the origin of that ballad, even though Federico tried to eliminate "anecdote" from the book and raise such experiences to a higher plane through creative poetic transposition.

Another professor who influenced Federico's academic career was Don Agustín Viñuales, an economics professor who had come to Granada to replace Don Ramón Guixé y Mexía. Don Agustín was one of the most authoritative economists in Spain, and served as Minister of Finance under the Republic. Sharp as a hawk, vivacious, rather slight, with a slender profile and a ready smile, he realized that Federico was an exceptional young man. A great friend of Don Fernando, in some ways he was his opposite. He was a modern spirit with a European education, like Don Fernando, and it was so easy to talk to him that, unlike Don Fernando, one easily forgot he was a professor. He was vibrant, elusive, cordial, reluctant to make moral judgments and ready to smile at any weakness. He was more a Dionysian and a cynic than a censor, but one had only to scratch Don Agustín to discover his principles and his noble, elusive spirit; just as, when one scratched Don Fernando one found his capacity for caring and for tenderness, his great robust Spanish soul, shaped by contention.

In 1923 Don Agustín Viñuales decided that Federico was going to earn a law degree. In his first period as a student, Federico had succeeded in passing (I know not how) a few subjects, including some difficult ones like Civil Law. But over half of his coursework remained. Don Agustín took up the "case of Federico" with his colleagues on the faculty. I believe

---

*The author is referring to "The Ballad of the Spanish Civil Guard."—*Tr.*
**Don Fernando's daughter, Laura de los Ríos (the author's wife) remembers Don Fernando's encounters with the Civil Guard (a rural constabulary closely allied with the *caciques*, or local bosses) as "a truly infernal part of my childhood [. . .] My father symbolized the struggle against caciquism, and after the popular revolt against one of these bosses, La Chica, in Granada in 1919, we received threats and anonymous letters." See Antonina Rodrigo's interview, "Laura de los Ríos" in *Triunfo*, Madrid, XXXVI (May, 1982), pp. 66-67.—*Tr.*

that his arguments went someting like this: "The family of this increasingly well-known young poet is demanding that he obtain a degree in
order to facilitate the practice of his true 'career,' that of literature.
The poet's general knowledge is far greater than that of the average student.
The humanistic tradition of our schools of law has always placed more
emphasis on cultural formation than on professional training. Federico is
an exceptional case, and it would be unjust to judge him by purely
academic standards. With the passage of time, the University of Granada
will not only be justified for having given him special treatment, but will
also take pride in it." Such were Don Agustín's arguments. In fairness to
everyone involved, I should add that in those days there was no lack of
the sort of automatic "passes" which allowed my brother to get through
subjects like Canon Law and Civil and Private Law ("Privil and Civate
Law," went the professor's spoonerism).

Don Agustín had no chance of achieving his goal without the active
collaboration of many different professors, for it was unthinkable that
my brother would ever study enough to pass the public, oral examinations which then existed. God knows with what reluctance Federico
enrolled in the University, but he willingly submitted to my tutelage in
studying for the examinations. It was my last year at the University
[1921-1922], and in some courses we took the exams at the same time.

The subject he was to be examined on by Don Agustín Viñuales
offered no difficulty at all. This professor was accustomed to begin the
exam on a subject of the student's choice. In Public Finance I had
prepared Federico on the subject of customs duties. My brother held
forth valiantly on the general part, and withstood a few more specific
little questions on other matters, but soon exhausted his knowledge of
the subject.

The exam was given by a tribunal, presided over by the full professor.
The session went on for several hours, with an audience of students who
came and went, awaiting their turn or figuring out what sort of questions
they might be asked and what sort of mood the tribunal was in. When it
was over, a beadle used to hand each student the little slip of paper on
which the grade was written, duly signed by the secretary of the tribunal.

I must tell of a very Viñualesque incident. Shortly before the emotional
moment when the grade slips were to be handed out, one of the beadles
called for Sr. García Lorca (I too went up to him), and he told my brother
that Professor Viñuales wanted to ask him what grade he thought he

deserved. Federico was a little taken aback, but, thinking that his exam had not gone so badly after all, he answered "High Pass!" And that was the grade he received.

One of the obstacles to Don Agustín's plan was that Federico still had to pass the make-up exam in Constitutional Law, a subject taught by Don Fernando. The ambitious official syllabus for each subject included an historical section demonstrating that the subject matter was as old as Man himself. In Constitutional Law this part concerned Greek political philosophy. The professor knew that Federico was an enthusiastic admirer of Plato's dialogues, which he read in editions borrowed from Don Fernando's own library. (We hardly ever left his house without a book under our arms.) Perhaps Federico had also happened to read, as I did, Machiavelli's *The Prince*. The examination began, I think, with a benevolent conversation about the Platonic dialogues, and then drifted gently towards the myths of antiquity, which Federico knew quite well. In those days, one of my brother's favorite books was a beautifully illustrated edition of the *Theogony* of Hesiod. The examination went so well that the student audience thought it unjust when Federico received the lowest grade: "Pass." I am convinced that nowadays any student showing the general culture and direct knowledge of texts that Federico showed would pass the examination triumphantly. By way of compensation for such severe grading, I should record the fact that, at that particular session, there was not a single "Fail."

The lack of "general culture" on the part of the students was such an obsession with Don Fernando that it became a part of university folklore. The year that I studied Constitutional Law with him, Don Fernando lectured on the Russian constitution, and the students were singing, to a popular tune, the following lyrics:

Entramos en clase,	We go to class,
me siento en un banco;	I sit down on a bench.
"a ver, lea sus notas",	"Let's see, read your notes,"
dice don Fernando . . .	says Don Fernando,
Y yo, ruboroso,	and I, blushing,
con miedo horroroso,	with fear and trembling,
la Constitución	begin to read
de la Nueva Rusia	the constitution
me pongo a leer,	of New Russia.
y un disparatón	A ghastly mistake

ha salido de mis labios sin querer.	has escaped my lips.
Entonces noté	Then I noticed
que Fernando de los Rios	Don Fernando was looking at me.
me miró.	And, as I lack "general culture,"
Como no tengo "cultural general",	the inevitable happened.
pues pasó lo que pasó.	

I am sure that Federico, although he played no part in these innocent jokes, knew this song, as he did another popular one, modelled on the "Response for Verlaine" of Rubén Darío, and which covered much of the university curriculum. Other songs were in circulation, including a very witty one on Penal Law, through which we managed to discover the identity of the two anonymous authors of the one about Constitutional Law. One of them, Antonio Morón, a member of the Back Corner group, died prematurely, after a curious, fleeting literary career in Madrid. In order to give a better idea of the atmosphere of the university in those days, I shall mention that once, when there was a faculty meeting, Don Agustín Viñuales sent the beadle to fetch me and, to my great astonishment, made me sing those songs, which had become very popular, in front of some of the professors to whom they alluded. They enjoyed every bit of it. Out of loyalty to my comrades, I allowed the authors to remain anonymous.

Another of the "obstacles" Federico had to surmount was Penal Law, taught by one of the most competent professors at the University, Don Antonio Mesa Moles, who was another friend of the family. Federico, who was sick of exams and of the whole situation, had decided not to take any more of them. We were in the courtyard of the University, when an unwilling Federico was summoned. Don Antonio Mesa himself came out looking for him, persuaded him to participate, and entered the room with Federico on his arm. After a few preliminary words, the professor asked Federico to give his opinion of the death penalty. I believe there was another question regarding the efficacy of correctional institutions in cases of juvenile delinquency, and how they ought to be organized. This exam, too, went satisfactorily, although I cannot say how Federico managed to defend himself, for I did not enter the room, and only overheard from the doorway.

I need hardly explain how, with my help, Federico managed to pass subjects like Process Law and International Law, subjects then without professors and taught by assistants. Now only Mercantile Law stood between him and the degree, and I had not had time to give him a general idea of what the course was all about. Federico did not show up for the exam, but in life he always had a lucky star (tragically disproven by his death). The professor in question made it known that, because he was to retire that very year, Federico's exam would be the last he would ever give, and he did not want to end his career by giving a "Fail." The deadline having already expired, my brother took the exam at a special session, without an audience. After a few general questions, he was invited to explain the first article of the Mercantile Code, which defines the concept "merchant." The examinee did not have a strictly legal idea of the concept, but he passed [1923]. Federico never again wanted to talk about his studies.

THE BACK CORNER AND THE ARTS CENTER:
THE INVENTION OF AN APOCRYPHAL POET

We young "intellectuals" belonged to a group that met in a café in the Plaza del Campillo. Our tables were located under the stairway that led up to the billiard rooms, and someone named this spot the "Back Corner."* The hours we lost—or perhaps gained—at those meetings cannot easily be calculated. One could go there for a coffee after lunch or an occasional apéritif, but the full meeting was at night, after supper. The history of the Back Corner would be the history of Granada's intellectual class at the time, for no one who was at all distinguished in art or literature failed to attend its meetings, whether as a regular member or an occasional one. In the summer the tables were placed outside in the shade of the huge plane trees that grew in the plaza. The city was vaguely aware of our discordant existence on the fringe of its established societies and institutions.

Earlier, during his student years, Federico had belonged to the Center of Arts and Literature,** whose president was Don Fernando de los Ríos. The painters that belonged to the Arts Center seemed to vacillate between a traditional realism and a tardy impressionism. In any event, it was a center of local culture that took in the entire creative life of

*El Rinconcillo, literally the "Little Corner."—Tr.
**Referred to hereafter as the Arts Center.—Tr.

Granada. It was nothing truly remarkable, but neither was it to be scorned.

I remember when the Center was located on the Street of the Catholic Monarchs, not far from the beautiful Plaza Nueva with its admirable Chancery building and the tiny, graceful church of Santa Ana, which Federico considered a symbol of the art of Granada. Back then, I too sometimes attended the Arts Center. Many different groups came together there: representatives of cultural institutions like the Institute and the University; those associated with the School of Arts and Trades; people with an interest in painting; journalists; and a few young university students who preferred the peaceful atmosphere of the Center to the more open, boisterous one of the Café.

The Trades School kept up a tradition of artistic craftsmanship among the working classes. Good furniture was made in Granada and old furniture was skillfully imitated. The city produced skilled woodcarvers (some of them truly excellent, capable of guiding the chisel with true mastery), workers who could reproduce the Moorish tiles of the Alhambra, sculptors who limited themselves modestly to the reproduction of Tanagra figures, terra cottas, or busts by Donatello. The city maintained (and still maintains) its ceramic factories, its looms, and the workshops that turn out carpets in the style of the Alpujarras.

There was a taste for decorative fabrics at the Center, and, needless to say, Granada's "art industry" produced the typical many-colored striped cloth for curtains. I think that the Center also helped foster small local industry and the cottage trade, as well as embroidery. Granada had a long tradition of embroidery, and my brother speaks of it, with tenderness and irony, in one of his best prose pieces, "Don Alhambro's Rooster,"* where he mentions a famous embroideress, Paquita Raya, who competed favorably against the skilled nuns in the city's convents:

> The nuns in the convent of Santo Domingo kept in a velvet case the two "master" needles of their Baroque school, the two needles with which Sister Golden Sacrament and Sister Silver Visitation had made such virginal marvels. That little case was the vestal icon that inflamed the starchy heart of the novices. It was a permanent elixir of thread and consultation.
>
> Paquita Raya had a more popular, more vibrant art, a Republican art full of open watermelons and apples that hardened on the fabric. An art of exact

*For complete text see *Obras completas*, Vol. I, pp. 1152-1158.—*Tr.*

82

realities and Spanish emotion. There was a great struggle between the two schools. All dark-skinned people were on Paquita's side. All blondes, brunettes, and a tiny group of albinos were in favor of the nuns.

It was my mother (who also did fine needlework) that told us about Paquita Raya. My brother captures the typical embroideress-nun in his ballad of "The Gypsy Nun":

Silencio de cal y mirto.	Silence of lime and myrtle.
Malvas en las hierbas finas.	Mallows in the fine grass.
La monja borda alhelíes	The nun is embroidering strawflowers
sobre una tela pajiza.	on a straw colored cloth.

This richly varied artistic tradition was discreetly present in our own home as well. There were striped curtains in one of the doorways, a little plaster pedestal holding a Tanagra figure, copper kettles and vases (authentic folk art), and a rich rug on the piano. Federico had a youthful spurt of enthusiasm for antiques in the popular style. His only spending money was the allowance my father gave him, and he limited his purchases to a few old ceramic plates and vases. I can also remember a pair of green glass objects which looked like columns and rested on small, heavy, flared bases. A woman known as "la Genoveva," who had an antique store not far from the Arts Center, affirmed that these were Arabic flatirons. Federico's flatirons gave rise to more than a few family jokes.

The manufacture of these "artistic" objects followed the city's changing tastes. When Granada developed a truer sense of "folk art," it did away with that tradition which, at its worst, had filled the houses of the rich with buffets and desks "in the style of the Spanish Renaissance," furniture with feet shaped like lions' paws, chairs whose backs were bicephalous eagles or even imperial shields that nailed themselves cruelly into one's back, chests with wrought-iron adornments and scenes of the Reconquest. There was much black ironwork, much red damask, and even stained-glass windows—that was *true* perfection! It would be unjust to blame all these aberrations on Granada, but to tell the truth the city's artisans were excellently prepared to perpetuate them.

One of the jokes that came out of the Back Corner was the invention of a poet whom we promoted as a representative of the "pseudo-Granadan" tradition. I do not know which of us thought of calling him Isidoro

Capdepón Fernández. The name Capdepón, a Catalonian surname, meant "bridgehead," and to this we added Isidoro, not very common in Granada, but not very rare either, and the more common and well-known Fernández, which made the name seem plausible. This was no onomastic masterpiece, to be sure, but the name sounded slightly ironic, was perfectly acceptable, and could pass for a real one.

No doubt the name influenced the very character of Capdepón's poetry. A different name would have produced a different poet. We sometimes had amusing conversations about names and surnames. I remember a lovely article which the poet José Moreno Villa wrote about nicknames and published in *El Sol*. The best ones, he said, were those Federico had told him about, and most of them were in use in Fuente Vaqueros.

These conversations about names could easily have given rise to other fictitious characters. On one occasion somebody said "The lines converge . . ." and perhaps it was Federico who shouted, "¡*Convergen!*, ¡hombre!, ¡*convergen!* That is the name of a foreign writer; or is he a Nordic composer?" And we tried out different versions: Konberghen, Khonvergen, etc. One of the members of our group has written that the name was mentioned in the local press. I do not remember if this is true. Konverghen's existence was a fleeting one.

Some of these names—the strangest ones—inspired Federico to make little sketches. Once he drew the effigy of the Frenchman Troplong (Too Long), whose name appeared on a law book one of the law students happened to mention. Impressed by the tremendous nasal quality of the last syllable, Federico gave him a nose that was somewhere between an elephant's trunk and a trumpet.

But the poet Capdepón acquired a real existence: he published poems from South America, where he had lived since his early childhood, and when he returned to Granada his trip was mentioned in the local press. Some of the members of the Back Corner, particularly José Mora, a professional journalist, had access to the press, and this made our task easier. Capdepón's fame extended well beyond Granada, and this proved to be his undoing.

It occurred to Capdepón to dedicate a sonnet to the Sevillian poet Don Juan Antonio Cavestany (our symbol of the highest, purest academic inspiration), reminding him of their meeting in Uruguay. I remember the final tercets of this sonnet, which have already been published.

Amigos fuimos en el Uruguay;
lustros pasaron desde entonces, ¡ay!,
que en acíbar trocaron nuestras mieles.

Hoy en Madrid, en tu presencia mudo,
te hago una reverencia y un saludo
frente al carro triunfal de la Cibeles.*

The sonnet was published. Unfortunately, it was published beside another sonnet, no less inspired, in which Cavestany answers Capdepón. A short while later there was a protest from the *real* Cavestany, who publicly declared he did not know Sr. Capdepón and that he had never been in Uruguay. According to Mora, Capdepón's sonnet (he should have said "sonnets;" he forgot about Cavestany's) was published in the newspaper *La Unión Mercantil,* of Málaga. Our Málaga "connection" was probably a young man named Marqués Mechant, who was then studying in Granada and writing his interesting book on the Spanish bibliographer Bartolomé José Gallardo.

Capdepón's dangerous brush with Cavestany was followed by another one in Madrid [1923]. The subtle poet and literary critic Enrique Díez-Canedo, who was familiar with Capdepón's poetry and personality, decided to nominate him for a vacant chair in the Royal Spanish Academy. If I am not mistaken another article to the same effect appeared in the magazine *España.*** It had probably been written by Antonio Espina, an excellent writer. These writers' sense of humor helped them introduce Capdepón to the world of letters in Madrid. He had already become well-known in our province. But Capdepón's growing fame brought about his

*We were friends in Uruguay, but many years have passed since then, and have made our honey as bitter as gall.
Today, in Madrid, in your silent presence, I bow to you and greet you before the triumphal car of Cibeles. [A well-known fountain in the center of Madrid.] The poem was first published by Mora Guarnido, p. 68.—*Tr.*
**Not one but three (!) articles on Capdepón were published in the prestigious weekly. The article signed by the novelist Antonio Espina reports on the "solemn reception" given Capdepón at the Royal Spanish Academy. The apocryphal poet spoke on "Rhetorical Menopause, or The Decadence of Civic Poetry in Today's Spain." See A. Soria Olmedo, "El poeta don Isidoro Capdepón (Historia de una broma de vanguardia)," *Cuadernos Hispanoamericanos,* 402 (December, 1983), pp. 149-152, and Antonina Rodrigo, *Memoria de Granada: Manuel Angeles Oritz, Federico García Lorca* (Madrid: Plaza & Janés, 1984), pp. 109-111.—*Tr.*

downfall, and besides, none of us had any interest in prolonging his life. He had merely been an innocent source of amusement.

There was a certain traditionalist, provincial note in Capdepón's poetry; his trips to South America had not completely converted him to Modernism. Come to think of it, Modernism was no laughing matter back then. We had editions of Rubén Darío, luxuriously bound in white suede, and had not yet abandoned the sad and languid gardens of Juan Ramón Jiménez. And yet, a strain of Modernism *was* detectable in Capdepón's art, as it was—much to their chagrin—in the poetry of many of the local "traditional" poets. Although Capdepón admired Villaespesa, he was neither as sentimental nor as new. The imaginary poet was not really inspired, I have to admit. He was but one more case of poetic mimicry.

In fact, Capdepón was hopelessly addicted to the worst of traditional rhetoric, the sworn enemy of any sort of authentic innovation. Many of his poems were written on café tables, by several hands. I remember one "excellent" sonnet . . . Capdepón is in Guatemala, remembering the Church of Saint Nicholas in Granada:

> En el cerro gentil de la chumbera,
> frente a la ingente mole plateada,
> altiva y colosal Sierra Nevada,
> una iglesia se yergue placentera.
>
> Su santo Nicolás allí venera
> la sublime piedad de mi Granada
> y le van a adorar, santa manada,
> desde el rico que goza, a la cabrera.
>
> ¡Oh, padre Nicolás! Hasta el lejano
> monte de Huatmozín llegan los ecos
> del pensil granadino que te adora:
>
> aquí los oye un español cristiano
> que, rodeado de guatemaltecos,
> piensa, gime, suspira, reza y llora.*

*On the lovely hill where the prickly pear grows, facing the huge, silvery, proud, colossal Sierra Nevada, rises a pleasant church.
There, its Saint Nicholas venerates the sublime piety of my Granada, and the holy flock (from the rich man to the simple goat girl) goes to adore him.
Oh Father Nicholas! The echoes of the Granadan garden [the parishioners] who adore you reach as far as Monte Huatmozín.
They are heard here by a Spanish Christian, who, surrounded by Guatemalans, thinks, sobs, sighs, prays, and cries.

I have published this sonnet because it seems worth saving from oblivion . . . or perhaps because I myself seem to have been one of the chief collaborators! I have devoted so much attention to this poet because, while going through Federico's papers, I have found a surprising number of Capdepón poems in his own handwriting. It is obvious that the poems were not written only by Federico; as I said, they were a group effort. But it is interesting to see Federico take a pencil in his hand and direct the course of the poem. With the manuscripts before me—scraps of paper, really—I can reconstruct the way these poems were created, and identify a few of the revisions made by Federico. A certain stanza which I contributed has been crossed out and another substituted that is certainly no better, but does match the poet's profile more closely. My contributions seem to emphasize the amatory element, and Capdepón was more discreet, more of a married man.

Capdepón shows, at least indirectly, the attitude which the Back Corner group took toward the currents of "official" art: the false classicism that brought public buildings under the spell of the "Renaissance style" I mentioned earlier; or, even worse, the mingling of that "Renaissance" with false Andalusian or Sevillian styles featuring little towers, niches, and fountains full of colorful tiles. Other public buildings succumbed to an analogous style we might call "false Modernism."

My file of Capdepón poems includes a sonnet in Federico's hand, dedicated to one of the architects who epitomized these tendencies. It has the following title: "Sonnet to the Illustrious Palacios, Author of the Portentous Building of the Circle of Fine Arts, Madrid, Which is Miraculously Supported On One Tiny Column." The sonnet reads:

¡Oh, qué bello edificio! ¡Qué portento!
¡Qué grandeza! ¡Qué estilo! ¡Qué armonía!
¡Qué masa de blancura al firmamento
para hacer competencia con el día!

La ciencia con el arte aquí se alía
con tanta perfección, según yo siento,
que en aqueste soneto sólo intento
tras mil enhorabuenas, dar la mía.

En Guatemala existe un edificio
de menor importancia en mi concepto,
y no obstante tuvieron el buen juicio
de nombrar general al arquitecto.

Mas en Madrid yo no he encontrado indicio
de que piensen honrar a tu intelecto.
Ya lo sabes, Palacios, ¡gran patricio!,
que a Babilonia antigua has resurrecto.*

Among these autograph manuscripts is a page-long biography of Capdepón which mentions his most popular work, *Breezes From Guatemala*,
and his inauguration into the Royal Spanish Academy.
Upon returning to Granada, Capdepón sings her beauty in an unfinished poem that goes on for fifteen stanzas:

> . . . Tanto me gustas, Granada,
> tan prendado estoy de ti,
> que yo ya no encuentro nada
> que complazca mi mirada,
> Granada, desque te vi.**

In some of these stanzas, the poet reveals his Modernist side. Granada,
transparent sultan, is beautiful:

> Más que el claror de la luna
> en noche de primavera,
> mucho más que el palor de una
> mano romántica y bruna
> que en mi frente se pusiera.†

Granada has won the admiration of "hundreds of intellectuals from
Spain and abroad":

*Oh, what a beautiful building! What a portent! What greatness! What style! What
harmony! What a mass of whiteness in the firmament, rivalling the day itself.
    Science is allied here with art in such perfection that in this sonnet I shall try only to add
my own congratulations to the thousand [you have already received].
    In Guatemala there is a building much less important, in my opinion, and yet they were
inspired to name the architect a general. But in Madrid I have found no sign that they plan
to honor your intellect.
    You know this, Palacios, great patrician, who have resurrected ancient Babylon.
    **. . . I like you so much, Granada, and am so much in love with you, that, since I saw
you, I find nothing I can look at with pleasure.
    †More [beautiful] than the brightness of the moon on a spring night, much more than
the pallor of a Romantic brown hand touching my forehead.

Aquí se han dado las manos
sobre tu Alhambra de trinos,
como si fueran hermanos,
melancólicos germanos
y bulliciosos latinos.*

But the noble city has fallen from her ancient splendor:

Granada, bella Granada,
emporio de ruiseñores:
hoy gimes abandonada,
la media luna enterrada
de tus príncipes mejores.**

Capdepón made a second and final trip to Granada, and there is proof
of this in another sonnet in Federico's own handwriting:

Heme otra vez. Segunda vez mi frente
recibe los efluvios de Granada,
odalisca que sueña recostada
sobre la falda de la mole ingente.

Pebeteros y aromas del Oriente
envuelven tu belleza nacarada
y el suspiro del ave en la enramada
al compás del sollozo de la fuente.

Deja a este bardo triste y sin ventura
al regresar de su postrer viaje
que en tu suelo reclame sepultura.

Que si en Colombia dejo mi linaje,
yo vuelvo a ti con mi emoción más pura
para morir como un Abencerraje.†

*Here melancholy Germans and noisy Latins have joined hands, as though they were
brothers, over your Alhambra of trills.
**Granada, lovely Granada, emporium of nightingales, today, abandoned, you weep for
the buried half moon of your best princes.
†Here I am again. For the second time my brow receives the exhalations of Granada, an
odalisque which dreams as it reposes on the side of a giant hill.
Incense burners and oriental fragrances envelop your beauty like mother-of-pearl and a
bird on the boughs who sighs to the time of the fountain's weeping.
Allow this sad, hapless bard, returning from his final voyage, to ask for burial in your
soil.
For, although I left my family in Colombia, I return to you with my purest feeling, in
order to die like an Abencerraje. [Moorish noble—Tr.]

Occupying both sides of the envelope of a letter sent to Federico by one of his friends in Madrid, is a fragment of a Capdepón poem about the decadence of art. The postmark on the envelope gives us the date of the poem: September 17, 1928:

¿Dónde están las febrífugas canciones
y los sonetos de pujante brío
que encadenando el estro a su albedrío
arrebataban nuestros corazones?
      ¿En dónde los poetas verdaderos?
¿Adónde la pureza de la lira
donde el alma de amor triste delira
en una apoteosis de luceros?
      En su estertor la lira agonizante
el ambiente llenó de imprecaciones.
Ya no cantan, valientes cual leones,
Lucrecio, Herrera, Campoamor y el Dante.
      Por doquier yace roto el sentimiento,
no queda del pasado apenas nada,
Euterpe se retira avergonzada
y ni el valle recoge su lamento.
      Se acabaron las Musas, los amores,
los artistas, las artes, los poetas,
ya no suenan las épicas trompetas,
el bosque se quedó sin ruiseñores.*

This is the end of Federico's text. But I remember that this poem, which was more ambitious than preceding ones, went on to include all the other arts. I also remember that when Federico came to sculpture he mentioned the name Archipenko:

*Where are the fever-chasing cantos, the sonnets of strength and vigor which, ruling inspiration at their will, swept away our hearts?
Where are the true poets? Where the purity of the lyre [that used to sing of] the very soul of love, delirious and sad in an apotheosis of stars?
In its death rattle, the dying lyre fills the atmosphere with imprecations. No longer do Lucretius, Herrera, Campoamor and Dante sing, as brave as lions.
Sentiment lies all around us in ruins, and hardly anything remains of the past. Euterpe hides away, ashamed, and the valley does not hear her lament.
The Muses are gone, as are the loves, the artists, the arts, the poets. No longer are the epic trumpets heard. The forest is bereft of its nightingales.

. . . And in their place triumphs an Archipenko
who sculpts in such an extravagant way.

. . . Y triunfa en su lugar un Archipenko
que esculpe de manera extravagante.

This is an important bit of information, because it shows at what an early date the Back Corner learned of this Cubist sculptor. I met Archipenko a few years ago in New York, and during our conversation I mentioned a pamphlet with reproductions of his work, published for one of his exhibitions in Germany. When I gave him the titles of some of the works he told me that the catalogue had been published for his first exhibition. He was astonished to think that his name could have been known in a remote Spanish city at such an early date. There is, however, an explanation. One of the members of the Back Corner, José Fernández Montesinos, was then a reader in Spanish at the Iberoamerican Institute, Hamburg. He probably sent us the pamphlet, though we might have gotten it from some other source. In our time, and even before, Granada had always made a respectable contribution to the diplomatic and consular corps. A little later, I myself would enter it.

INTERPRETATION OF GRANADA

The rural surroundings of Federico's childhood, Fuente Vaqueros, in which all his works are rooted, yielded to the marvellous urban setting of Granada. A certain lyrical strain in my brother's work reflects the soul of Granada.

Granada's historical symbolism seemed to rob it of the vitality of the other great Andalusian capitals: Sevilla, Córdoba, Málaga. Granada represents the hopeless end of an historical cycle, one which draws to a close with the conquest of the city by the Catholic Monarchs [1492]. But Granada also represents a starting point for the creative affirmation of the Spanish Renaissance, which spilled over, culturally and politically, into Europe. An overwhelming feudal power was imposed on a population of Arabs and Jews harshly converted to Christianity. The modern city has its beginnings in this conflict. On one of the city's hills, only a tiny door separates the Renaissance Palace of Charles V, with its imperial "Roman" solemnity, from the Alhambra, with its exquisite arches and glazed tilework. In the city itself, illustrious specimens of Christian architecture overshadow the Arabic design of narrow streets and delicate arcades resting on slender columns. Closed convents, some of them extremely poor, are lodged in intimate courtyards with lovely Arabic lines where, surrounded by old laurels, fountains weep over their age-old abandonment. Federico and I once visited the home of a beggar who received us in a tiny whitewashed patio that seemed a miniature replica of the Alhambra.

The fact is that the creative impetus of the forces of the Empire began to withdraw, little by little, towards the northwest—towards Sevilla, the great port of embarkation for America, as is proven by the shortness of the cathedral tower and by the Emperor's unfinished palace, which has no roof in our day and lies open to the elements. It is not strange that even Góngora saw Granada as a melancholy memory of the past:

. . . Those ruins and remains
which Genil enriches and Dauro bathes . . .

. . . Si entre aquellas ruinas y despojos
que enriquece Genil y Dauro baña . . .

No doubt the great Baroque poet was thinking of the tombs of the Catholic Monarchs and of the man who forged their military grandeur, "The Great Captain,"* a Cordovan (like Góngora himself) who lies buried in a church with the great proportions of a cathedral, San Jerónimo. This splendid example of Isabeline Gothic, which lay abandoned in our time, impressed us with the strength of its walls, the richness of its ornamentation, and the intricate oriental look of its royal shields.

The same contrast between strength and ornateness is apparent in the Alhambra. Beside the Alcazaba (the most complex European fortress of the fourteenth century) one finds an exquisite, decadent Arabic palace that is strikingly different from the robust art of Córdoba or the corporeal and gracile presence of the Giralda of Sevilla. It is the delicate palace which seems closest to our spirit.

I believe that what we perceived in Granada was a certain spiritual frustration and a tendency to dwell on the conflict and melancholy of the past. The city's spirit seemed to have taken refuge in forgotten little corners; or on the high ground where Granada looks out over her lands, longing for escape; or in the gardens where the little waterjet seems afraid to shoot upwards and the funereal cypress traces its dark silhouette

---

*Gonzalo Fernández y Aguilar (1453-1515), known as Gonzalo de Córdoba, earned the title "El Gran Capitán" during his brilliant campaign in Italy against the French (1495-98).—*Tr.*

against the high, transparent sky. The city withdraws into its own cautious intimacy. The style of Granada has been expressed lucidly by Federico himself.

Granada loves what is tiny. . . . The language of the people puts even verbs in the diminutive. . . . Granada, quiet and refined, girded by her sierras and definitively at rest, seeks her horizons in herself. . . . [The diminutive that is typical of Granada] tries to limit time and space, the sea, the moon, the distances, and even the prodigious action. We do not want the world to be so big, or the sea to be so deep. Immense terms must be domesticated and made smaller.

Granada cannot leave her home. She is not like other cities that are on the edge of the sea or the shores of great rivers, cities which travel off and return enriched by what they have seen. Solitary and pure, Granada makes herself very small, she girds up her extraordinary soul and her only escape is her deep natural port—the stars.

. . . The little palace of the Alhambra, a palace which Andalusian fantasy invented by looking through the wrong end of the binoculars, has always been the aesthetic axis of the city. Granada still seems unaware of the Palace of Charles V and of her well-drawn Cathedral. There is no Roman tradition, no tradition of the clustered column. Granada is still afraid of her great cold cathedral tower, and she withdraws into her ancient little alcoves with only a pot of myrtle and a jet of icy water. There she carves little ivory flowers inlaid in hard wood.

Although there are many fine specimens of Renaissance architecture, that tradition seems to slip quietly away. Granada pokes fun at the large dimensions that were fashionable during the Renaissance, and she builds the incredible little tower of Santa Ana with all the city's poise and ancient grace—a tower more fit for doves than for bells.

. . . Granada is apt for dream and for daydream. On every side she borders on the ineffable. . . . Her voice is one which descends from a little mirador or rises from a dark window. It is a poignant, impersonal voice, full of indescribable aristocratic melancholy. . . . To hear that voice we must delve deep into ourselves, explore our own intimacy and secrecy, adopt a definitively lyrical attitude.

. . . Just the opposite of Sevilla. Sevilla is Man in all his emotional and sensual complexity. Sevilla is political intrigue and the arch of triumph. Don Pedro and Don Juan. Sevilla is full of humanity and her voice draws tears because all understand it. Granada is like the narration of what already happened in Sevilla.*

On another occasion the poet spoke of "Holy Week in Granada":

The traveler who has no problems and is full of smiles and the screams of locomotives goes to the carnival of Valencia. The bacchant goes to the Holy Week of Sevilla. The man burning for nudes goes to Málaga. But the melancholic and contemplative man goes to Granada, to be all alone in the breeze of sweet basil, dark moss, and trilling nightingales exhaled by the old hills near that bonfire of saffron, deep gray, and blotting-paper pink—the walls of the Alhambra.

To be alone . . . To understand not the water's play, as at Versailles, but the water's passion, the water's agony.

. . . The uninformed traveler will get the feeling that Granada is the capital of a kingdom with its own art and literature, and he will find a curious mixture of Jewish and Moorish elements which seem to have been blended by Christianity but are really alive and incorruptible in their ignorance of one another.

Neither the prodigious mound of the Cathedral nor the great imperial and Roman seal of Charles V have effaced the little shop of the Jew who prays before an image recast from the seven-branched candelabrum, nor have the sepulchres of the Catholic Monarchs kept the Crescent from showing at times on the breast of Granada's finest sons. The dark struggle continues without expression. Well, not really without expression. On the Colina Roja are two dead palaces, the Alhambra and the Palace of Charles V, which continue to fight the fatal duel that throbs in the heart of every Granadan.**

This Colina Roja had been the scene of a conversation [1526] leading to the most important innovation in the history of Spanish poetry. It was there, amid the myrtles and fountains of the Alhambra, and the murmur of courtly conversation, that a great Venetian ambassador [Andrea Na-

*The author is quoting from a lecture Federico gave about the Baroque poet Pedro Soto de Rojas. The lecture was read in Madrid (October, 1926) and in Havana, Cuba (March, 1930).—*Tr.*

**Lorca read this speech on the radio a few months before he was assassinated. For the complete text, see *Deep Song*, pp. 54-56.—*Tr.*

vagero] had invited the Spanish poet Juan Boscán to experiment with certain Italian and classical genres and meters. Boscán's friend Garcilaso de la Vega would use these forms to craft poems of such high perfection that only those of the Italians themselves were comparable. Who would have imagined that one night here in the gardens of Granada Spanish Renaissance poetry would begin to overtake all other European poetry, and that these Italian forms would provide a channel for the inspiration of an entire Golden Age: for sonnets sculpted with impeccable elegance or intense pathos, the lavish poetry of certain Sevillians, the dark inner trembling of Saint John of the Cross. Later, from the high ground of the Huerto de los Mártires, Saint John of the Cross would gaze into the abyssal night of his poetic inspiration. Federico remarks (and perhaps his intuition was correct) that it was here in Granada that "the 'meseta' poetry of Saint John of the Cross fills with cedars and cinnamons and fountains, and Spanish mysticism can receive that oriental air, that 'wounded stag,' (wounded by love) who 'comes to the hill.'"* The imaginary presence of these poets tensed Federico's soul whenever he visited the Alhambra as a young man.

As symbol and key of two social classes (the victorious aristocracy, on the one hand, and the humble serving class on the other) Granada offers two great names to the Renaissance tradition: Don Diego Hurtado de Mendoza and Fray Luis de Granada. Don Diego, who was an historian, poet, and ambassador of Charles V, adopted the Italian tradition without renouncing the Spanish one and cultivated the fine arts and literature with the style of a great lord. He was to be overshadowed by a writer of more universal appeal, the son of a washerwoman, Fray Luis de Granada, one of the most widely translated authors of the Castilian tongue. Fray Luis, who combined classical and medieval culture into a great synthesis, is at his best when discussing the place of small and even tiny things in the universe. It was precisely this interest in small things which Federico considered to be characteristic of the city. For Fray Luis, God's wisdom and providence are more resplendent in tiny things than in large ones. He was, as Federico wrote, a "humble, retiring, fastidiously refined man, a master 'looker,' as are all true Granadans." His observations on the spider, the mosquito, and even tinier beings, are unforgettable. I wonder if Federico, in his first poems, is not somehow evoking the

---

Deep Song, p. 54. He is quoting from one of the "Songs of the Soul and Her Spouse."—Tr.

work of Fray Luis (along with that of certain modern poets). For like Fray Luis, Federico focuses his attention on insects and other small animals, placing them on a scale mounting to a mysterious world beyond the reach of the senses. I remember that in our little library there was an old edition, bound in vellum, of the *Ladder to Paradise* of St. John Climacus, translated by Fray Luis de Granada.

Fray Luis' marvellous description of the pomegranate (*granada*), the fruit which symbolizes the city, is an especially good example of his fine powers of observation; and Federico devotes a poem to that fruit in his first book of verse. But let us read Fray Luis' description of the peacock. I shall include only the part referring to the eyes of his tail feathers:

For a moment let us ignore those hairs which go right up the shaft of the feathers until the end (and are hooked and beautifully colored), and let us come to the eye which is at the end of the feather and has an immense variety of colors. These colors are so fine and so lovely that none of the dyes which men have invented can equal them in their luster and subtlety. For within the eye is an oval of brightest green, and within the oval is another with almost the same shape of a very delicate purple color, and these are surrounded by other very beautiful circles which greatly resemble the shapes and colors of the rainbow. Then there is the beautiful hair, which also has many colors, where the feather ends. And in this eye or circle that we were describing, there is something no less admirable: the hairs and designs which make up the figures are so closely interwoven and so perfectly equal that the figure does not appear to be made up of different threads, but looks like one continuous piece of silk.*

During the Baroque period, which left its mark on the city's architecture, Granada would once again make an important contribution to Spanish literature. The center of a poetic school, Granada would even produce an excellent woman poet. The most illustrious voice of that movement was that of Don Pedro Soto de Rojas, whom Federico considered a symbol of the aesthetics of Granada:

At a time when Góngora was launching his proclamation of pure, abstract poetry, which was received avidly by the most lyrical spirits of his day, Granada could not remain inactive in the struggle that was reforming the

*From *Introducción del símbolo de la fe*, Part I, Chap. XXII, sec. II.—*Tr.*

literary map of Spain. Soto de Rojas embraces the difficult, strict, Gongorine order. But while the subtle poet of Córdoba plays with oceans, forests, and the elements of nature, Soto de Rojas shuts himself up in his garden to discover water-jets, dahlias, goldfinches and gentle breezes—the Moorish and half-Italian breezes which still rustle the branches, fruits, and copses of his poem.

In a word, his chief characteristic is the aesthetic "preciosity" of Granada. He arranges his Nature with the instinct of someone arranging a domestic interior. He flees from the great elements of Nature and prefers the wreaths and fruitbaskets he can make with his own hands. And this is what has always happened in Granada. Beneath the impression made by the Renaissance, native blood was still producing its own peculiar fruit.

. . . This is why, in the seventeenth century, Soto de Rojas (who had returned, weary and disillusioned, to Granada from Madrid) writes these words on the title page of one of his books: "Paradise Closed to Many. Gardens Open to Few." In my judgment, this is the best, most exact definition of Granada: Paradise Closed to Many.*

The Baroque title of Soto de Rojas' book seemed enormously appealing to us when Federico wrote those words. It was the heyday of Góngora. Federico's communicativeness and vitality sometimes made him want to give lasting expression to his literary enthusiasm. It was after he read Soto de Rojas' book that he wrote the lecture from which I have just quoted, on the aesthetics of Granada. The complete manuscript is lost. We also decided to place a commemorative plaque on the house where the poet had probably lived [1926]. It turned out to be an admirable carmen on the heights of the Albaicín, known locally as the "House of the Masks" because of the carving on the façade. The garden—the supposed "paradise"—was enclosed by part of an ancient rampart built by the Arabs. From the wall, overgrown with wild flowers, one looks out on a splendid landscape, then bathed in a sunset I have never forgotten.

As homage to Soto de Rojas, Federico also wanted to prepare a critical edition of the *Paraíso cerrado*, and the project was undertaken by one of the scholars in our group. But in fact we never managed to raise enough money to publish it. Not many patrons could be found in Granada.

*From Lorca's lecture on the Baroque poet Soto de Rojas. The Spanish text is found in C. Maurer, ed., *Conferencias* (Madrid: Alianza Editorial, 1984), Vol. I, pp. 127-143.

In the immediate literary past, no writer from Granada excited our enthusiasm. Perhaps only Pedro Antonio de Alarcón, the Romantic-Realist novelist, really deserved any serious consideration. True to the tradition of Granada (he was born in beautiful Guadix), Alarcón is at his best when he writes imaginative short stories or the sketch of manners. The enthusiasm felt by Manuel de Falla for *The Three-cornered Hat* (1874) made Alarcón even greater in our eyes. I would even say that Falla's work, based on Alarcón's delightful tale, is one of the threads Federico wove into the dense fabric of *The Love of Don Perlimplín*. The slightly caricatured figure of the old Corregidor in *The Three-cornered Hat*, his style of dress, and his decidedly erotic inclinations are transformed by Federico and transferred to other poetic contexts: first to Don Mirlo of *The Shoemaker's Prodigious Wife* and then to Don Perlimplín. The strange, shifting landscape of Guadix and its surroundings would also influence the setting of *Blood Wedding*.

Speaking of *The Three-cornered Hat*, Federico used to admire the clever way Don Manuel simulated the cry of a bird by rubbing a piece of cork on glass bottles of different sizes. It also amused my brother to discover the origin of certain rhymes that accompany the comical movements of the Corregidor when he comes secretly onto the stage. Don Manuel never said so, but those rhythms originated in the imitative nature of a children's game we used to play:

Hacen así	The washerwomen
así las lavenderas,	do this,
así, así, así,	do this, do this, do this.
Hacen así	The ironing women
así las planchadoras,	do this,
así, así, así . . .	do this, do this, do this . . .

The lines go on and on, adding seamstresses, hairdressers, cooks, etc. It was a children's game which we had heard in Valderrubio. I think the Corregidor takes a step every time the song says "do this." The rest of the words accompany his movements of listening, hesitation, looking round, etc. The matching of rhythm, movement, and dramatic situation appears, sometimes with great obviousness, in the dialogue of my brother's plays, though I doubt he was consciously imitating Falla.

In Alarcón's day there was a group of writers from Granada known as

"La Cuerda Granadina,"* one of whose members was the notorious Manuel Fernández y González [1812-1888]. He was born in Sevilla, but passed for a Granadan, for he studied and lived there before he set up shop in Madrid. This colorful character deserves more than passing mention. He symbolized the liquidation of the historical novel, and he brought that genre to an end not without a certain charm and great inventiveness when it came to plot. Some of his novels, like *Pastrymaker to His Majesty, The King's Cook*, and a third one set in Granada, *The Moorish Bandits of the Alpujarra*, were extraordinarily popular. Whatever talent he had was wasted on the genre he cultivated: the novel in installments. His powers of invention were stimulated by a desire to make money (he probably didn't make very much) and by the demands of a disorderly life. It is said that he wrote more than three hundred novels.

He did not actually write those novels, he dictated them. It is also said (for this local glory had his own legend) that he dictated to several secretaries at once, as if he were playing chess. He found that dialogue took up more space than narration or description and he tried to stretch out the dialogue with exclamations and monosyllables, one to a line. Once, while dictating, he made one of his characters exclaim, "¡Jesús, mil veces!" (Jesus, a thousand times!) He paused and asked his secretary, "Should I simply write out 'Jesus' a thousand times?" In his office was a plaster bust of Miguel de Cervantes, and one day he stopped in front of the bust and said, "Miguel, Miguel. You too have talent!"

Besides the group of local writers known as La Cuerda there was also a literary society called The Lyceum, which met in a spacious building adjoining the Cervantes Theater. (The Theater was said to have taken over part of the shady little Plaza del Campillo in a burst of illegal growth.) The gentlemen and artists of the Lyceum had been responsible for the coronation of Don José Zorrilla as Spain's poet laureate (1889). The ceremony, which had repercussions all over the country, took place in the majestic circular courtyard of the Palace of Charles V. Perhaps the city was trying to repay Zorrilla for the poems he had devoted to her. In the late Romantic style of those poems is a formal opulence that hints at the poetic renewal that was to come. The old author of *Don Juan Tenorio*, a spectacularly popular work, decided to rest on his laurels and

---

*Literally, the "Rope"; the writers were known as "knots" on the rope. The group was founded by Liberal writers and politicians in Granada around the middle of the nineteenth century. It fizzled out in Madrid in the 1870s.—*Tr.*

stay in Granada for the rest of his life. The gentlemen of the Lyceum had to remind him that those laurels were purely symbolic. The story of this coronation was passed down to us by word of mouth—such was its solemnity and importance. The Lyceum grew decadent, its literary tradition disappeared, and it turned into a bourgeois casino.* As a child I used to climb its curving white marble staircase holding my father's hand and watch him skillfully playing omber beneath the huge glass windows. I don't think that Federico (who was older) ever visited the Lyceum back then. In its great salons other, more distinguished groups organized formal balls. I remember how frustrated I felt, in early adolescence, at not being able to attend those balls because I did not have the required tuxedo.

At Carnival time, there was always a formal ball in the salons on the upper floors of the Cervantes Theater and a masked ball downstairs in the auditorium. The latter was a bacchic, noisy event open to all sorts of unholy people. Carnival was celebrated in a spectacular way, with parades, floats, battles of flowers, and popular musical ensembles with improvised instruments and drums made from rough cowhide. The different schools of the University sent their "estudiantinas," and the students dressed in their traditional suits, their black capes, and colorful ribbons. They carried the special banners of the different schools: red for Law, blue for Letters, yellow for Medicine, etc. The "estudiantinas" (student bands) were made up of flutes, bandurrias, guitars, and triangles. There were all sorts of masks, and the most popular figures were the harpies who dressed in old sheets, curtains, and rags.

It would be too easy, and a shade inaccurate, to say that all this uninhibited merriment resembled a scene from Goya. The stream of people slowly made its way to the picnic grounds of the Bola de Oro, and on the way one heard the shrill music of fife and drum and the song about the strong woman in the Paris Circus (rat-a-tat!) who lifted fourteen horses (rat-a-tat!) and an orangutan in her bare hands. The din

*During his trip to Buenos Aires in 1933, Federico told the following story to the journalist Pablo Suero: "Shortly after the fall of the monarchy [1931], the peasants of Granada set fire to the aristocratic Casino. The whole city heard the alarm and went to watch, and my father, my brother Paco, and I were among the crowd. The flames were threatening to destroy the entire building.

"My brother and I looked on calmly, almost joyfully, because something we detested was being destroyed. 'What a shame!' my father said suddenly, and I knew how sorry he felt—he had been going to the Casino for years and years. My brother and I looked at each other and one of us—I forget which—said, 'I'm glad!'" *Obras completas*, Vol. II, p. 1020.—*Tr.*

of the improvised bands blent with the crystalline sound of the bandurrias and triangles.

Federico never took part in these musical ensembles, and he was probably not yet a distinguished enough member of the Arts Center to form part of its float. One year that float was titled "The Turkey Man," and there was an enormous figure of a peasant with a crazy straw hat, surrounded by a number of members disguised as turkeys. One event I always went to see was the battle of the flowers and streamers, but I did this on my own, not in the carriage with my mother and sisters. Everyone in Granada regretted the end of Carnival.

From an early age Federico liked to wear disguises. He liked the idea of not being recognized as he strolled along with some friend, for example, Ismael [de la Serna] who later designed the cover of his first book [1918]. I don't think Federico cared about tricking his friends by disguising his voice: what he really enjoyed was the simulation, not the dissimulation, of disguise.

My father considered disguises to be degrading, and felt great aversion to them. Even so, he allowed my mother and the sewing woman to improvise Pierrot suits for us. I can remember my mother's beautiful, skillful hands making the ruffled collars from abundant white tulle.

Perhaps it was Federico's early fondness for disguises which led to the thematic appearance of masks and disguises in several of his plays. Of course, the disguise has a long history in the theater. In my brother's creative world, tradition and personal experience are equally important. Some of his characters seem to straddle the fine line that separates the person from the mask. It is not a matter of the disguise as a dramatic device—there is a deeper poetic meaning.

OLD ARTISTS OF GRANADA

The Cuerda de Granada was followed by the Confraternity of the Avellano, founded by Angel Ganivet, the hairy Spaniard who was to make Granada a part of the great literary renaissance that swept the Spanish-speaking world toward the end of the century. The Modernist movement represents the Hispanic expression of the great spiritual crisis occurring in Europe and America at the close of the nineteenth century. The crisis affected large areas of thought, political and religious attitudes, and literary sensibility. In Spain this renewal tended to be more intimate and less ornate, less cosmopolitan and more interested in questions of national identity than in America, and it influenced all the literary genres: not only poetry but also the essay, the novel, the theater, and even non-literary arts. Falla, Gaudí, Picasso, Zuloaga—all belong, chronologically, to Modernism.

The Spanish representatives of this literary renewal are known as the "Generation of 1898," a term which has sometimes been identified with, and sometimes opposed to, the term of Modernism. Perhaps the first important encounter among the writers of 1898 occurred in Madrid in 1891 when the young Ganivet met the Basque Miguel de Unamuno. Both young men were applying for university chairs in Greek, and between them they were to create the modern Spanish essay.

Ganivet's career as a writer began with a little book entitled *Granada the Beautiful* (a book with the small dimensions that Federico considered typical of Granada). It was an interpretation of the spirit of the city, not dissimilar to what my brother was to do, in a more poetic way, in some of his own works. I believe this was the only work of Ganivet Federico ever paid any attention to. In it, Ganivet reminds the people of Granada of the physical deterioration of their city and, thus, of their spirit. Federico alludes to this little book in his prose, and follows Ganivet by making water the expressive symbol of Granada. In fact, the very name "Confraternity of the Avellano" carries an implicit homage to water, for the Avellano is the name of one of the fountains in the Darro valley, where the members often met, presided over by Ganivet himself.

Though they were very old in our day, we were able to meet some of the members. Not Ganivet, surely, for he had committed suicide at age thirty-three by throwing himself into the waters of the Dwina (in 1898, the very year Federico was born). A few of these local writers, refined old men, came occasionally to our tertulias. Some had been affected by Modernism, and others were interested in local customs, as was Ganivet himself. We regarded them all with respect and sympathy.

One was Don Nicolás María López, Ganivet's friend and correspondent, who lived in a *carmen** on a narrow street in the Albaicín. Don Nicolás was so courteous that when it was time to paint the façade of his house he asked his neighbor across the street what color he preferred. This group of local writers, some of whom belonged to distinguished, well-to-do families, also included men of science like Gago Palomo who led a secluded life in his *carmen* in the Albaicín but is said to have contributed to international symposia on astronomy. It was also said that he had discovered new stars with rudimentary optical instruments.

There was also (inevitably) a learned local historian, Don Francisco de Paula Valladar, who published a historical and literary magazine named (what else!) *The Alhambra. The Alhambra* had a history that went all the way back to the time of Romanticism, and in it the great Espronceda had published two of his most important works (one was *The Student of Salamanca*, 1839). It was impossible to mention any aspect of Granada's past without hearing Don Francisco say (and as he said it, his heavy,

*"The word *carmen*, from the Arabic, denotes a hillside villa with an enclosed garden hidden by high walls from inquisitive eyes, and corresponds to the Islamic notion of the inner paradise, a reflection of heaven." Gibson, *The Death of Lorca*, p. 8.—*Tr.*

nearly black beard would tremble): "I already mentioned it in my *Alhambra*." Federico did a funny imitation of him. But in fact Don Francisco was nearly always right. And it is remarkable that *The Alhambra* managed to survive for more than half a century. By contrast, when we tried to publish a literary magazine [*gallo*, 1928] we could not make it last more than two issues.

But we did not really consider ourselves successors to the old Confraternity of the Avellano, a group with which we had only fleeting direct contact. Our real predecessors were the tangential, residual elements of that group we met at the Arts Center. These men influenced the non-literary education of my brother far more than did the old writers of the Confraternity. I am referring to men, some quite young, who were not even writers, but rather painters or sculptors without any great aspirations who earned their living as professors at the Trade School. They were amateurs, who often combined their interest in art with some other profession, for example tailoring. The Catalonian artist Santiago Rusiñol, a writer with Modernist leanings who was well known as a painter of gardens, entered into contact with our Back Corner group. Once, when he was discussing artistic matters with a local painter, another man came up and, scarcely able to hide his irritation, reproached Rusiñol's interlocutor for not having finished a suit he had ordered long before. Rusiñol asked him in astonishment, "You mean you are a tailor?" The other man replied, timidly, "Only an amateur."

These people, who lived on the very borderline of artistic creation, were partly responsible for Granada's eternal provincialism in matters of art. And yet, in the best of cases, they were attractive individuals who embodied certain aspects of Granada's spirit—for example, her popular habits of speech. Federico himself never lost (at least not the way I did) his unmistakable local accent.

I should also mention Paco Vergara, a professor—I think he taught drawing—at the Trade School. Vergara had an unlimited supply of stories, which he told with singular wit and style. He could do perfect imitations of the speech of different social classes and regions of Granada, even to sounds and resonances. One imitation in particular seemed to bring out all his powers of mimesis and observation: he liked to mimic the sound of a pair of old ladies, in the middle of winter, coming into one of those icy, deserted conventual churches one finds in Granada. One heard the squeaking of the door on its hinges, the thud made by the heavy leather curtain in the vestibule, the duo of coughs, the murmur of the nuns in the choir stalls, the harsh and sometimes unchurchly exclamations of the sacristan.

Some of his stories revealed the psychology of certain types of local people, or their language, or their provincial social milieu and would hardly seem funny to those who know nothing of our city. The best of these stories cannot even be reproduced in writing, for they end with a burst of spicy language. By the way, Federico, who spoke very carefully, did not enjoy vulgarity in the speech of others, except for extreme cases of true linguistic inventiveness.

The Back Corner group came into tangential contact with certain figures from the city's immediate past. One was Vicente León, then an old man living by himself. Whenever he fell ill, he hung a sign from his balcony saying that the apartment was for rent, and left his door open so that people would come in and keep him company. There was always some kind housewife to make him coffee and take him a glass of water for his aspirin. When he was really sick and had lost his wits, Don Vicente asked for some very strange medicine. One day, instead of asking for "scrambled eggs" he requested "a couple of scrambled bulls." These, he thought, would help him recover his strength.

These local characters, who became proverbial in the city, made friends with the Impressionist and Post-Impressionist painters, both Spanish and foreign, who were attracted to Granada by her beauty, landscape, and light. They often met at the Polinario Tavern, located on the very grounds of the Alhambra, with its patio shaded by a grapevine, its little fountains, and remains of Arabic arcades and columns. The owner, who was known as "El Polinario" formed part of the tradition I have been describing—he was something of a painter and not a bad guitarist. On the upper floor of the tavern he had a little art gallery, with works by the Spaniards Rusiñol and Darío de Regoyos and a splendid canvas by John Singer Sargent.

El Polinario's son, Angel Barrios, was an excellent guitarist and an inspired composer, who had studied under Manuel de Falla. He was an extraordinarily interesting person, a good friend of ours, and he belonged to the same popular/learned tradition as his father. We saw much of him at the Back Corner. Federico was much amused by a speech defect of his, rather common in the lower classes of Granada: the substitution of "l" for "r." "Is today Flyday?" he would ask. Angel had a certain Moorish air, or so we imagined, and a sensual mouth with thick protruding lips. Paco Vergara used to call him "Roundbeak." The first time Federico went to

Madrid he stayed at the same boarding house as Angel Barrios, and my brother told me that when Barrios invited him to a first drink he raised his glass to the glory of art and shouted, "Long Live Alt, what the hell!" (and "what the *hell*" is a euphemism). Barrios had founded a trio composed of a guitar (which he played), a bandurria (played by a blind man covered with pockmarks named Recuerda) and a lyre. Granada always had a fine tradition of guitar and bandurria players, who played at popular dances, still called by the traditional name of "lantern dances," and at parties in houses of ill repute. We sometimes ate dinner at one of the restaurants in the infamous Manigua neighborhood and invited one of these musicians to share our table. The main dish was often a very classical one: green beans, from local gardens, fried with ham from Trevélez, a village of the Sierra Nevada where hams are cured with snow. My father was a great lover of Trevélez ham, and so was Federico.

I remember the bandurria player from one of those occasions, Zapata. It was he who introduced us to the literary genre known as the *cerrajería*,* an absurd song whose rhymes seem to occur at random, as though obeying subconscious associations, a sort of folkloric Pre-Surrealism. Zapata sang us many different *cerrajerías*, one of which I remember especially well and still like to sing. It later became the theme song of the numerous Spanish students who lived together at the Engineering School in Toulouse, the university at which I studied Public Law on a scholarship. The *cerrajería* went like this:

Macacafú, macacafú,	Macacafú, macacafú,
macacafú, macacafú, margá.	macacafú, macacafú, margá.
Si te gusta comer a la pimén,	If you like to eat pep—,
si te gusta comer a la tomá,	if you like to eat toma—,
si te gusta comer a la alcachó, fa, fa.	if you like to eat articho, cho, chokes.
Chiribí, chiribí, margá.	Chribí, chiribí, margá.
Chimpón, polaví, polaví, polaví,	Chimpón, polaví, polaví, polaví,
polipolipón, chimpón.	polipolipón, chimpón.
Manguanguay de la vida culinay,	Manguanguay gourmet.
que manguanguay, que manguanguay;	Manguanguay and manguanguay.
manguanguay de la vida culinay,	Manguanguay gourmet.
que manguanguay, macacafú.	Manguanguay, macacafú.

Cerrajería is a locksmith's shop. What locksmiths have to do with the genre the author is describing is uncertain.—*Tr.*

Eme a: ma.	Em Ay: may
Eme e: ma-me.	Em Ee: may-me
Eme i: ma-me-mi.	Em Ee Eye: may-me-my
Eme o: ma-me-mi-mo.	Em Oh: may-me-my-moh
Eme u: ma-me-mi-mo-mu.	Em You: may-me-my-moh-you.
Macacafú.	Macacafú.

The song contains allusions to tropical America: Cuba and Puerto Rico. *Macacafú* may be a reference to the macaque monkey. There are other allusions to slightly absurd characters: Margá is General Margallo and Polaví is General Polavieja.* I do not believe Federico appreciated these *cerrajerías*, a subordinate and vulgar form of folklore. If he ever remembered the *macacafú* it was only to tell how one of the waiters (a serious man, with a deep, dark voice, who wore a black tie, black beard, black mustache and loved to read philosophy) used to sit down beside the blind singer and devour one *macacafú* after another. Federico had a great talent for noticing these tiny, comical situations, and he took great delight in them.

These *cerrajerías* were similar to certain children's swing songs we used to know. At the risk of ruining the chronological order of my story (this book is only a collection of memories, and does not pretend to be a biography), I should say that as an adolescent Federico especially loved the swing. (It was almost an obsession.) He shared that love with us three younger children, especially with Isabel. When we made trips to the country, one of the first things we did was to make a swing with the thick cords used in farm chores like the wheat harvest. We used to hang these swings in an old abandoned stable, which we had cleaned and soaked down. Sometimes we took turns swinging. But Federico liked to swing by himself; he would rock rhythmically for a long time, allowing his imagination to take flight, and sometimes he would hum to himself.

Federico said, years later, that some of those simple swing melodies had their origins in remote antiquity. At the piano he knew how to modulate them introducing certain small changes that produced strange, delightful harmonies. One of the swing songs he sang was this one:

---

*Both generals served in Cuba. Juan García Margallo (1839-1893) died in action in the Moroccan wars. Camilo García Polavieja (1838-1914) served as governor general of Cuba and of the Philippines.—*Tr.*

Ya viene la vieja	The old woman is coming
por las escaleras,	down the stairs
con un racimo de uvas	with a bunch of grapes
y otro de ciruelas.	and a bunch of cherries.
¡Apeón!,	Step it up!
que viene la vieja	Yes, down she comes
con un tizón	with the fire tongs,
y baja a la niña	down to the girl
del mecedor.	on the swing.
¡La chica!	The little one!
¡La grande!	The big one!
¡La campanilla del estudiante!	The little bell of the student!

The exclamations "The little one!" and "The big one!" accompanied one short and one long shove on the swing, and then came the moment called "the slip-away," when the swing was slowing to a stop.

From the words of these swinging games we can see that in the village they were played by children, while in the city they were also played by older girls and boys. There were lovely melodies, although not all of them were very old:

Mamayuyui, papayuyui,	Mommy-hah! Poppy-ho!
mi madre tiene un colchón,	My mother has a matress
y lo tiene *guardaito*	and has it stowed away
pa cuando me case yo.	for when I get married.

Some of these lyrics seem to have been invented in a happy burst of improvisation:

La niña que está en la bamba	The girl who is on the swing
con la toquilla *encarná*	wearing a red shawl
es la novia de mi hermano,	is my brother's girlfriend;
pronto será mi *cuñá*.	soon she will be my sister-in-law.

. . . or this one, equally pretty, with its confidential air:

| De aquellos tres que vienen | Of the three men who are coming |
| ¿cuál es el tuyo? | which is yours? |

| El de la capa larga | The one with the long cape |
| y el pelo rubio. | and the blond hair. |

The swing was in vogue among adults in the eighteenth century as may be seen from the paintings of Goya and others. And yet, some of the swinging or rocking songs take up themes that go back to the Middle Ages:

En los olivaritos,	In the olive groves,
niña, te espero,	girl, I await you
con un jarro de vino	with a jug of wine
y un pan casero.	and *casero* bread.*

A los olivaritos	I go to the olive groves
voy por la tarde,	in the afternoon,
a ver cómo menea	to see how the air
la hoja el aire.**	is moving the leaf.

We find the very same theme in a well-known parallelistic song from the Middle Ages:

De los álamos vengo, madre,	I have come from the poplars, mother,
de ver cómo los menea el aire.	to see how the air is moving them.
De los álamos de Sevilla,	The poplars of Sevilla
de ver a mi linda amiga.	to see my pretty friend.
De los álamos de Granada,	The poplars of Granada
de ver a mi linda amada.	to see my pretty love.

In the song from Granada, the poplar has been replaced by the olive grove, and the mention of *casero* bread could very well refer to the famous dark bread of the village of Alfacar, the only bread in Granada that bears that name.

Casero means home made.—*Tr.*

**There is a reminiscence of this little poem in the first scene of the second "engraving" of Lorca's play *Mariana Pineda.* In a ballad recited by Clavela and the daughters of Mariana we find the lines: "En el olivarito / me quedaré a mirar / cómo el aire menea / las hojas al pasar." ("I will stay in the olive grove and watch how the wind shakes the leaves when it goes by.")—*Ed.*

The form of the song beginning "In the olive groves . . ."—a *segui-dilla**—makes one suppose that it is relatively modern. But today the critics are inclined to believe that the *seguidilla*, which was very popular in the eighteenth century, may have its roots in antiquity. The use of the word *hoja* in the singular (*hojas* would be normal) brings to mind older songs, like this one from Hurtado de Mendoza:

Aquel árbol que vuelve la hoja   That tree which turns its leaf
algo se le antoja.   is trying to say something.**

The connection between the swinging songs and these older songs was noticed by Federico in one of his lectures, "How a City Sings from November to November."† Federico had a habit of establishing connections between the past and the present. This never involved meditative reflection; it was instinctive, as though he felt the call of distant times. It happens above all in his first period as a poet, but also in his later theater. We can see this dimension of his spirit in the series of poems entitled "Palimpsests," published in *First Songs*. There the poet gives plastic expression to the hidden but vital trace of the passage of time:

I   I

Ciudad   City

El bosque centenario   The centenary forest
penetra en la ciudad,   penetrates the city,
pero el bosque está dentro   but the forest
del mar.   is in the sea.

Hay flechas en el aire   There are arrows in the air
y guerreros que van   and warriors
perdidos entre ramas   lost in the branches
de coral.   of coral.

*A popular verse form that often consists of four lines of 7, 5, 7, and 5 syllables respectively, with assonant rhyme.—*Tr.*
**Literally, "fancies something."—*Tr.*
†A lecture on the folksongs of Granada, based on the idea that "a man from Granada blind from birth and absent from his city for many years would know the season by the music he heard sung in the streets." See the bilingual edition by C. Maurer, *How a City Sings From November to November* (San Francisco: Cadmus Editions, 1985).—*Tr.*

Sobre las casas nuevas	Over the new houses
se mueve un encinar	moves a forest of holm oaks
y tiene el cielo enormes	and the sky has huge
curvas de cristal.	glass curves.

II	II
Corredor	Corridor
Por los altos corredores	Down the high corridors
se pasean dos señores.	go two gentlemen.
(¡Cielo	(New
nuevo.	sky.
¡Cielo	Blue
azul!)	sky!)
. . . se pasean dos señores	. . . two gentlemen
que antes fueron blancos monjes.	who were once white monks.
(Cielo	(Middle
medio.	sky.
¡Cielo	Purple
morado!)	sky!)
. . . se pasean dos señores	. . .two gentlemen
que antes fueron cazadores.	who were once hunters.
(Cielo	(Old
viejo.	sky.
¡Cielo	Gold
de oro!)	sky!)
. . . se pasean dos señores	. . . two gentlemen
que antes fueron . . .	who were once . . .
Noche.	Night.

And yet, in a way, Federico was an anti-historical being, at least in the years of his early youth. I believe that, back then, he was unable to feel time as history; he felt it as an elemental, shaping force. To him, the living mystery of a perishable individual flower or the rock beside the water were more vital manifestations of time than the flux of great events. Much later, in one of his final poems,* the poet would say,

> Stone is a shoulder to carry time
> with trees of tears, and ribbons and planets.
>
> La piedra es una espalda para llevar al tiempo
> con árboles de lágrimas y cintas y planetas.

From adolescence on, Federico's personality held the speechless attraction of a creature immersed in a world full of hidden resonances. But his world was totally simple and *natural*, in the deepest sense of the word. Perhaps this was the key to his great personal charm.

It would be absurd to say that Federico was not "intelligent." He has left us literary interpretations and criticism which, though they lack the rigor of the professional, cast new light on different facets of poetry, dance, and painting. We need only remember his "Ode to Salvador Dalí," written at an early date [1925-26]: it shows a deep understanding of abstract painting and of Dalí before he had traded his fame for simple notoriety. The "Ode" is an elevated epistle in the classical mold, and in it the authoritative voice of the poet rises to levels of noble objectivity.

The poet was capable of penetrating shrewdly into the intellects of others, and even of probing his own mind, as in the lecture which he gave in the Ateneo de Granada [October, 1928], entitled "Imagination, Inspiration and Evasion," a long analysis of the mysterious process of poetic creation, where Federico brilliantly explains the functioning of his own creative mechanism. Federico's speeches, lectures, and interviews allow us to reconstruct his esthetic ideas with perfect coherence.**

My brother's critical attitude, his artistic judgments, the coherence of his criteria, and his perception of the phenomena of reality—all this was based on lucid intuition, sparked by imagination. Perhaps there is no truer means of literary criticism, nor a more valid way of acquiring knowledge. I said before that in a certain sense Federico was an anti-historical or extra-historical being; what I mean is that he was the *result*

---

*"Lament for the Death of Ignacio Sánchez Mejías."—*Tr.*
**This was done brilliantly by Marie Laffranque in *Les idées esthétiques de Federico García Lorca* (Paris: Centre de Recherches Hispaniques, 1967).—*Tr.*

of certain forces, to which he merely submitted. He expressed both a subterranean tradition rooted in ancient times and a vibrant present enhanced by his own vitality. This element of living fact, of phenomenon, placed Federico at the opposite end of the scale from the historian, for *he himself* was a fact worthy of being recorded historically. For this reason, it would be entirely false to say that Federico did not leave a very great mark on the history of contemporary Spanish poetry. He used to tell the story of the captain who said, "Let us depart for the Thirty Years War." Federico is the last poet of his generation whom one could accuse of harboring such an attitude.

His rapid comprehension of literary currents and tendencies, and the intelligent way in which he accommodated himself to his own poetic nature would never have allowed him to become an "ideologue." Federico was the antidote to ideology. He would have been incapable of reading a book of philosophy, even the most easily accessible to a man of average culture. As for ideas, he gave them passion and substance. In this he resembled Unamuno, who was much more extreme, and in fact my brother felt deep admiration for the great teacher, whom he visited more than once in Salamanca.

For these reasons, it would be difficult to illustrate Federico's biography with pithy sayings that show his ingeniousness, wit, and mental prowess. All his contemporaries praise Federico in the same way: they emphasize the indefinable grace of his presence.

THE BACK CORNER: A FEW OF ITS MEMBERS AND ACTIVITIES

Our group at the Back Corner broke away from the aforementioned Arts Center which had become set in its provincial ways and hostile to any new trends in art. Suffice it to say that while Federico was ardently defending the new painting,* the Center was holding an exhibition parodying Cubism and even Impressionism. The participants were the best-known painters in Granada, devoted to the realistic reproduction of scenes with "local color." Many of their works struck a pathetically decorative "Moorish" note. Wasn't the Alhambra in Granada? Their paintings filled with parrots, fruit baskets, and, of course, turbans.

Before Federico established himself as a writer, the most distinguished figure in our group, a sort of honorary president, was Paquito Soriano, who, as time went by (and after marrying one of his cousins) slowly returned to bourgeois conventions and more traditional attitudes. This coincided with the slow disintegration of the Back Corner whose most active members were now absent. I remember that someone (perhaps it was Juan Benítez, the music professor) said one day at a plenary session of our circle, "This group is like a Roman candle: the day it explodes, I don't know where it will end up." How right he was. The group's two

*The author is referring to a slide show Federico gave in October, 1928, titled "Sketch de la nueva pintura." For the text see *Conferencias*, Vol. II, ed. cit., pp. 33-49.—*Tr.*

painters were soon to make their way to Paris: Ismael de la Serna, who gained fleeting fame in refined Parisian circles, and Manuel Angeles Ortiz, the distinguished disciple of Picasso. Others wound up in South America [José Mora Guarnido] and Germany [José Fernández Montesinos], and one of them, Miguel Pizarro, in Japan.

Paquito Soriano Lapresa, who is mentioned more than once in my brother's works, deserves special attention. Contrary to what the diminutive "Paquito" might have led one to believe, he was a very fat man, with a white, round face, and hair as prickly as a sloe plum. His soft, abbatial hands looked very pale as they rested on the ebony cane he almost always carried. On his right hand he wore a ring with an enormous, dark, oval stone. On the whole, Soriano's decadent manner (shared by Ismael in matters of dress) stood in sharp contrast to the simplicity of the rest of the group.

Soriano often wore a tailcoat and dickey to our meetings. I cannot remember anyone else his age who would have dared to dress so formally every day. I say "anyone his age" because sometimes (perhaps on the days when there were faculty meetings at the University) Fernando de los Ríos would come to class wearing tails. And the professor of Arabic, Don Pascual Meneu, who arrived in Granada somewhat later, would regularly report to the University wearing a frock coat and top hat. I remember that Don Pascual, as a protest against the quality of the water at the College of Arts, would arrogantly cross the city with a water jug dangling from his right hand. Sometimes, as a protest against the restrooms at the University, he carried a utensil much more private in nature. None of which kept him from being an excellent and enthusiastic professor.

To reach the Back Corner Paquito Soriano had to come down our street, the Acera del Casino, which was right in the center of the city and which basked in the prestige of the Casino, an elegant club that always put out tables and comfortable wicker chairs on both sides of the sidewalk. Soriano would go strolling by in his tails. At Christmas he would carry a pair of *carrañacas* (two long strips of wood with serrated edges adorned with colored paper and strips of tin, which make noise when rubbed together). At Carnival time he would wear a green pepper on his nose. Such was the humor exuded by the calm, abundant humanity of Soriano.

Soriano, who was sedentary by nature, used to make imaginary trips to distant countries: advanced and liberated Scandinavia or scorching Central Africa. Such divagations and imaginings arose from an intellectual exoticism that was a fundamental part of his personality, held in check by a keen sense of humor that flowed ceaselessly through his melodious, rather high-pitched voice. He was always breaking into shrill laughter and at those moments his massive figure and double chin would begin to tremble, as would his round, white, neatly shaven face.

Soriano had his lyrical side, and he loved the nocturnes of Chopin, the crystalline notes of Debussy, the distant gardens of Juan Ramón Jiménez, with all their sentimental sensuality. He introduced us to the writings of Fráncis Jammes, whose young heroines (Pömme d'Anis, Clair de Ellebeuse, Almaïde d'Etremont) were proverbial amongst us, and to other French authors who cultivated a more or less exquisite eroticism. We were also fond of the Russian novel and short story: Chekhov, of course, and Andreyev, Turgenev (we all read *Spring Rain*), and, somewhat later, Proust, Strindberg, and the "Ballad of Reading Gaol" of Oscar Wilde. These were some of our favorite writers at an age when all of us read avidly and made frequent trips to the sizable library of Paquito Soriano, who, as the only son in a well-to-do family, could spend money on books on diverse subjects, enriching the collection formed by an older brother, who had died years before and whom we had never known. Soriano used to bring foreign magazines to our gatherings, and we never went without *La Vie Parisienne*. Through the advertisements of this magazine Soriano struck up correspondences with foreign women. He would sometimes read these letters in the Back Corner, and once he brought us the portrait of a splendid Swedish woman. I suspect that Soriano never sent his own photo to the women who wrote him.

Another source of reading material of a very different nature was the excellent library of Don Fernando. We too bought books, and eventually we had our own account in the Prieto bookstore, on Mesones Street. Our love of reading, especially Federico's, made my father complain that we were abusing the freedom he had granted us. It seems to me that this authorization was discreetly limited to textbooks and to those books we might consider useful, plus a few for mere pleasure. It was here that Federico went overboard, though I should add that, by way of compensation, my father never had to buy him a single textbook I still have a receipt from the Prieto bookstore listing *Riders to the Sea,* which some have supposed that Federico read.

Soriano dabbled amiably in many different subjects, and refused to undertake any of them with even a shade of constancy. His wit was such that he could convert any scrap of information into a dissertation on

Bantu languages or the chirimoya fruit, astronomy or music. He would often listen to a symphony with the score in his hand, though I doubt he could read it. He spoke with the same assuredness and precision in private as he did in public. His political opinions were a bit whimsical: he belonged to the Socialist Youth, but he said he sympathized with the syndicalist movement, which tended towards anarchism. In fact, he said that what attracted him to syndicalism was its apoliticism, but on other occasions he spoke of his "mystical respect for the law." For the law and, I would add, for parliamentary procedure. I remember general meetings at the Arts Center when Paquito Soriano would stand up and demand the floor in order to discuss "old business" rather than the topics proposed by the board of directors. He demanded strict compliance with procedure, which he knew by heart, down to the last section and subsection. Armed with his "points of order," he often came close to paralyzing the meeting.

Federico used to tell how he and a friend had paid Paquito a surprise visit and had found him dressed as a priest in a splendid old cassock, reading from an antiphonary placed before him on a lectern. It is difficult to say whether all this was a pose. Soriano had a fine sense of humor, and perhaps he simply liked to get dressed up to amuse himself.

Paquito Soriano was a perfect dilettante, gifted with a sharp wit and well-suited for polemics. His great powers of speech far outstripped his writing ability. He never attempted to write a single line of literature, and I cannot remember that he ever wrote any of us a letter. Some of the younger members at the Back Corner spread the rumor that there were spelling mistakes in a note Soriano once wrote in the café. But none of us questioned his skill at choosing the right word or positioning a creative epithet. The only text of his that I can remember was an open letter published in a local newspaper in which he reminded his readers of the ancientness of the Archdiocese of Granada, one of the first regions in Spain to be converted to Christianity. The ancient Roman city of Illiberis had witnessed the first national council. Soriano concluded that Granada deserved to be upgraded in the ecclesiastical hierarchy. If this was impossible, then at least its archbishop, Monsignor Meseguer y Costa, should be elevated to the cardinalate. The Roman Curia probably paid little attention to that brief letter in a provincial newspaper, but a little while later Archbishop Meseguer was, in fact, made a cardinal. And some people remembered the letter, which the Back Corner had taken so lightly.

Other members of the group helped create the friendly atmosphere that drew us together every day. It would be difficult to imagine a more closely-knit group, with fewer personal clashes and rivalries, a group regularly joined by promising new members, over whom Federico presided, disinterestedly and happily.

The Back Corner made itself known by means of certain collective acts. Besides the ceremonies honoring Soto de Rojas, we put up a tile plaque in honor of Isaac Albéniz. It was placed on the house of the official architect of the Alhambra, where we supposed the composer had once lived. We used to order these plaques from the ceramic factory in Fajalauza, one of the artistic industries of Granada which had maintained its folk tradition (a tradition which has since become quite—perhaps too—fashionable). The plaques were skillfully drawn from old models by the etcher Hermenegildo Lanz, a member of our group and a loyal friend.

One of the people who first encouraged Federico in the Back Corner was Melchor Fernández Almagro, today a member of the Royal Academy of Letters and the Academy of History, an excellent historian and intelligent critic, somewhat older than we, whom we used to call by the diminutive "Melchorito." Unlike Paquito Soriano, Melchor has fully developed his talent. He is one of the most gifted literary critics and best writers in Spain, and as historian of the contemporary age he has left books that will become classics. I must add, sadly, that when he writes on recent events, the harsh circumstances imposed by the Civil War and its cruel and useless aftermath have limited his thought and expressiveness, depriving him of historical objectivity: this is the sad consequence of a regime that cannot be censured, even in its greatest excesses, while its opponents, left defenseless, are fiercely attacked.

Melchor's pleasantness was unequalled. He was blessed with a prodigious memory, and there was no anecdote, no happening, no imputation, scrap of gossip or love affair that he did not, and does not, remember, regardless of whether it concerned the living or the dead. When he wants to he can spin a delightful history in miniature out of a tiny detail.*

This is not the right moment to list all of the others in our group. The mention of Fernández Almagro seems justified because he was the first to move to Madrid, and he served as a contact for Federico on his first visits to the capital. Melchor probably spoke of Federico in the elegant

*This chapter seems to have been written several years before Fernández Almagro's death in 1966.—Tr.

social milieu he liked to frequent. His penchant for faithfully chronicling social and political life had drawn him into the circle of what were then the ruling classes. His personal qualities must have been a great help— his vast knowledge, his pleasant conversation, and, perhaps, his being a descendant of Diego de Almagro, who had conquered Perú with Pizarro. To be sure, we had our own Pizarro, Miguel, who had not succeeded as a writer, and whom Federico called in a little poem, "an arrow without a target," eternally Platonic, in love with a distinguished and beautiful woman from Granada, María, the daughter of a local politician, Don Nicolás Cuadrado. Miguel used to call her by the name of the heroine of *Spring Rain*, Macha Nicolaevna. He was a handsome, slender, dark-skinned lad, and I remember his lovely voice as he recited, with theatrical gestures, the most melodious poems of Rubén Darío, including, naturally, the "Triumphal March."*

*Late in his life, when he was living in exile in North America, Miguel Pizarro (1897– 1956) began to write poetry. His book *Versos* was published posthumously, with words of introduction from Federico García Lorca and Jorge Guillén (Málaga, 1961). Pizarro left an unpublished play entitled *Los despatriados* (*The Exiles*). *Versos* begins with the poem Don Francisco mentions ("Miguel Pizarro! / Arrow without a target!").—*Ed.*

MANUEL DE FALLA

Our circle at the Back Corner was strengthened by the presence of Manuel de Falla [1920]. I do not remember how it was that the great composer came into contact with the group; quite possibly, it was through Don Fernando de los Ríos. One of the members has written that it was because of an accidental encounter, while Don Manuel was taking his daily walk through the woods of the Alhambra. Don Manuel lived in a small house (a *carmen*) at the foot of the Colina de los Mártires, with a little garden hidden from public view, a fountain with a water jet, and a splendid view of both the Sierra and the city. To young men like us he seemed an example of modesty, even timidity. His stark, white bedroom, with a cross over his humble bed, looked like a monastery cell. Don Manuel was also a model of extreme, almost excessive neatness. He smiled easily, though at times he could look very grave. His gaze was quite profound, and his hard, brilliant eyes sometimes gave him the appearance of a carved figure.

He was somewhat timid, but he also felt great spiritual fervor. At certain moments his well-drawn features would be motionless, and a faraway look would come into his eyes. But then suddenly he would "return," smile, and listen courteously.

Through Falla we found it much easier to meet people from outside Granada. Travelers were often attracted to the city's beauty, and if they belonged to the world of art they rarely left without paying a visit to the great composer. It was a time when first-class concerts were given in Granada, and through Falla we were able to meet illustrious musicians. Some of them made prolonged visits, for example Wanda Landowska, whom Don Manuel's old serving-woman used to call "La Handoska," to the maestro's great amusement.

It was we who had sent him this excellent servant. She was the aunt of our cook, and through her we learned small amusing details of the maestro's daily life. His obsession with germs made him impose rules of domestic hygiene to which the poor woman was totally unaccustomed. The house was radiantly clean. Don Manuel used to time himself as he brushed his teeth, turning this operation into a meticulous exercise. He was unable to work when he knew there was a fly in the room—the insect had to be tracked down and swatted. Such mannerisms were part of the order and cleanliness that governed his life—a fragile life which he defended out of a sense of duty.

His musical ability, which Don Manuel recognized but did not proclaim, was a gratuitous gift, a grace which he felt he would have to account for someday. Modestly, he used to speak of music not as an art, but as a profession [oficio]. The great demands he made on himself arose partly from this attitude, which must have influenced the way Federico thought about his own "profession" of poetry. Federico's joy and vitality were counterbalanced by the steadfast labor of Don Manuel, who was reflexive and responsible, but also full of passion.

Falla's attitude makes me remember the lesson of poetic rigor taught to the poets of Federico's generation by Juan Ramón Jiménez. The philosopher José Ortega y Gasset had sent a similar message to these young men: "Let us cultivate, above all, the art of rejection." But to Federico, Don Manuel was a closer, more vivid and beloved model than either of these two. Don Manuel's attitude was neither an intellectual pose nor a purely esthetical matter. It involved neither ivory towers nor impregnable towers of pride and disdain. Don Manuel was an example of fervor and modesty. How different he was, in his thirst for perfection, from Juan Ramón Jiménez. The poet from Moguer felt an obsessive passion for Art (with a capital "A"), but this had little to do with Falla's total "professional" dedication. Don Manuel was not unaware of his gifts as an artist, but he felt neither proud nor responsible for them. "Those of us whom God has gifted," he used to say, "must cultivate their gift." He was an artist "by the grace of God," but he believed one acquired personal merit only by perfecting one's gift. One became worthy of it through hard work. Falla's dedication revealed Benedictine patience and Franciscan simplicity. Devoid of any sort of false modesty, he took satisfaction in the work he was able to accomplish. A work that was perfect—i.e. finished—did not need to be tampered with. He was a responsible "maestro," a master, and every one of his works is literally a masterpiece.

Juan Ramón Jiménez once wrote a lovely little poem alluding to the very essence of the poetic work:

> No la toques ya más,   Touch it no more,
> que así es la rosa.   the rose is like that.

Rather than reveal confidence in the finished work, this little poem reveals insecurity. It is less a norm than a fearful precautionary warning—a warning that the successful poem is capable of still further perfection. The little poem seems full of unsatisfied longing: the work has been abandoned and the poet feels it to be distant and vulnerable. I have long suspected that these two famous lines (whose syllabic structure makes them seem like the first half of a *seguidilla*) were originally a hendecasyllable:

> No la toques ya más, que así es la rosa.

Perhaps this was the beginning of a poem, or the last line in a stanza. I cannot, of course, prove this hypothesis. But were it true it would be a miraculous admonition. Poetry herself (in the form of a detached verse) would be warning the poet of the dangers of an over-anxious "revisionism." My suspicion *deserves*, at least, to be true. It would illustrate, in poetic terms, the impassioned almost morbid relation between the poet of Moguer and his own work.

These two Andalusian mentors, born of ancient races (the poet with his Nazarene beard and bluish eyepits; the composer as cleanly shaven as a monk, bald and ivory-skinned) had certain traits in common. The two delicate, highly precise organisms were alike in their meticulousness, their fear of disease, their horror of dust, and their total intolerance of noise. The poet was much more sensitive: he was also tormented by extreme sensitivity to lights, fragrances, and colors. These traits form part of the legend of Juan Ramón and are universally known. But Falla hid such oddities, and they were scarcely known outside his home in Granada.

Juan Ramón is known to have lined the walls of the workroom in his Madrid apartment with cork. He probably regretted that he could not insulate it as perfectly as an acoustical laboratory. Falla struggled against the noises of Granada, defending himself from pianos, both distant and near, whose owners agreed not to play during the maestro's hours of work. On one occasion, on the feast of Corpus Christi [1936], a sort of amusement park had been set up. There were shooting galleries and other noisy contraptions, including a big merry-go-round that revolved to the music of a huge, shameless organ which could be heard day and night. The merry-go-round had been installed in the Embovedado, the lower part of the city, just in front of our house. Falla lived in the Antequeruela, in the high part of Granada, far from the source of the noise. After a bitter inner struggle, the composer complained to the City Hall. The Mayor of Granada, my brother-in-law Manuel Fernández-Montesinos, who was assassinated around the same time as my brother, was a friend of Don Manuel. Ironic and temporizing, Montesinos decided to try to reach an agreement with the owner of the merry-go-round. Both Falla and he went to speak with him. The mayor proposed that the apparatus be turned down to a *pianissimo*, if possible, or be used without any musical accompaniment whatsoever during the maestro's hours of work, which Falla had already cut back to a minimum. The good man agreed. But Falla wished to pay him an indemnity, and asked him to calculate how much business would be lost during those hours without music. Needless to say, the calculation had to be exact—otherwise Falla would not be Falla. The owner wanted no part of it—I remember with what irritation he fled from the idea of such a calculation. Without knowing Falla, it would be hard to imagine how he must have agonized over that decision, and how those carnival noises must have bothered him, despite the fact that they were coming from far across the city, attenuated by the distance and ironically distorted by the wind.

Federico loved to tell stories like this one about Falla. Perhaps that very merry-go-round, or some similar one, installed during the carnival at Corpus, gave rise to this little poem, written by my brother years before the incident I have been describing:

Los días de fiesta	Holidays
van sobre ruedas.	go gliding by.
El tiovivo los trae	The carrousel brings them
y los lleva.	and takes them away.

| Corpus azul. | Blue Corpus Christi, |
| Blanca Nochebuena. | white Christmas Eve. |

Los días abandonan	All other days
su piel, como las culebras,	shed their skin like a snake,
con la sola excepción	but not holidays.
de los días de fiesta.	

Estos son los mismos	These are the same ones
de nuestras madres viejas.	our old mothers had.
Sus tardes son largas colas	Their evenings are long
de moaré y lentejuelas.	trains of moire and spangles.

| Corpus azul. | Blue Corpus Christi, |
| Blanca Nochebuena. | white Christmas Eve. |

El tiovivo gira	The carrousel turns,
colgado de una estrella.	hanging down from a star.
Tulipán de las cinco	Tulip of the five
partes de la tierra.	parts of the earth.

Sobre caballitos	Upon little horses
disfrazados de panteras	disguised as panthers,
los niños se comen la luna	children eat the moon
como si fuera una cereza.	as if it were a cherry.

¡Rabia, rabia, Marco Polo!	Take that, Marco Polo!
Sobre una fantástica rueda	Upon a fantastic wheel
los niños ven lontananzas	the children see remote
desconocidas de la tierra.	unknown parts of the earth.

| Corpus azul. | Blue Corpus Christi, |
| Blanca Nochebuena. | white Christmas Eve. |

Falla's Catholic orthodoxy and scrupulous fulfillment of his religious duties did nothing to dampen his cordial relations with our young group, so indifferent to matters of religion. We admired his charitable soul, his true Christianity, and the consistency of his conduct and his principles. One day Federico told me with great enthusiasm of having been at Falla's house when some prisoners escaped from a nearby jail. The guards had fired into the air to frighten them. The news of the escape spread through the neighborhood like wildfire. After a while there were noises and loud shouting and it seemed that the escapees were being chased through the streets near the maestro's house. Alarmed, the maid dashed over to bolt the door. Don Manuel shouted, "Open it! Open the door! They are being chased by the police!" Falla's instant, spontaneous reaction, his hard threatening look and energetic voice made a deep impression on my brother.

Falla must have been horrified by the catastrophe of the Spanish Civil War, the brutal persecution and assassination of many of his friends in Granada. He had already been deeply saddened by the unlawful acts and political tension that preceded its outbreak. My family told me gratefully of Don Manuel's frequent visits after the assassinations of my brother and brother-in-law. In a neighborhood that had been terrorized, such visits to a politically "marked" family were deeply appreciated.* Falla left Spain to flee from the horror, and only his body returned. My sister Concha told me that before Falla left Granada, the so-called "authorities" tried to honor him at a public ceremony, and that Falla refused. His letter of refusal was published in a local newspaper, buried among the advertisements.

Falla showed his prodigious energy whenever he directed his own

---

*Another touching incident, described by Ian Gibson in 1973, years after this chapter was written, deserves to be mentioned here: "[In 1939, after arriving in Buenos Aires, Falla told José Mora Guarnido that] some months before the rising, he had been visited by a group of young Falangists who wanted him to compose a hymn for their organization. He had refused as politely as possible, explaining that his Catholic conscience forbade him to compose music that might be used to inspire violence. But the young men had insisted, and eventually he agreed to instrumentalise a popular Spanish song to which they could put any words they chose. When the rising started Don Manuel, terrified, shut himself up in his *carmen*. There he learned of the assassinations that were taking place in Granada, and indeed he can hardly have failed to hear the sinister firing from the cemetery every morning. Then one day they told him that Federico had been arrested. Falla, a gentle, timid man, knew that he must try to help his friend and accordingly set out for Falange HQ in search of the young men who had gone to see him about the hymn. Perhaps they could do something. When he found them he begged their assistance, and two of them accompanied him to the Civil Government. The building was packed with people and Falla sat on a bench while one of the Falangists went to make enquiries. When he returned his eyes were full of tears. It was too late, Lorca had been shot that morning." I. Gibson, *The Death of Lorca*, p. 108.—*Tr.*

music. I will never forget the rehearsals of his *Concerto* in the Casa de los Tiros in Granada. Don Manuel wanted to obtain a certain tempo and he made the Orquesta Bética de Cámara (a group he himself had founded) repeat the piece over and over, until the musicians and composer were all exhausted. Falla sat mopping his shiny brow and bald head with a handkerchief. It was hard to believe that this fragile little figure could possess so much stamina. Perhaps his example influenced the intense way that Federico directed his own works, *Blood Wedding* for example.

Falla always wanted to write something with Federico, and I suspect that my brother sometimes wrote with the maestro in mind. During the act of creation every writer thinks, more or less consciously, of an ideal reader, and on one particular occasion that reader was Manuel de Falla. Falla and Federico had probably conversed on the subject of the Holy Eucharist, and Federico decided to write a Catholic poem, "Ode to the Most Holy Sacrament of the Altar" [fragments of which were published in December, 1928 in the *Revista de Occidente*. The dedication read, "In honor of Manuel de Falla.]. Federico naively supposed that the theme would please his old friend, but Falla had a very different idea of the nature of religious art—Falla, who hoped some day to acquire sufficient inner concentration and fervor to write a Mass! The easy, self-confident tone of Federico's "Ode," and the idea of expressing the Eucharistic symbols in bold, surrealistic metaphors (some of them of a purely mechanical character: the host as a "pressure gauge," or a "little tambourine of flower" or a "bull's-eye of insomnia") must have seemed little less than sacrilegious to Falla. Showing the energy and the respect for others which were so typical of him, Falla wrote the following letter to Federico:

Granada, 9 February 1929

Dear Federico,

You had never told me about the work you were preparing, and thus I did not know you were thinking of dedicating it to me.

I learned of it from Pepe Segura, who has just returned from Madrid. Just as I was trying to obtain a copy of the *Revista*, I received the one which Adolfo Salazar had sent me so I could read his article.

And therefore, please do not find it strange that I haven't written to you until now, thanking you for your dedication. I feel very honored.

I have no need to tell you, who know me so well, how we differ with respect to the subject of your "Ode." Were I to write on the same theme, I would do so with my spirit *on its knees*, and I would beg that all Humanity be made divine through the grace of the Sacrament. And then I would make my offering: gold, frankincense and myrrh. Pure and unalloyed. I know you understand me, Federico. Please pardon me if something I say bothers you. I would be very sorry if that were the case.

Certainly, as happens in all your works, this one contains parts that are beautiful and undeniably well-expressed. But, you being who you are, I could not hide, as I would from others, my exact impression. That would be contrary to the friendship and the loyalty I owe you. I shall place my hope in the definitive version and in the rest of the poem.

Remember me fondly to your father and to Paco. Your whole family is well. I had the pleasure of seeing them today.

A hug of gratitude from

MANUEL DE FALLA

For the moment the poem was abandoned,* as were other odes with the same structure and analogous tonality, like the "Ode to Sesostris."**

Falla had a way of allowing his friends to share his musical "profession." He commissioned the figures and stage settings of his *Master Pedro's Puppet Show* from our mutual friend Hermenegildo Lanz, a fellow member of the Back Corner. I will tell later [pp. 142-147] of the almost childish enthusiasm he devoted to a little show we put on at our house to celebrate the Feast of the Epiphany. He once persuaded me to translate from the French Jean Aubry's poem "Psyché," for which he had composed music [1924]. I was never able to do so, given the difficulties of the project and the composer's insistence (perhaps only natural) that the Spanish text reflect the exact meaning of the French. The first stanza was so difficult to translate, despite the (unsatisfactory) help of the maestro himself, that I have never forgotten it:

Psyché, la lampe est morte: éveille-toi. Le jour
Te considère avec des yeux noyés d'amour
Et le désir nouveau de te servir encore.

*The "Ode" contains four parts. The manuscript of the two final sections is dated in New York, 17 December 1929. The letter Federico probably wrote in reply to Falla has never been found. We do know that the friendship of the two artists was unclouded by this incident.—*Ed.*

**The manuscript of "Oda y burla de Sesostris y Sardanápalo" was published for the first time in 1985 (ed. Miguel García-Posada. La Coruña: Esquio-Ferrol).—*Tr.*

With a few exceptions, none of the members of the Back Corner spent as much time as Federico and I at Falla's. I cannot remember that the sedentary Soriano ever climbed the street to the composer's house. There, at Sunday gatherings, after the simple tea served by María del Carmen (the composer's devoted sister), we often listened to him play the piano. On the piano, framed in black, were the drawings which Picasso had made for *The Three-cornered Hat*. Those drawings influenced the ones Federico would do later, sometimes even for plays which he never wrote.

DEPARTURE FOR MADRID

Don Fernando de los Ríos guided my brother toward the Residencia de Estudiantes, and there he found a more refined atmosphere than was available to other students and youth from the provinces who, for diverse reasons, went to Madrid.

The Residencia was a sequel to the Institución Libre de Enseñanza,* and in its organization and spirit one could detect the influence of the Institución's founder, Francisco Giner de los Ríos. The director of the Residencia, Alberto Jiménez Fraud, had worked closely with Giner. This relationship became even closer when Don Alberto married Natalia Cossío, daughter of Don Manuel Bartolomé Cossío, for the latter had been Giner's favorite student and was the continuer of his work. Don Manuel was a brilliant art historian—it was he who had "discovered" El Greco. The natural elegance, beauty, and distinction of Natalia Cossío must have done much to improve the social conduct of the young "Residents"; she used to invite them, individually and in groups, to the director's house, which was impeccably furnished and located on the very campus of the Residencia.

*A small secondary school founded in Madrid in 1876 with far-reaching effects on modern Spanish culture. The Institución promoted the ideas of co-education, laicism, physical education, the pedagogical use of manual labor and travel, etc.—Tr.

Don Alberto was the sort of Andalusian who is refined and retiring, quiet and courteous. He had a miraculously invisible way of making his authority felt. Almost never that I can recall was a Resident called into his presence and reproved, even gently, for a breach in the rules. Discipline was accepted voluntarily: one behaved oneself, and that was that. No set of rules could have elicited better conduct from the students. What is remarkable is that the Residencia hardly existed as a pedagogical institution. Its enemies liked to say that it was simply a distinguished boarding house, and they were right. The Residencia was a tightly knit community devoted to a certain way of life, and its program merely offered a series of opportunities to practice that mode of life.

When Federico left for the Residencia [1919] we had been living on the Acera del Casino for many years. I can remember the preparations for that trip—one of them was putting name labels on Federico's shirts and collars. It was I who drew the letters, in indelible Chinese ink, for I had excellent handwriting and a steady hand. I remember printing in neat tiny letters not only his initials but also rhymed couplets, where Aeolia rhymed with magnolia, dahlia with Natalia. I have never seen Federico so furious. My contributions had to be carefully cut away. With infinite patience and, I think, a smile of complicity, my mother cleverly mended the holes where the offending couplets had been. I have already recorded one or two practical jokes which Federico played on me. Let this one serve as compensation.

At the time it was not unusual to travel to another city to study, but students almost always attended local institutions. For example, it would have been totally unthinkable for a student from Sevilla to attend the University of Granada, or vice versa. Nor did the prestige of one university or department ever attract students from distant regions. What mattered wasn't where one studied, it was earning a degree, and a degree from one university was just as official as one from another. And thus Federico's trip to Madrid was never spoken of at home as a *study* trip. It was thought of, somewhat vaguely, as a literary one. In the provinces, Madrid enjoyed considerable prestige as a center of cultural activity, and that idea was well-founded. Apart from what I have already described, intellectual life in the provinces did not have much to offer. There was also the silly idea that one could not really be a writer, a painter, or a poet until one "triumphed" in Madrid. To publish a poem or an article in a local newspaper was within almost anyone's reach, but to publish in the *Heraldo de Madrid* was something else again. Sometimes, very rarely, a local author would manage to have his work performed in a theater in Granada by a prestigious company. But this was practically unheard of. The real place to triumph was the capital. We often discussed such provincial superstitions in the Back Corner.

Federico told me that, once, upon returning from one of his trips to Madrid, he had run into the owner of a stationery store in the center of Granada. This man had made himself locally famous on account of what he had once said to a politician of liberal persuasion, a great lover of the city, and protector of her people: Don Natalio Rivas. When Don Natalio was quite old (I suppose his intelligence was beginning to wane) he became an advisor to Franco. Don Natalio never missed a chance to find jobs—not very well remunerated ones, to be sure—for his political friends or, simply, his friends. He was always placing them in the town government, the city hall, the trade schools, the national government, etc. For Don Natalio was a man of influence. Once, when he had just scored a big political success—I can't remember whether it was a speech in the Cortes defending the interests of Granada, or a promotion to Minister in a liberal cabinet—his friends, i.e. half of Granada, offered him a tumultuous banquet. Naturally, there were speeches. Many of them. Diverse and sundry local characters rose to toast the illustrious patrician, and among them was Don Eladio Pericás, the man I mentioned earlier, the owner of the stationery store. Don Eladio's speech was extremely brief. With his glass held high he looked at the illustrious politician and said: "Don Natalio, see if you can get good jobs for *all* of us!"

One day, as I was saying, this same Pericás crossed paths with Federico, and they exchanged the following words. My brother did a wonderful imitation of Don Eladio as he told me of this conversation:

"Son, are you coming from Madrid?"

"Yes, Sir. That's right."

"And did you triumph there?"

"I don't know. I think so."

"But did you triumph officially?"

"Oh, well, I don't know about *that*!"

II. FEDERICO'S THEATRE

Lorca and his star, Margarita Xirgu, after the première of *Yerma* at the Teatro Espanol in Madrid, 1934.

Scene from Act III of *Mariana Pineda* at the Teatro Goya in Barcelona, June 1927, starring Margarita Xirgu, set by Salvador Dalí.

Scene from Act II of the Buenos Aires production of *The Shoemaker's Prodigious Wife* (1933), starring Lola Membrives. The Shoemaker is reciting the ballad quoted on pp. 178–180.

THE BUTTERFLY'S EVIL SPELL

The Butterfly's Evil Spell was first performed on March 22, 1920, at the Eslava Theater, Madrid. It is a dramatized fable that comes from a lost early poem.* A wounded butterfly falls into a field of cockroaches. One of the roaches, Curianito, an imaginative character who is somewhat of a poet, falls in love with her. The Butterfly recovers her ability to fly, and the lover is left alone. Perhaps the play ends with the suicide of the leading character. I am not sure, for the manuscript, which was lost for a long time, is missing the final pages, and I cannot remember the ending.

The poet was twenty-one years old when the work was first performed. The Eslava Theater was then one of the most prestigious in Spain. Catalina Bárcena, the leading lady, was famous all over the Spanish-speaking world, and the director of the theater, Gregorio Martínez Sierra, the author of *Cradle Song,* was a vital part of the Modernist movement. Martínez Sierra's interest in reforming the theater helps to

---

*See Lorca's poem, "Los encuentros de un caracol aventurero" ("The Encounters of an Adventurous Snail") published in *Book of Poems,* ed. Mario Hernández (Madrid: Alianza Editorial, 1984), pp. 50-59. A recently discovered letter from Gregorio Martínez Sierra to Lorca reveals that they originally thought of staging *The Butterfly's Evil Spell* as a puppet play (Gibson, *Federico García Lorca,* p. 256).—Tr.

explain the attention he paid to my brother, who was very young and totally unknown.

Martínez Sierra, who felt a noble desire to promote new talent, had also written the text of Falla's *El amor brujo,* the work which made the great composer universally popular. The part of the Butterfly, which includes a dance we might call "the dance of the wounded butterfly," was performed by Encarnación López ("La Argentinita"), who was just beginning her career. I mention this because, later on, both Federico and Manuel de Falla would collaborate closely with her.

The memory of *El amor brujo (Bewitched Love),* whose title has a Modernist flavor (remember *El embrujo de Sevilla* [*The Bewitchment of Seville*], the Modernist novel by the Uruguayan Carlos Reyles) helped determine the title given to *The Butterfly's Evil Spell.* The poet did not choose the title himself. His own title—*The Lowest of Comedies*—had been rejected.

Martínez Sierra was probably right to reject it. Spanish theater possessed a well-defined hierarchy: there was the more or less classical theater; drama; the high comedy; the popular one-act musical comedy, full of local color called *el género chico* ("the little genre"); and, finally, minor spectacles that went from the spicy one-act farce (*sainete*) to the variety shows with dancers and music-hall songs. This last variety of entertainment was beginning to be known as *el género ínfimo* ("the lowest genre"). No doubt the title which Federico had proposed—*The Lowest of Comedies*—gave no hint of Martínez Sierra's intentions of reform and innovation.

Today, looking back over the years, we can find among the *sainetes* and even among the music-hall numbers little masterpieces of musical movement, intention, irony, and charm. No one enjoyed them more than Federico. In his "Talk About Theater"* he clearly recognizes that every sort of theatrical spectacle can possess value and even dignity. His later collaboration with La Argentinita, who began more as music-hall performer than as a dancer, may have originated in that first artistic encounter in the Eslava Theater and in the failure of *The Lowest of Comedies.*

And a failure it certainly was! The cockroaches' appearance onstage, in a work with poetic intentions, written by a novice for characters with very complicated costumes, was too much for the Madrid audience of

*Translated in *Deep Song,* pp. 123–126.—*Tr.*

1920, or for any other audience. The stage decorations were ordered from a Uruguayan painter of avant-garde tendency, Rafael Barradas. In order to keep things in perspective with the roaches, he painted daisies as large as tree trunks. But that wasn't all. What he wanted to do, he said ironically, was to interpret nature through the eyes of a cockroach. The decorations were rejected, and new ones were ordered from another "novel" stage designer, Mignoni.

It is impossible not to feel a little melancholy on remembering those moments when a yearning for reform, inexperience, and adolescent ambition blended together into a little drama that also had its bitterly comical moments. Federico told me with great relish how the audience roared with laughter when the Scorpion said, "I'm going home now/and eat ten flies." The actors, some of whom were excellent, fought off that laughter with intrepid professionalism. Also, Federico was already a man of many friends. He was living in the Residencia de Estudiantes, and almost the whole of that institution installed itself strategically in the highest seats in the theater, in order to ward off any sort of attack. This only made for a noisier failure, not only inside the theater, but also at the exits.

It is not that the piece had no precedents. A little earlier, the Spanish theater had witnessed an adaptation of *Chantecler*, by Edmond Rostand. But Federico's work was unrelated; it grew out of his own personal experience and inspiration. In fact, this very first attempt at theater is a perfect example of the unity of his work and the relation which exists between his plays and his poetry.

The purely chronological fact that he was famous as a lyric poet before he was famous as a playwright has made some people mistakenly suppose that his theater was an offshoot of his lyrical works. This error arises from a false critical focus. Federico is not a poet who *goes* to the theater (perhaps this is true in cases of "poetical theater"); he was an artist with a dramatic vision of the world who tried to express that vision by means of the theater from the very first, uncertain strokes of his pen. It is true, on the other hand, that he found his own lyrical language before he ever acquired dramatic vision and technique. He says in the prologue of *The Butterfly's Evil Spell*, "Poetry that asks why shooting stars exist is very harmful to souls that have not yet blossomed." In his posthumous play *The House of Bernarda Alba*, Adela, the youngest character, asks, "Mother, why do we say, when there is a shooting star, or a bolt of lightning . . ."

In the prologue of *The Butterfly's Evil Spell,* the old Sylph-Poet, who seems to have "escaped from one of the great Shakespeare's plays," announces, "The kingdom of the animals and plants is near at hand." The "Ode to Walt Whitman," published as part of *Poet in New York,* ends with the following words:

> ... and a black child [will] announce to the rich white men
> that the kingdom of the wheat has come.

> ... y un niño negro anuncie a los blancos del oro
> la llegada del reino de la espiga.

These precise correspondences (and we could easily add many more) between theater and poetry, and between adolescence and maturity, prove that in Federico's first works we can already see his true profile as a writer.

No one who has read his first book of verse, *Book of Poems,* will fail to observe the similarity between *The Butterfly's Evil Spell* and the animal poems (some of which are even written in dialogue); in both works the poet personifies natural elements. These echoes are also heard in his later theater: the personification of light in *Blood Wedding;* the importance of the horse in that work and in *The House of Bernarda Alba;* the role of the butterfly in *The Shoemaker's Prodigious Wife,* etc. Without understanding the personification and presence of the natural elements, it would not be possible to grasp certain aspects of his later works.

But the animal poetry of *Book of Poems* is often successful, whereas, despite the tender, ingenuous poetry of certain passages, *The Butterfly's Evil Spell* is not really a viable dramatic work.

The author himself was aware of this. He was guided more by instinct than by a carefully thought out knowledge of the nature of the theater as a genre. Some have said that Federico was so discouraged by the rush of the rehearsals that he wanted to withdraw the play, and that, trusting in my father's generosity, he was ready to propose refunding what the company had spent on it. It is not hard to imagine the state of mind of this unknown author: how hard it would have been to withdraw his work from the Eslava Theater (of difficult access even to famous playwrights). There was also the fear of a noisy failure (which, at heart, he knew he deserved) balanced by the thrill of putting himself to the test, rather than simply fleeing. The decisive factor was the firmness of Martínez Sierra, who had never ceased to believe in the possibilities of this work and in his own ability to "discover" new talent. Interestingly enough, it was the young poet, rather than the veteran author, director, and impresario, who was proven right.

Federico surprised his friends and the actors by the calmness with which he accepted his failure. Perhaps the jeers and foot-stomping of the audience convinced him of his own strength and made him decide never to make facile concessions. I have no doubt that he remembered those moments years later in the Author's speech in *The Shoemaker's Prodigious Wife*. There Federico defends the rights of the theater and tries to justify fantasy and even the absurd as theatrical values, threatened by commercial theater:

> Esteemed audience. (*Pause*) No, "esteemed" no. Just "audience." It is not that the playwright does not consider the audience "esteemed." On the contrary. It is just that the word conceals fear and trembling, and a sort of plea for the audience to be generous with the actors' and the author's imagination. The poet does not ask for benevolence, he asks for attention. It was long ago that he surmounted the thorny barrier of fear that authors feel for their audience . . .

The *Butterfly's Evil Spell* lasted for only two performances, and this may have been a record. Failed works usually lasted for three. I was in Granada when the work was performed. We knew that Federico would not communicate the results, which the family was avidly awaiting, if they were not positive. My father had asked a close friend of his, a banker who happened to be in Madrid, to send us a telegraph saying whether the work was a success or a failure. My parents, my sisters, and I were gathered in the living room and now, as I evoke that lovely room, I remember its Art Nouveau style, its wavy, dark wood molding that stood out against rich wallpaper with huge flowers and brilliant gold leaves, its sculpted white marble fireplace, its door (I have never seen one so richly carved) with birds and monkeys in high relief. After a long time—it was probably after one o'clock in the morning—the telegram arrived. Don Manuel Conde (for that was the name of the family friend) had composed it with tact. But it contained more truth than he realized: "The work did not please. All agree Federico is a great poet."

THE PUPPET PLAYS

Puppet theater is twice as profound as normal theater. For in the guignol, the theatrical character, who is the incarnation of a real being, is replaced in turn by the puppet. When the puppeteer pokes his huge head through the curtains of the stage, with a puppet dangling from either hand, we witness a rare artistic event. It was probably Cervantes who was the first to be aware of the complexity of this phenomenon, and to exploit its poetic possibilities.

This popular form of theater, which we think of as primitive—an elemental form of art—takes pleasure in exposing the complicated workings of dramatic fiction. I am thinking, above all, of the relationship between the author, the characters, and the audience. One essential part of this "simple" spectacle is that the puppeteer speaks and argues with his characters, even before they come onstage, and thus he himself turns into *two* characters, and makes the puppets independent of the hand that works them and the voice that gives them life. This is what Federico manages to do in the *Retablillo de Don Cristóbal*,* in the initial dialogue between the director and his two characters, Don Cristóbal and Miss Rosita:

---

*Literally, *Don Cristóbal's Puppet Show*, referred to hereafter as the *Retablillo.—Tr.*

"Come out, the audience is waiting!"

"I'm coming."

"What about Rosita?"

"I am putting my shoes on. (*Snoring is heard*)

"What's this? Are you snoring, Don Cristóbal?"

"I'm coming, Mr. Director. I was just taking a leak."

"Be quiet, and watch your language."

This sort of fictive play was also used by Federico in the prologue of *The Shoemaker's Prodigious Wife*, with its dialogue between the Author and the Wife. To make the dialogue more life-like, Federico himself played the part of the Author on the night of the première. Sometimes it is the character himself who addresses the audience. I remember how amused Federico was by a story told by someone from our Back Corner group. Some naughty children with a pea-shooter were firing garbanzo beans or cherry pits at the puppets. Don Cristóbal turns to the audience and says, "I am going to insult the mother of the next kid who shoots." The audience angrily protests, and the puppeteer himself has to ask them to pardon his character: "Esteemed audience. Please pardon Don Cristóbal for what he said. But try to understand that there are a lot of sons of b--- in this theater."

The same situation, elevated to the level of poetry, occurs in Cervantes' "Master Pedro's Puppet Show." It is true that in the story I have just told there are realistic elements extraneous to the story itself. But the mere *possibility* of such occurrences (and Cervantes understood this perfectly) is enough to affect the dramatic character of the puppet show. The extra-artistic element is but one more aspect of the complex relationship between the author, his characters, and the audience—a relationship which, as I said earlier, helps define this form of minor theater.

Puppet plays were probably important during the period of our classical theater. One need only read the chapters of *Don Quijote* that tell of "Master Pedro's Puppet Show"* to see how lively and full of action these shows must have been. Some of the movements were narrated rather than executed, but even so, it must have been very hard for the puppeteer to keep up with the manipulation of the figures. The same man was responsible for accompanying those movements with sounds and music, drums and bells. The stage was lit up by a profusion of little candles. The

*Chapters XXV and XXVI of the first part of *Don Quijote.—Tr.*

figures were made of cardboard and, judging from the way they are described, were fairly detailed. We do not know much about Master Pedro's repertory; what he performs for Don Quijote is a theme taken from a ballad from the Carlovingian cycle. But this particular sort of puppet show (the *retablo*) has not come down to us. When Federico titles one of his works *Retablillo* he is simply remembering Cervantes. And when Antonio Machado evokes distant memories in his *Solitudes* and catches sight of

> delicate little figures
> that the puppeteer places on his stage [*retablo*]

we can assume that those delicate little figures, and the word *retablo* itself, allude to a purely literary experience. We cannot suppose that Don Antonio ever saw the "little figures" or the *retablos* during his life in Castile and Andalusia.

The puppets that have subsisted in popular tradition, those that Federico and Machado were familiar with as children, are the roughly executed *cristobalitos* or *cristobicas** with heavy wooden heads, too hard to be broken under Don Cristóbal's billyclub. The voice was simulated with two little pieces of reed, tied together by a thread. Between the reeds was a tiny piece of vibrating tissue—one usually used the skin of an onion or a little piece of tripe, such as the skin from the sausage called *chorizo*. It is not easy to speak through this device without making a whistling sound. I have tried often, with only moderate success.

THE GIRL WHO WATERS THE BASIL
AND THE INQUISITIVE PRINCE

The Feast of the Epiphany is one of the great traditional holidays of Spain. And the theme of the Three Wise Men, an extremely poetic one, has always captured the popular imagination. The Three Kings are the equivalent of traditional characters from other lands, and, as everyone knows, on January 6 they leave gifts for children on the balconies and beside the hearth. It is a holiday exclusively for children. In Granada it was especially important, for the Three Kings "really" appeared. Leading

---

*The generic name for puppets, formed from the Andalusian diminutives of "Cristó-bal" (Christopher), the traditional villain.—*Tr.*

a train of maids and dignitaries, horses and camels, and carts laden with toys for poor children, they crossed the city by the light of torches and flares. This parade, which later spread to other cities, was organized by the Arts Center, where Federico began his career in music and literature. In 1923 we celebrated the Feast of the Epiphany at home. Federico had organized a theatrical performance for our youngest sister, Isabel. A swarm of boys and girls, friends of hers, gathered in our house, together with many adults. The stage was set up in the wide doorway between the front parlor (where the actors and musicians were) and the drawing room, where the audience waited impatiently. The chief collaborator, especially on the musical part, was Manuel de Falla.

First on the program was an interlude of Cervantes titled *The Chatterboxes*, a work with a minimum of dramatic action, as is typical of this sort of minor theater.* The influence of this work on one of Federico's plays is easy to detect. A gentleman comes upon a ruffian in the street, and the latter turns out to be an unbearable chatterbox. The knight decides to take him home and keep him there, so that he will out-talk his wife, the "greatest chatterbox in the world." The authorities, who are hunting for the ruffian on account of certain minor offenses, discover him in the gentleman's house and try to take him away. But the gentleman intervenes and tells them of the good that the ruffian is doing. The forces of law and order, who are generous and compassionate (Cervantes' idea of what they *should* have been like) accede to the gentleman's request. Their leader lays down only one condition: the chatterbox must come and live with him and cure his own wife, who suffers from the same defect. The little work comes to an end, as do all the others of its genre, with joyful songs and dances, much to the dismay of the wife who was given voice and action by my sister Conchita.

The humor of that "interlude" comes to a climax with an insuperable war of words between the two chatterboxes. They are constantly interrupting each other, and neither is able to catch his breath. Their long-winded speeches contain a mechanical association of ideas, a dizzying automatism that is simply hilarious. Cervantes would not be the great writer he is if, even when using a simple scheme like this, he were unable

---

*Recent scholarship has cast doubt upon the attribution of this work to Cervantes. For example, Eugenio Asensio in his introduction to the *Entremeses* (Madrid, 1971, pp. 14-15) and in his *Itinerario del entremés* (Madrid, 1971, pp. 26-28 and 99). In 1923, of course, no one doubted that *The Chatterboxes* was the work of Cervantes.—*Ed.*

to portray the distinctive personalities of his little characters. The gentleman is irascible and witty, the wife is insulting and authoritarian, the representative of justice is tactful and circumspect, the maid obedient but quick to answer back.

For this occasion Federico wrote a work whose complete title was *The Girl Who Waters the Basil and the Inquisitive Prince*. This little work was adapted from a children's story. In the souvenir program we made for the occasion, it is defined as an "old Andalusian tale" divided into "three engravings and a color print." *Mariana Pineda* would later be divided into three "engravings" instead of acts.

It seems to me that Federico wrote the work using fragments from an old story he had half forgotten. I say this because I do not remember that the story ever formed part of our repertory of folklore (though, admittedly, Federico knew more than I). Some of the questions, including the one that is alluded to in the title, have a markedly traditional flavor, and this suggests that not everything was invented by the poet. The program says that the story has been "put into dialogue and adapted for the 'Billy-Club Theater of Andalusia' by Federico García Lorca."

With the help of my sister Concha, who shared Federico's fine memory and so many of his other qualities, I have managed to reconstruct the plot of the story just as it was performed.*

The Girl, a puppet who was worked by my sister, appears in a window singing "El Vito" with the lyrics Federico was to make popular years later:

Tengo los ojos azules	My eyes are blue,
y el corazoncito igual	and my heart is the same
que la cresta de la lumbre.	as the tip of the flame.

The same words and music are sung repeatedly by Doña Rosita in *The Billy-Club Puppets*; we may suppose that the Girl was an early version of her. The Prince, who was worked by Federico, asks the Girl:

| Niña que riegas la albahaca, | Girl who waters the basil, |
| ¿cuántas hojitas tiene la mata? | how many leaves does the plant have? |

*An unauthorized version of this puppet play was published in 1982 in the magazine *Titere, Boletín de la Unión de Titiriteros y la Asociación de Amigos de la Marioneta*. See Gibson, *Federico García Lorca*, p. 675.—*Tr.*

The Girl replies with an equally difficult question:

Dime, rey zaragatero,	Tell me, you troublemaking king,
¿cuántas estrellitas tiene el cielo?	how many little stars does the sky have?

The Girl closes the window and the Prince sadly withdraws. In order to speak to her again, he disguises himself as a fishmonger and, now that he is on the same social level as the Girl, an idyll begins: the Girl pays for the fish with kisses. They repeat the scene with the questions, but when the Prince is asked how many stars there are in the sky he answers:

[As many as] the kisses you gave the fishmonger.

Los besos que le diste al pescadero.

The Girl does not return to the window, and the Prince begins to pine away. There is a meeting of wise men to cure him. The Girl disguises herself as a magician with a black cape and a conical hat spangled with silver stars, and comes into the palace saying:

Soy el mago de la alegría,	I am the magician of happiness.
que traigo el trompetín de la risa.	and I bring the little bugle of laughter

I think it is the Girl herself who suggests that the only way to cure the Prince is to have him marry the Girl who waters the basil. I remember there was a final idyll in a fantastic garden with the "tree of the sun" and the "tree of the moon"; we still have these decorations at our country house in Granada, the Huerta de San Vicente. This scene must have been the "color print" that puts an end to the work.

But without a doubt, what most amused the children was that, between acts, Don Cristóbal himself (played by Federico) came out and began to converse with the audience, calling the children by their names. This moment of spontaneous communication with an audience of children— or an audience which the show had *turned into* children—made a deep impression on the poet. Much later, in 1934, thousands of miles away in the Avenida Theater of Buenos Aires, Don Cristóbal would come back onto the stage, worked, once again, by the poet. He would begin his performance with these words:

Ladies and gentlemen: This is not the first time that I, Don Cristóbal, the drunken puppet who marries Doña Rosita, have accompanied Federico García Lorca onto the stage—a stage where I can only live, and never die. The first time was in the poet's house—do you remember, Federico? It was springtime in Granada, and the drawing room of your house was full of children saying "The puppets are made out of flesh. Why do they stay so small? Why don't they grow up?" The great Manuel de Falla was playing the piano, and Stravinsky's *Soldier's Tale* was heard in Spain for the first time. I still remember the smiling faces of the newsboys whom the poet had asked up from the street, and the curls, ribbons, and smiling faces of the rich children.

The *Soldier's Tale* served as background for Cervantes' *The Chatterboxes*. It was arranged by Falla for clarinet, violin, and piano. Federico's own little play was accompanied with music of Debussy, Albéniz, Ravel, and an anonymous Spanish dance of the seventeenth century. But in Federico's mind, and perhaps also Falla's, the *pièce de résistance* was the staging of the *Mystery of the Three Kings*, which the program announced in these words: "Now comes the greatest event of all." The chief merit of this anonymous thirteenth-century work is that it is the first known play of the Spanish theater. It would be curious to know how long it had been since it had last been performed—perhaps not since the Middle Ages. To be sure, this performance was a minimal one: the stage was probably less than a meter and a half wide, and the curtain was made from two red and white peasant kerchiefs.

The figures and the decorations were made by the painter Hermenegildo Lanz, from whom Falla would later commission the sets, costumes, and puppets for the Paris première of *Master Pedro's Puppet Show* in the salon of the Princess of Polignac, American patron of the arts and owner of the Singer Sewing Machine company. In making the cardboard decorations and figures, Lanz followed the splendid miniatures in the "Albert the Great codex" which is in the library of the University of Granada.

The musical accompaniment was performed by a little orchestra composed of a violin, a clarinet, a lute, and a piano, the latter played by Falla. Among other pieces of old music were a few *cantigas* of Alfonso the Learned, which we learned to sing acceptably after much practice, and two liturgical pieces from a Catalonian codex, the *Llivre vermeill*, which were sung by Isabel and her friend Laurita de los Ríos. To make the instruments sound older, Falla covered the strings of our baby grand piano with tissue paper. After much experimentation the piano sounded like a harpsichord, much to the delight of the maestro. This first experiment in puppet theater, staged for an audience of children and friends, must have made Federico remember the première of *The Butterfly's Evil Spell*. Many years later, when writing a didactic prologue for the *Retablillo de Don Cristóbal*, he addresses it to an imaginary audience of children.

During that celebration of the Feast of the Epiphany my brother probably sensed that his art was vaguely connected to a tradition several centuries old. The spirit of Cervantes himself seemed to smile upon that roomful of giggling children.

THE BILLY-CLUB PUPPETS. TRAGICOMEDY
OF DON CRISTÓBAL AND MISS ROSITA

There are several versions of this play, and I shall have to begin by describing them carefully. First, there is a typescript in the possession of an actor, with a note saying that it was used for a performance in the Zarzuela Theater, Madrid, at the end of 1937. I was absent from Spain at that time, and have no direct knowledge of the performance. This script was also used as the copy-text for the first edition of *The Billy-Club Puppets* published in Buenos Aires in 1949 and incorporated, in 1960, into the fourth Spanish [Aguilar] edition of Federico's *Complete Works.**

I myself have two other manuscripts, one of them unfinished. It is impossible to tell from the handwriting, or any other evidence, which is the earliest, so I will simply call them Ms. A and Ms. B. They are interesting as early versions of the published play.

Ms. A is dated August 5, 1922: five months before the private performance of *The Girl Who Waters the Basil*. It is divided into two sections of unequal length. The first section corresponds, with slight variants, to Scene I of the published version. The second section bears the title "Act

---

*It was thus the source used by James Graham-Lujan and Richard L. O'Connell in their version in *Five Plays by Lorca* (New Directions, 1963).—*Tr.*

Two" and is divided into two scenes corresponding, with a few variants, to scenes V and VI of the published version. Ms. A is only half as long as the published version, but it is perfectly viable and complete.

Ms. B contains a new plot. It begins with a "Foreword" spoken by Mosquito, corresponding to the prologue in the published version. It is not explicitly divided into scenes, but the changes in the stage settings show that it follows scenes II, III and IV of the published version. Ms. B has no ending. We can suppose that the ending is missing because a natural denouement had already been written (in Ms. A). The published version is simply a combination of Ms. B (scenes II, III and IV) and Ms. A (scenes I, V and VI). Only the poet could have combined the two manuscripts—some of the substitutions, omissions, and additions bear his unmistakable mark. Besides, all the revisions improve the text. What is extremely interesting is that the final version—the published one—possesses a perfect, organic unity, obtained merely by superimposing two independent texts, without either of them borrowing anything from the other. It is even more remarkable that Ms. A is (as I have said) complete in itself. This version moves even more smoothly and rapidly than the published one, and in this sense perhaps it is superior.

There is also a lost manuscript of this work. Federico wanted to add songs and dances and, if I remember correctly, this version was based on the complete text—the one which has been published. Federico asked the Philippine composer Federico Elizalde to collaborate with him, and I remember the two of them sitting at the piano of the Hotel Majestic in Barcelona. My sister Isabel, Federico, and I had gone to Barcelona to attend the première of *Doña Rosita the Spinster* (1935).

The *Billy-Club Puppets* does not contain any clear indication as to the nature of the characters, and more than once I have been asked if it was best to perform the play with marionettes or with people. In the final version the poet seems to want the little characters to be performed by people, and this would mean inverting the procedure typical of the traditional puppet theater—instead of puppets playing the roles of people, people would act as puppets. This inversion would be much to Federico's liking. When Ms. A and Ms. B were combined, the plot became much more complex, and perhaps this is why in the final version the characters are apparently to be played by people. But there is no reason why the play cannot be done by puppets. At certain moments, two expert puppeteers would be required.

Of the two manuscripts, A seems more intended for puppets than B.

In the sixth and final scene (which comes from Ms. A), shortly before the work ends, the stage notes indicate that the characters are indeed puppets: "Various puppets enter. . . . The central door opens up, and we see puppets carrying torches." There are no previous indications of this sort, although the situation, movements, and acting have a certain puppet-like quality. Those who have read the work will remember that its denouement revolves around the fact that Don Cristóbal is nothing but a mortal puppet, i.e. his mechanism is capable of breaking down. The other characters recognize objectively that he is only a puppet, and automatically place themselves on another level of reality. But on the whole, the author has given the *Tragicomedy* an ambiguous quality, allowing for both possibilities. This is part of its charm. It is interesting that in the first scenes in Ms. A and Ms. B there are never more than two characters on stage at the same time. The play grows progressively more complicated but not so much as to be unworkable in a simple puppet theater.

This ambiguity is kept up by means of what the characters themselves say. In the first scene, for example, Don Cristóbal looks at Doña Rosita and says: "I'll definitely take her. She is probably one meter tall. Women should have exactly that height, no more, no less." It is a height equally distant from normal human height and from that of the traditional puppets of Andalusia. In the denouement the author establishes and maintains the puppet-like nature of Don Cristóbal, alluding to his wooden head, a head made from cheap poplar wood, with knots that exude resin, etc. But when it comes to actually defining him, one of the characters in the manuscript says, "Cristobita was a puppet!" The published version says, more ambiguously, "Cristobita was not a person." The correction shows that Federico wished to maintain the confusion, and this is also shown by the appearance, or simple mention, of characters with diverse origins, for example Figaro, a character who is delightfully minimalized in the work, or the allusions to the family of Don Cristóbal, who says he is going to tell Rosita:

> . . . the story of Don Tancredo mounted on his pedestal. You know? Hah!
> And the story of Don Juan Tenorio, a cousin of Don Tancredo and mine.
> Yes sir! A cousin of mine!

Don Juan is well known, but not Don Tancredo, a real character who became famous, almost legendary, because at the beginning of the bullfight he would appear "mounted on his pedestal" in the center of the ring, dressed in white, like a statue from the third act of José Zorrilla's *Don Juan*. The bull went for him like an arrow but Don Tancredo stood so still that the animal always stopped a few inches in front of him and merely sniffed and backed away. The least movement on Don Tancredo's part would have cost him his life. I do not think he ever had an accident. This maneuver, which is no longer performed, was still extant during our youth—Federico and I actually saw it.

Some of the puppet characters are invented ones. The name of Scare-Clouds, which alludes to someone's height, and that of Tire-Souls,* which refers to the slowness of someone's speech, were the nicknames of real people from Fuente Vaqueros. I am surprised there is no Bed-On-His-Shoulder, the village nickname for someone who often changed his residence. Federico delighted in these nicknames, which seemed to reveal the creativity of his village.

The main characters—Don Cristóbal, Miss Rosita, the Mother, Mosquito—are traditional ones. There is another traditional character, Currito from the Harbor, of whom we learned from Uncle Frasquito—the same uncle who taught Federico the song "El café de Chinitas." I still remember a certain scene which Federico reproduces in my uncle's very words when Currito first appears.

"Yes, it's Currito from the Harbor."
"Why you mischievous little devil! How fat you've gotten!"

The plot of this play (aside from the wedding of the main characters) is totally invented. And yet I could identify more than a few lines and songs that come from the traditional puppet theater; for example, the following song, which the priest intones at Don Cristóbal's funeral:

> Cantemos o no cantemos,   Whether we sing or not,
> cinco duros ganaremos.   we are going to earn 25 pesetas.

This innocent burst of anti-ecclesiastical satire appears in the original manuscript, but not the published version. It was probably removed by the censors.

Cansa-almas, called Wearisome in Graham-Lujan and O'Connell's translation (see *Five Plays*). Scare-Clouds is called Quakeboots.

Another traditional scene is the one where Doña Rosita tries on boots for her wedding. Interestingly, this scene, which has the same innocent picaresque flavor as the one I have just mentioned, appears in an interlude by Cervantes entitled *The Hawk-Eyed Sentinel*. The fact that in both works a character disguises himself as a shoemaker seems to confirm Federico's double (popular and learned) sources. The appearance of this motif in both the popular puppet theater and in Cervantes, who was so fond of puppets, suggests that the popular puppet theater may have a more complex origin than has been supposed.

The early date of this minor work gives it special importance for the study of the evolution of Federico's theater, especially with respect to the creation of his dramatic language. There are very strong lyrical overtones (they are strongest in Ms. B), and much use is made of the oddities and peculiar expressions of Andalusian Spanish. Federico was extremely skillful at recreating such modes of speech and this aspect of the work deserves a separate study. What I would like to examine now is the way in which Federico uses words to give a special rhythm to the characters' actions. The work begins with these words from Rosita:

> (*Counting her stiches*) One, two, three, four . . . (*She pricks herself*) Ouch! (*Sucking her finger*) This is the fourth time I have pricked myself on the final *r* in the words "To my beloved father."

Rosita has begun counting the stiches and matching the "one, two, three, four" to the movements of the hand hovering above the cloth. This gives the feeling that she is counting time, so that there is a very strong sensation of time at the very beginning of the work. The number *cuatro* (four) in the initial series links up with the sentence "*Cuatro veces me he pinchado ya . . .*" (This is the fourth time I have pricked myself). That sentence continues an action that began before the curtain went up (a typical feature of Federico's theater, as we shall see later). But the action is suddenly broken off—"One, two . . . (*She puts down the needle*)"— giving way to the true action: "Ah, how I would love to get married." This initial monologue is interrupted in turn by a whistle, at which Rosita exclaims, "Oh-ho-ho, it's my boy!" and then a rapid movement "(*She runs to the balcony*)." The movement towards the balcony has barely begun when it is interrupted by the voice of the father, who calls from another room in the house ("Rositaaaaaa!") and this creates a new emotional situation: in a stage note the author says, "*She is frightened.*"

Rosita answers ("Wha-a-at?") and this triggers a tiny series of actions, specified in the stage note: *A louder whistle. She runs and sits down to her knitting, but blows kisses towards the balcony.* Then the father enters, and the dialogue begins.

This series of interruptions of time, of emotion, and of physical movements (from the moment Rosita pricks herself and stops counting, until the moment when the father's entrance interrupts the kisses she has been blowing toward the balcony) nearly exceeds the space allotted to it. Gestures, words, and movements must be endowed with musical rhythm. The "one, two, three, four" with which the play begins seems to set up the rhythm for the ensuing action.

This deliberately rhythmical movement is more than simply interesting, it introduces the very theme of the "tragicomedy." Rosita struggles with love, on the one hand, and the impositions of her family, on the other. She is at the center of things, beckoned, almost simultaneously, by one call coming from off-stage (the whistle of her lover from the street) and another coming from inside the house (her father's voice). The symbolic objects in the play will be the embroidery frame, the window, and the door.

The language sometimes produces the materialization of non-material things that is so typical of Federico. Through the mouth of Mosquito he says in the prologue, "Hush, so the dregs of the last whispers will settle down." The whistle I mentioned earlier, a whistle heard in the following scene as well, will bound off the dramatic space. After whistling again Cristóbal says, "The whistle has struck her windowpane like a little pebble of music." Analogous procedures help create the spatio-temporal settings that make this play a little jewel. In it we find diverse levels of comical and lyrical language. This is how the poet revived a genre that was extremely impoverished, almost extinct, when it reached his hands.

RETABLILLO DE DON CRISTÓBAL

Ten years later, after he had had more experience in the theater and had written both major works and a cycle of minor ones like *The Shoemaker's Wife* and *Perlimplín*, the poet returned to Don Cristóbal. In this play we no longer find the exquisite lyrical intentions that had characterized the interpretation of popular art under the aegis of Juan Ramón

Jiménez (a tendency which can probably be traced back to Giner de los Ríos).* What the poet now prefers is crude, raw, even salacious language. This style is closer to genuine popular theater. The author does not even construct a plot; the play is no more than a series of scenes held together by the main character. There are more authentic expressions and an increase in the amount of verse. The poet makes use of the absurd chains of verse that are often found in children's rhymes.

The freer and apparently simpler treatment makes for the shortest piece in Federico's theater. And yet, the complex relation between the author, the audience, and the characters is much more evident than in the earlier play. Not only does the Director speak to the puppets, he also addresses the Poet. And the Poet speaks with the other characters, who can now be clearly identified as puppets—the author has not wanted to take refuge in any sort of artistic ambiguity.

This little work begins with a prologue that is almost didactic in character. Despite the freedom of its language, none of Federico's plays has more markedly *critical* intentions. It is the most "exemplary" play he ever wrote, not only because of what is said against theatrical convention, but also because the indecent language is such an obvious way of breaking with it. The whole play is a defense of creative freedom.

The work breaks off abruptly in the middle of a somewhat incoherent plot. With one word, the Director brings the action to a halt and addresses the audience:

(*He sticks his huge head out into the theater*) Enough! (*He takes the puppets and lets them dangle from his hand, showing them to the audience*). Ladies and gentlemen: Those who live in the country often hear plays like this one beneath the gray branches of the olive trees, or in the dark air of abandoned stables. Amid mules' eyes hard as fists, the tooled leather of Cordovan harnesses, and tender clumps of wet wheat, one can hear joyful, charmingly innocent bursts of strong language. These are the words we cannot stand to hear in the atmosphere of the city, dark with alcohol and decks of cards. Such words seem fresh and innocent when spoken by the puppets of this charming very old rural farce. Let us fill the theater with fresh wheat, and let us have strong language to chase away the boredom and vulgarity to which we have condemned the stage.

*See page 130.—Tr.

In the figure of the Poet we find the lyrical profile of Federico. When the Director buys him for five pieces of gold, the Poet says, "I don't want gold coins. Gold seems like fire to me, and I am a poet of the night. Give me silver ones. Silver coins seem like the moon is shining on them." Those who know Federico's poetry will recognize the writer of so many poems about night, and the connection between the moon and the coin:

Cuando sale la luna,	When the moon comes out,
de cien rostros iguales,	moon of a hundred equal faces,
la moneda de plata	the silver coin
solloza en el bolsillo.	sobs in the pocket.

They will also recognize the writer who never lost sight of the educational role of the theater, who tried to raise his audience to the level of Poetry, and make middle class people think of the countryside where he had discovered pure forms of art. And they will recognize a man of good will, who believed in the innate goodness of that "mischievous little devil" Don Cristóbal, and in his possible salvation.

The play also gives us a glimpse of the poet's face—his brown face, with its salient cheekbones, a face made fuller by the passage of time. This is how the Director portrays him.

You fake! If you don't keep quiet, I will go up there and split that big cornbread face of yours!

In just a few pages the play gives us the profile of the poet and the man. This is how the true artist leaves his mark on his work: in big things and in small, and even (without narcissism) by knowing how to laugh at his own image.

MARIANA PINEDA

Dated January 8, 1925, *Mariana Pineda* had been read in its entirety to a group of friends in 1924. It was not until October 1927, that it was performed in Madrid by the actress who would be the leading lady in most of my brother's plays, Margarita Xirgu. The time that usually elapsed between the writing and the publication of his works was an essential part of my brother's life in art. Those works did not remain unknown, but were often read to small groups of friends, and even to large audiences, before being printed. This gave Federico, among the poets of his generation, the reputation of a popular bard, one which the poet deserved because of the masterfully simple, completely unhistrionic way he read his poems and dramas. He had a rough, almost husky voice, warm and full of nuances. Never, either in his recitals or in his singing, could he have been a professional. I think he took the stage as an actor on just two occasions: once to read the prologue in *The Shoemaker's Prodigious Wife* on the night of its première (and this was because he did not have to act, but merely to read the part of the Author) and once in a performance of La Barraca,* where he played the part of Shadow in

---

*La Barraca (literally "shack," "hut") was a government-subsidized theatre group which toured Spain giving performances from the classical repertory. Shortly after founding La Barraca (1931), Lorca told the American journalist Mildred Adams: "The theatre is

Calderón's *auto sacramental Life Is a Dream*, with the veils of his costume covering his entire body.

Despite his skill as a conversationalist and raconteur, Federico never trusted the spoken word. He wrote down all of his lectures before he read them; even the little talks that he gave in Spanish villages as director of La Barraca were carefully written, as though addressed to the most sophisticated of audiences. As far as I can remember, he improvised on only one occasion, the banquet offered him by a group of Catalonian intellectuals after the success of *Doña Rosita the Spinster*. Despite promises to the contrary, there were speeches, and in the end my brother had to make one himself. God knows what an effort he must have made, aided by his charm and the natural expressiveness of his language and gestures.

The time which elapsed between the writing and première of *Mariana Pineda* is partly attributable to political circumstances. Mariana Pineda was a heroine of liberty, and Spain was then governed by the dictatorship of Primo de Rivera (1923–1930). Liberty was a touchy theme. There was even the possibility that the play would be banned altogether. This is the reason which Martínez Sierra gave, years later, to one of Federico's biographers, as an excuse for having rejected the work: "*Mariana Pineda* is not a political pamphlet against the Primo de Rivera dictatorship, but it certainly seemed like one." Margarita Xirgu wanted to take the risk, and in fact one of the reasons for the work's success may have been the political moment at which that hymn to freedom finally appeared.

Mariana Pineda's tragic life must be viewed in the context of the political actions and reactions of nineteenth-century Spain, an epoch that made the best of the Spanish Romantics, Mariano José de Larra, exclaim, "Spain, like a new Penelope, merely weaves and unweaves."

During the ominous reign of Ferdinand VII, that lovely woman was sentenced to death in her native Granada after the authorities found in her house a half-finished flag that was to have served as the banner of an

---

especially adapted to educational purposes here in Spain. It used to be the most important means of popular instruction, popular exchange of ideas. In the days of Lope de Rueda it was just such a theatre on wheels as we are planning now. It went to all the villages, and gave all the famous old plays [. . . .] Outside of Madrid today the theatre, which is in its very essence a part of the life of the people, is almost dead, and the people suffer accordingly, as they would if they had lost eyes or ears or sense or taste. We are going to give it back to them in the terms in which they used to know it, with the very plays they used to love." See "The Theatre in the Spanish Republic," reprinted from *Theatre Arts Monthly* in *Obras completas*, Vol. II, p. 979.—*Tr.*

insurrection against the abject tyranny of the King. She was promised life and liberty if she would reveal the names of the leaders of the insurrection. Mariana preferred silence and death. She was executed by garroting in a public square on May 26, 1831, at age twenty-seven. But in fact Mariana had already been kept under surveillance and subjected to house arrest for the possession of certain incriminating documents. She served as a liaison between the conspirators and the political prisoners. One of the leaders of the conspiracy was a relative, Fernando Álvarez de Sotomayor; Mariana concealed his name during her imprisonment and trial. By disguising himself as a Capuchin monk, he was able to escape from the prison to which he had been sentenced for his revolutionary activities. The heroine smuggled the monk's habit into the jail at great personal risk. They had decided that the escape would take place on a day when one of the prisoners was to be executed, and friars from several different orders were to be entering and leaving. The original story, told by Sotomayor himself and revealing Mariana's participation, has come down to us.

Certain other remarkable details about Mariana's death have turned it from history into legend, and in fact a children's ballad sung in Granada served as the starting point of Federico's work.* But Mariana Pineda really has *two* legends. In the first of them she is a pure symbol of political freedom. I could not express this tradition better than did a certain political figure from Granada, who wrote and published the following, before dying recently at a very advanced age:

When I was very young I met certain old people [for example, his father, who was an ardent liberal and an eyewitness to these events] who were living in Granada and lived through those days of sadness. But I never heard any of them say, even as gossip, that Mariana, in her heroic deed on behalf of Liberty and her Fatherland, had been moved by the slightest shade of personal interest—nor even by anything as human as the love felt by a woman for a man.**

*In Lorca's day the ballad of Mariana Pineda was sung by Spanish children as accompaniment to "circle games." For an excellent study of the popular origins of *Mariana Pineda*, with many versions of the ballad, see Sandra Cary Robertson, *The Resurgence of the Theatre of Popular Poetry: Federico García Lorca and Rafael Alberti, 1923-1935* (PhD. thesis, University of California at San Diego, 1984), pp. 169-190.—*Tr.*

**Natalio Rivas, in the prologue to C. G. Ortiz de Villajos, *Doña Mariana Pineda. Su vida—su muerte* (Madrid: Renacimiento, 1931), pp. 13-14.—*Tr.*

The second legend supposes that Mariana acted out of love. It doesn't take much imagination to turn Mariana's story into an idyll. Consider the few details I have given about Mariana's cousin: he was young, handsome, and aristocratic, and Mariana had been a widow since the age of eighteen. There is thus a political legend, the one written down, and a sentimental one, the one carried about on the wings of the wind. Why not admit that both are true? After all, they are not incompatible. Was Mariana a liberal or a woman in love? Couldn't she have been both?

The key to this historical and legendary problem would be the record of her trial. And I say *would* be because the proceedings have been stolen from the archives of the Chancery of Granada. There are two versions of why this theft occurred. First, the ideological version: the trial was so monstrous from a legal point of view, and it cast the King's "justice" in such an unfavorable light, that the proceedings were destroyed by someone who was anti-liberal and reactionary. Second, the sentimental version: so clearly did the trial reveal Mariana's love affair that the ideological symbolism of her death was in danger. The pious hand of some liberal removed it from the eye of history.*

Aside from a few documents found in the City Hall of Granada, the only primary source is the book of Don José de la Peña y Aguayo, published in 1836 with the title of *Mariana Pineda*. I have conversed personally with the descendants of this Peña, who was a liberal lawyer and a friend of Mariana, and who adopted her daughter after her death. From these conversations, and in view of the fact that he was able to consult the trial proceedings shortly before they disappeared, I have decided that it was probably a liberal who stole the proceedings.

Federico has been reproached for having accepted the amorous version, the one most befitting a Romantic heroine (let us remember the historical date of this episode). But he had reasons other than style or plot. The author believed that his Mariana was the one which best matched the historical facts. This is what he himself says on the matter:

. . . Surrounded by a multitude of poetic shades, Mariana had been asking for justice from the mouth of a poet. . . . They compared her to Judith, and she searched in the shadows for the hand of her sister Juliet. Around her wounded neck they placed the golden necklace of the ode, but she was

*The author is summarizing the two versions presented by Ortiz de Villajos, pp. 67–73. Most of his historical information on Mariana Pineda comes from this book. A more recent account is that of Antonina Rodrigo, *Mariana Pineda* (Madrid: Alfaguara, 1965).—*Tr.*

asking for the freedom of the madrigal. While everyone sang of the eagle that cuts through the iron bars with one sweep of its wing, Mariana was bleating like a lamb, abandoned by all, sustained only by the stars.

Fulfilling my duty as a poet, I have contrasted a living, Christian Mariana, resplendent with heroism, to the cold one on the pedestal, dressed as a foreigner and a freethinker.

Margarita [Xirgu] has fulfilled her duty as an actress, and by means of her voice and her gestures has given substance to this lovely, torn shade, marrow and symbol of Liberty.

The poet believed that the ideological myth had been concealing a Mariana who was both more human and more real. His play follows reality more closely than has been supposed. Federico made use of historical or biographical facts, and even in the parts written in verse we can find literal quotations from the historical Mariana, for example these words, which she spoke after the death sentence was read to her: "I have a very short neck to be executed like this." Mariana refused to let them remove her stockings (one of the precautions taken against suicide) saying that she wanted to "pull up her socks" before she went to the scaffold. It is also an historical fact that the executioner, who was extremely nervous, put the hood on her backwards, and she herself rectified the error and turned it around. Federico was unable to utilize these facts, but he did show her coquetry and the interest she took in her dress. Poeticized in the play, these scarcely credible details seem to have been invented by the poet. But poetry contains more truth than is supposed by those who do not believe in it. Moreover, in no country as in Spain have poetry and history so often crossed paths. *Mariana Pineda* carries on a tradition that begins with the *Poem of the Cid*; it is but another case where, to find historical truth, it is probably least risky to follow the path of poetry.

Even what is most conventional in the work, the amorous harassment of the heroine at the hands of the implacable Pedrosa, chief of the city's police, is not an invention of Federico, but part of the traditional story of her life; it has found its way into her biographies, although with certain qualifications. And yet, despite its (somewhat dubious) truth, and despite having been hallowed by tradition,* this detail adds a melodramatic note

---

*In one of the popular ballad versions studied by Robertson (p. 176), "the political context of [Mariana's] death has disappeared, and the situation is expressed as an individual conflict of sexual interest." Mariana tells Pedrosa: "Yo no muero porque yo soy libre, /

to the work, one which the poet probably would have toned down had he been older.

At any rate, I would dare to say that this work has never been given a really careful reading. The playwright is fully present, not merely as possibility but as reality. What makes *Mariana Pineda* important as an artistic achievement is that in it Federico discovered his dramatic language. That language must be judged in relation to the purpose of the work, which is pointedly subtitled "Popular Ballad in Three Engravings." It is thus the dramatic evocation of a Romantic situation that has been subjected to a process of stylization, as revealed in the words "ballad" and "engraving." The poet felt that it was no longer possible to write a drama in the style of the Spanish Romantics or even the Neo-Romantics who were still producing successful plays in Madrid.

> I am not saying that my work belongs to the vanguard . . . it falls somewhere in the second line. But I believe that it has certain unusual vibrations. My play is naive, like the soul of Mariana Pineda, and I wanted to give it the atmosphere of an engraving, using all the lovely commonplaces of Romanticism. It is obviously not a Romantic drama because today one can no longer seriously do a pastiche, that is, a drama of the past. I saw two ways to carry out my intentions. The first was by treating the theme with the truculency and crude coloration of the broadside ballad, but of course no one could do this better than Don Ramón [de Valle-Inclán]; the other, the one which I followed, answers to my own vision, a nocturnal, lunar, childish vision.

If the drama has any Romantic intentions, we will have to put the adjective in quotation marks. As in painting, there has to be a certain distance between the spectator and the subject matter being dramatized. The poet had planned to "frame" the stage setting of the prologue in black, as though it were an engraving, and I believe this was actually done by Salvador Dalí for the première.* If one overlooks this technique, it is easy to arrive at a mistaken judgment. As always happens in art, a work

---

*An interesting letter from Dalí to Lorca concerning the settings for *Mariana* may be found in Gibson, *Federico García Lorca*, pp. 473-474.—*Tr.*

---

ni tampoco que soy liberal; / sólo muero porque no has podido / de mi cuerpo tu gusto lograr." ("I die neither because I am free nor because I am a liberal; only because you have not succeeded in taking your pleasure with my body.")—*Tr.*

may be rejected, but only on the author's terms. An artist does not fail by *being* a Romantic or a Cubist, rather *as* a Romantic or as a Cubist. In any case, *Mariana Pineda* is not a Romantic play, nor could it have been. It is the *intentional stylization* of a Romantic play. It is on this freely chosen interpretive ground that the poet must be judged, whether favorably or unfavorably.

One of the methods which Federico selected to give his work a Romantic atmosphere was the renewed use of verse. This is the only play except *The Butterfly's Evil Spell* written entirely in verse. The language has an elevated, lyrical tone. The critics have pointed out, and perhaps they are right, that the theater of Lope de Vega may have served as a distant model, especially the work where his lyricism flows most freely, *The Knight of Olmedo*. It is true that among all the works of that fabulously prolific creator of the Spanish theater, this was Federico's favorite.

More lyrical than Romantic, if we want to speak precisely, or Romantic *because* it is lyrical, if we choose to simplify, *Mariana Pineda* shows us a Federico who had already mastered his means of expression. This is not surprising, for by now he had done so in poetry. For some, there is no purer note in Federico's poetry than the minor lyricism of the *Songs*, which were published in 1927, the same year that *Mariana* was staged. And despite the more or less evident influence of his masters, one can already find, in this minor lyrical mode, the unmistakable profile of the poet—for example, in the brief "Rider's Song," one of the most popular poems in the book.* Similarly, one might say of *Mariana Pineda* that, although parts of it are tinged with a certain adolescent naïveté (which perhaps Federico never lost), it contains dramatically successful moments that the poet would never surpass—that is, if we accept the work on its own terms, those of the author. We could cite the ballad of the bullfight at Ronda, or the ballad about the death of Torrijos, considered by critics in Spain and abroad as completely successful poems. I agree with them. But I also think that the *discovery* of the poetic value of those narrative moments (so akin to those found in Lope and in the classical Spanish theater) has been aided by the poet's fame as a writer of ballads, and the fact that the *Gypsy Ballads* may be the best known book of Spanish, perhaps even European poetry. Discoveries made *a posteriori*

---

*See Francisco García Lorca and Donald M. Allen, eds., *The Selected Poems of Federico García Lorca* (New York: New Directions, 1961), pp. 39-40.—*Tr.*

are always the easiest. But let us try to view the poet's work from *Mariana Pineda*, and not *Mariana Pineda* from the later works.

The best moments of *Mariana,* in my judgment, are those in which the characters' feelings grow so intense that they allow, and even demand, an increase in the poetic tension. I have already spoken of the narrative and historical part of the play. A good narrative style is expected of *any* playwright. What is more remarkable is Federico's way of bringing about emotional climaxes.

No doubt it was a dangerous undertaking, in a work written in verse, with a Romantic, lyrically stylized atmosphere, to place the two lovers face to face: Mariana and Sotomayor. This danger was made even greater by the fact that they were real, historical characters: love and liberty mingling in a passionate idyll. Especially noteworthy is the convincing dramatic stance of the two characters, whether united or apart, with Sotomayor looking to freedom and Mariana looking to love. In the sober depiction of that meeting we find some of the best lines in the play, and their poetic texture in no way lessens the dramatic tension.

> Like two white rivers of blushing silence
> your arms encircle my weary body.

> Como dos blancos ríos de rubor y silencio,
> así enlazan tus brazos mi cuerpo combatido.

A careful reading shows that the work reaches its poetic height at the moment of its resolution and, so to speak, Mariana's marriage to death. At the risk of lapsing into melodrama and sentimentality, the poet decided to reproduce certain historical circumstances: a new invitation to betray Sotomayor in exchange for a pardon a few minutes before her life ended; the fact that Mariana left for the scaffold from a convent where she had been imprisoned during her last days. All this must have been welcome material in the hands of a poet who wanted to lead the predominately lyrical work to a dramatic resolution.

The convent scene makes *Mariana Pineda* pivot around a final departure, as does *Cradle Song* by Martínez Sierra. A departure towards life, in one case, and towards death in the other. Although Federico was dealing with an historical situation, there is no doubt that he remembered Martínez Sierra's work when he wrote the ending of *Mariana*. Perhaps this was not the best solution for him to have followed, for he now had to raise the dramatic tone from idyllic sentimentalism to something tragic and pathetic. And yet I think this is where the work shows its greatest artistic strength. In these final scenes we witness a transformation of character. The author delves deep into Mariana's emotions and preserves her as an historical symbol. Abandoned by her comrades and conscious of her sacrifice, she sees herself as the incarnation of liberty on some ineffable eternal level where death, too, is a liberation.

> Do you love liberty more than you love your Marianita?
> Well, then, I will be the very liberty that you adore!

> ¿Amas la libertad más que a tu Marianita?
> ¡Pues yo seré la misma Libertad que tú adoras!

Love, freedom, and death are fused into one poetic symbol.

> To die! What a long sleep without dreams or shadow.
> Pedro, I want to die for what you do not:
> for the pure ideal that burned in your eyes.
> Liberty! So that your lofty light will never go out
> I offer myself entire. On with it, heart!
> Pedro, see what my love for you has made me do!
> When I am dead, you will love me so much that you will be unable to live.

> ¡Morir! ¡Qué largo sueño sin ensueños ni sombra!
> ¡Pedro, quiero morir por lo que tú no mueres,
> por el puro ideal que iluminó tus ojos!
> ¡Libertad! Porque nunca se apague tu alta lumbre
> me ofrezco toda entera. ¡Arriba, corazones!
> ¡Pedro, mira tu amor a lo que me ha llevado!
> Me querrás, muerta, tanto, que no podrás vivir.

These last words vibrate, however remotely, with something that keeps the human figure from dissolving into an abstract value. This final act of female vengeance is not devoid of greatness.

Mariana's farewell, the last words she speaks, express her dramatic transformation with rare poetic intensity. And yet even in this situation the poet does not lose his eye for the insignificant, anecdotal detail: a sort of talisman that always kept him in touch with reality.

I give you my heart. Give me a bunch of flowers.
I want to make myself look pretty in my final hours.
I want to feel the hard caress of my ring
and put on my lace mantilla.
You love liberty more than anything,
but I am Liberty herself. I give my blood,
which is your blood and the blood of all creatures.
No one's heart will ever be bought!
Now I know what the heart and the tree say.
Man is a captive and cannot free himself.
Liberty. Oh true and lofty Liberty,
light up your distant stars for me. [. . .]

I am Liberty because love wanted it so!
Pedro! Liberty, for whom you abandoned me.
I am Liberty, wounded by men.
Love, love, love, and eternal solitude.

¡Os doy mi corazón! ¡Dadme un ramo de flores!
En mis últimas horas yo quiero engalanarme.
Quiero sentir la dura caricia de mi anillo
y prenderme en el pelo mi mantilla de encaje.
Amas la libertad por encima de todo,
pero yo soy la misma Libertad. Doy mi sangre
que es tu sangre y la sangre de todas las criaturas.
¡No se podrá comprar el corazón de nadie!
Ahora sé lo que dicen el corazón y el árbol.
El hombre es un cautivo y no puede librarse.
¡Libertad de lo alto! Libertad verdadera,
enciende para mí tus estrellas distantes. [. . .]

¡Yo soy la Libertad porque el amor lo quiso!
¡Pedro! La Libertad, por la cual me dejaste.
¡Yo soy la Libertad, herida por los hombres!
¡Amor, amor, amor y eternas soledades!

The desolate solitude on which the work ends accentuates the feeling
of loneliness that surrounds Mariana from the very beginning. One of
Federico's biographers has written: "The most moving thing about this

first of Lorca's great characters is the sense of loneliness which the spectator perceives from the very first time he sees her come on stage. That loneliness stays with her until the very end."*

In *Mariana Pineda* Federico was to find many of the techniques he would use in his later work, such as beginning the drama with a prologue, a procedure he used as early as *The Butterfly's Evil Spell,* and which he would employ in almost all his later plays. In *Mariana* the prologue is balanced by an epilogue, which occurs when the character has already left the stage. In it one hears the same children's ballad that was heard at the very beginning. The play ends with a scene having no movement whatsoever, a true "engraving."

Despite the work's untrammeled unity, one hears language of every sort, from colorful images and daring metaphors foreshadowing those of the *Gypsy Ballads* to the plain, simple language of popular songs and refrains, regional expressions, and stress patterns taken from popular speech. All these elements are fused together into a polished, unified style. And this is accomplished without the author's resorting to the facile dialect used by so many other playwrights (nor did he use dialect in any of his other works). The bullring, in the ballad of the bullfight at Ronda,

| giraba como un zodíaco | was revolving like a zodiac |
| de risas blancas y negras. | of white and black laughter. |

And before abandoning the hope that her lover will save her, Mariana says:

| Él vendrá como un San Jorge | He will come like a Saint George |
| de diamantes y agua negra . . . | of diamonds and black water . . . |

Following a certain ballad technique which seems to draw on an ancient lyrical tradition, the poet finishes off these verses with an image that melts the Romantic tension into pure lyricism. Mariana awaits her beloved in the morning,

| cuando sobre el cielo oscuro | when the lemon grove barely shines |
| brilla el limonar apenas | in the dark sky |

*J. Mora Guarnido, *Federico García Lorca y su mundo,* p. 135.—*Ed.*

165

| y el alba finge en las olas | and the dawn feigns, in the waves, |
| fragatas de sombra y seda. | frigates of silk and shadow. |

Amid the melancholy with which Mariana often expresses her loneliness, we hear the tender, delicate lyricism of *Songs*, in forms so pure and refined that, had they been distinct poems, they would surely have been included in that book, despite the uncompromising rigor with which Federico and I made the final selection. I do not know how many poems, which have since been lost, were sacrificed with almost certain injustice. It is the tone of *Songs* (a book whose brevity must have seemed typically Granadan to Federico) which we hear in the following words by Mariana:

Si toda la tarde fuera	If this whole afternoon were
como un gran pájaro, ¡cuántas	like a great bird, how many
duras flechas lanzaría	hard arrows I would shoot
para cerrarle las alas! [. . .]	to close its wings! [. . .]
¡Con qué trabajo tan grande	How hard it is for the light
deja la luz a Granada!	to leave Granada.
Se enreda entre los cipreses	It tangles itself in the cypresses
o se esconde bajo el agua.	or hides beneath the water.
¡Y esta noche que no llega!	And this night which never comes!
¡Noche temida y soñada	Night I have feared and dreamt of
que me hiere ya de lejos	wounding me from afar
con larguísimas espadas!	with its long swords.

In *Mariana* we can also hear echoes of the superior, more perfect tonality of *Book of Poems*. And this is not surprising, given the fact that many poems in that book are in dialogue (remember the origin of *The Butterfly's Evil Spell*). We also find the direct popular inspiration of children's ballads, the passionate, sensual, dramatic emotion the poet feels towards the themes of love and death, the flight towards pure song that has not been trimmed down into particular poems—song that seems more appropriate for extroverted expression than for other more intimate lyrical forms. Listen to these words of Mariana, which have the tone of the book I have just mentioned earlier:

> Sleep peacefully, my children,
> while I, lost and mad, feel

the rose of blood in my breast
burn with its own living glow.
Dream of the vervain and the garden
of Carthage, fresh and luminous,
and the painted bird that rocks
in the boughs of the green lemon tree.*
For I too am asleep, children,
flying through my own dream,
like the seeds that fly on the wind
never knowing where they are going.

Dormir tranquilamente, niños míos,
mientras que yo, perdida y loca, siento
quemarse con su propia lumbre viva
esta rosa de sangre de mi pecho.
Soñar en la verbena y el jardín
de Cartagena, luminoso y fresco,
y en la pájara pinta que se mece
en las ramas del verde limonero.
Que yo también estoy dormida, niños,
y voy volando por mi propio sueño,
como van, sin saber adónde van,
los tenues vilanicos por el viento.

Perhaps this diversity of poetic strains and their unification into one sustained chord have not been duly observed, nor have other things that later became hallmarks of Federico's vision of the theater, the use of dramatic time and space, for example. Some scenes, and even subordinate characters, anticipate those of *Doña Rosita the Spinster*, a work to which *Mariana* bears a faint resemblance, due, among other things, to the atmosphere. Both works have a certain melancholy tone consistent with their origin in Granada.

Granada had never had a poet capable of expressing and interpreting her in an intimate spiritual way—perhaps not since the prodigious ballad of Abenámar, which depicts, in the poetic light of dawn, the towers of the Alhambra, still held by the Arabs:

*She is echoing several traditional Spanish children's songs.—*Tr.*

| ¿Qué palacios son aquéllos? | What palaces are those? |
| ¡Altos son y relucían! | They are high and they were shining! |

In the ballad the King woos Granada as though she were a proud woman, and this motif has its roots in Arabic poetical tradition. It is an example of the interpenetration of history and poetry which I referred to earlier; for scholars have determined that the light which bathes the ballad is that of the morning of July [27], 1431.* With this example before us, we can truly speak of the "historical" drama *Mariana Pineda*.

The characters have their origin in reality, not only those which are historical figures, like Mariana, Sotomayor and Pedrosa, but also those who belong to the world of Granada, like the nuns of the convent. Another character taken from reality is the adoptive mother of the heroine, a predecessor of the Aunt (also an adoptive mother) who is so skillfully depicted in *Doña Rosita the Spinster*.

I cannot explain why the protagonist of *Doña Rosita* is named after a flower, nor why one of the characters from *Mariana Pineda* bears the name of Clavela. I do remember my mother telling us about someone named Isabel la Clavela, but I cannot remember her. I know she was a village woman, and Federico has kept her first name, and her poetic last name in the play.

The great care with which the work was written is shown by the small number of careless errors that crept into the work, and God knows how many can be found in plays written in verse, even in the most careful ones. To me the language of the scene between Fernando and Mariana in the first act is much less controlled than the rest of the play. That scene (VII) also contains a bit of obvious padding and a factual error concerning the color of a flower:

Por ese amor verdadero	Because of this true love
que muerde mi alma sencilla	that bites my simple soul
me estoy poniendo amarilla	I am turning yellow
como la flor del romero.	like the flower of the rosemary.

*For a commentary, see C. Colin Smith, *Spanish Ballads* (Oxford: Pergamon Press, 1964), p. 127: "In this famous ballad King John II of Castile questions Abenámar (Yusuf Ibn-Alahmar), pretender to the throne of Granada and supported by the Christians, about the buildings of the city which they can see from a hill outside it. It was on 27th June 1431 that the Christian army came within sight of the city. [. . .] The personification, and the pleasant fiction of the city being the 'bride' of her ruler, are borrowed from Arabic poetry and for long led scholars to assume that the ballad was translated from an Arabic original. . . ."—*Tr.*

The mistake was noticed, if I remember correctly, by Enrique de Mesa, an excellent poet who wrote the theater reviews in one of the Madrid daily newspapers. It would not have taken a poet with a liking for the country, especially the mountains, to notice this mistake, for the flower of the rosemary is traditional in Spanish poetry. Góngora himself has a pretty *letrilla*, one of his best know poems, which begins like this:

Las flores del romero,   The flowers of the rosemary,
niña Isabel,   Isabel, my child,
hoy son flores azules,   are blue today,
mañana serán miel.   tomorrow they will be honey.

It is hard to imagine how Federico could have made such a mistake. He must have been carried away by the sound of the lines. The plant was "familiar" to him in more than one sense of the word: Romero is the second last name of my mother. Federico had even glossed Gongora's *letrilla* in his "Little Song from Seville" in *Songs*, explicitly mentioning the true color of the flower.

Federico was drawn to the theater by vocation. It was an inauspicious moment for that artistic genre, looked down upon by those searching, both in Spain and elsewhere, for "pure poetry." As everyone knows, it was under the tutelage of Juan Ramón Jiménez that poetry came to be considered one of the most demanding forms of purism. For a poet to write plays was considered an act of treason, even in the country that had produced one of the three great theatrical traditions of Europe, and even when its earliest authors had considered the theater to be one of the highest forms of poetry (from Juan del Encina and Gil Vicente to Lope de Vega, when the theater reached maturity). It was not that there was no theater written by poets—there *was* during the Modernist period— only that it was looked down upon. And it was not that the theater was limited as a literary genre, only that, as such it was considered incompatible with the idea of the "immense minority" which Juan Ramón thought of as the poet's ideal following.

It is true, on the other hand, that Antonio Machado, the most essential and profound of our poets, collaborated with his brother Manuel on a theatrical work staged some time after *Mariana Pineda*. But listen to what Manuel Machado (the more elegant and more Modernist of the brothers) wrote in 1920, when he reviewed *The Butterfly's Evil Spell* in the Madrid daily *La Libertad*. After praising the quality of the verse and objecting, with good reason, to the lack of direction and technical skill, he said:

> Sr. Lorca should not take this as harsh criticism. For it is neither necessary nor desirable to write plays. A synthetic-poetic sense of life and of its great ideal problems can and should adopt a nobler and more perfect form than that of theater. The supreme art is to write beautiful verses. [And here he adds, perhaps out of compassion:] Sr. García Lorca has come close to that ideal.

None of this had the slightest effect on Federico's destiny as a playwright. On the contrary: despite the disdain shown by Juan Ramón and others for the "treason" of the young author, *Mariana Pineda* helped strengthen his dramatic vocation. And thus he added a new chapter to the history of the Spanish theater.

THE SHOEMAKER'S PRODIGIOUS WIFE

The première of this play took place on December 24, 1930 at Madrid's municipal theater, the Teatro Espanol. Because the theater was subsidized by the government, the companies that performed there were required to put on a certain number of plays by Spanish authors. Across that stage came the most important theater of nineteenth- and twentieth-century Spain; and from the Romantic period on, the "blue room" of the Español, which was always full of writers and artists, had been the meeting place of the most famous *tertulia** in the Madrid literary world.

The writing of *The Shoemaker's Prodigious Wife* was a more complicated process than has been supposed. The poet himself says in an interview, "I wrote the play in 1926, a little after finishing *Mariana Pineda*, but it was not performed until 1930, by the company of Margarita Xirgu." Angel del Río, who was an eyewitness, asserts that Federico wrote much of the play in New York in 1929-1930. We can assume that the poet was revising the earlier version, and that this revised text is the one that Margarita Xirgu presented in 1930 in Madrid.

When Federico visited Argentina (a major event in his theatrical career), the play was presented again, in a new version. Federico modified the "Violent Farce" (that was how he subtitled the play), adding songs and dances written especially for the leading lady, Lola Membrives. These additions brought out the play's vaguely ballet-like air, the musical line of its plot, and its stylization in the manner of comic opera, and also sharpened the profiles of the characters. On the occasion of this new production, Federico remarked in an interview (*La Nacion*, November 30, 1933) :

> The work which I put on in the Teatro Español in Madrid was a chamber version. That production was a more intimate one, but it robbed the play of its true rhythmic perspectives. In reality the true première is here in Buenos Aires. The play is now bound together with songs from the eighteenth and nineteenth centuries, danced with extraordinary charm by Lola Membrives and her company.

The poet's remarks can seldom be taken at face value: perhaps because he was a poet Federico has a tendency to exaggerate. He sometimes looks at things mimetically, through the eyes of his listener, allowing the listener's point of view to filter poetically into his own words. Too many of his remarks have been taken literally. As I said earlier, perhaps it was he himself who began to create his own legend, attributing to himself childhood illnesses which kept him from speaking until age four, lameness, Jewish or Gypsy blood, etc. For him the frontier between reality and fantasy was never a very firm one. Just as there was much life in his poetry, there was much poetry in his life. He was always drifting off towards some imaginary plane of his own. The trouble is that where facts were involved, such imagination might easily have been confused with deceit. And thus it is sometimes moving to see Federico suddenly pull up short in the middle of an interview in order to re-establish a fact or insist on the authenticity of an opinion.

This problem of authenticity and this interplay between fantasy and reality have much to do with the character and basic theme of the work we are examining. In the last analysis, *The Shoemaker's Prodigious Wife* is a personal projection of the most universalized theme in Spanish literature. The fact that both personal and universal elements are present in this light-hearted work is highly significant: through some mysterious design, *the poet himself* embodies certain luminous facets of Spanish art.

When I said that Federico's words should not be taken at face value, I was referring to what he said of *The Shoemaker's Wife*: it is simply not true that the work had lost all its "rhythmic perspectives," nor can we believe that the version staged at the Teatro Español was a "chamber version." In precisely the same interview, he adds, "What is typical of this simple farce is the lively, closely-knit rhythm of each scene, and the use of music." The music was added later, but not all of it—there were already songs in the Madrid version, and the rhythm lies at the very heart of the work, and could in no way have been added later. [. . .]*

The existence of a first version, written in 1926, seems certain. The poet himself tells us:

> It was the summer of 1926. I was in the city of Granada, surrounded by black fig trees, spikes of wheat, and little crowns of water. I felt as though I were holding happiness in my hands. I felt I was the intimate friend of all the roses in the garden. I wanted to set a dramatic example, as simply as possible, giving fresh coloration to [a play which might have] contained only disillusioned phantasms.

We might doubt the poet and qualify his remarks when he is referring to factual matters, but we would be ill-advised to mistrust him when he expresses himself in poetic terms. Behind the roses, spikes of wheat, fig trees, and water I can recognize our country house in Granada. It was at the Huerta de San Vicente (for I believe the poet is telling the truth), and not amid the skyscrapers, anguish, and sleepless nights of New York City, that this work was born.

Once again, in 1930, Federico joins hands with Margarita Xirgu and rises to the boards. But by now his poetic personality is well-established. Perhaps he is still not completely conscious of his mastery of poetry, but the aura which has surrounded him from his first works is now more visible. No matter how much he would protest, later on, about being pigeonholed as a certain type of author, he was known now as the writer of the *Gypsy Ballads*.** Margarita Xirgu felt greater admiration and

---

*I have taken the liberty to omit two pages of information on the different manuscript versions of the play. A more recent and complete account may be found in Mario Hernández, ed., *La zapatera prodigiosa* (Madrid: Alianza Editorial, 1982).—*Tr.*

**As early as January, 1927 Lorca wrote to his friend Jorge Guillén, "This gypsy *myth* of mine annoys me a little. They confuse my life and character. This isn't what I want at all. The gypsies are a theme. And nothing more. I could just as well be a poet of sewing needles and hydraulic landscapes. Besides this gypsyism gives me the appearance of an uncultured, ignorant, and *primitive poet* that you know very well I'm not. I don't want to be typecast. I feel as if they're chaining me down." David Gershator, tr., *Selected Letters*, p. 94.—*Tr.*

affection for him than ever. Federico helped direct the play, out of a desire (stimulated, perhaps, by his visit to New York the year before) to bring about changes in theatrical technique, and the actress was ready to accommodate him. One day Margarita told my mother, "If Federico wants us all to roll on the floor, we will do it."

In order to better understand the relationship of the author with his actress, and of both of them with the audience, perhaps we ought to explain the importance of the *estreno*, or première (the Spanish word *estreno* has no exact equivalent in other languages). The *"répétition générale"* in the French style is but a timid *estreno*, and in France the "première" performance can also be the last. In Madrid, there was no such thing as a theater half full of invited guests—the phenomenon known in Spanish theater jargon (no matter how illustrious those guests were) as "typhus." In a theater stricken with typhus, the *estreno* would have been a sham. Packing the house with a kindly audience would have been unthinkable in a city like Madrid, which had developed a special "first-night" audience which included a group known as the "catcallers": self-appointed critics, failed authors, and those who were simply resentful and envious. Perhaps this group is the Spanish answer to the French *claque*, brought in by the theater company to falsify the performance. At any rate, an *estreno* was at least as dangerous as a bullfight.

This may have been a good thing, for an author's reputation was thus directly created by the audience, rather than by the critics. I must say there were good drama critics on all the major newspapers. (In those days the press editorialized freely, dealt more in opinion than in information, and did not distinguish so markedly between writers and journalists: Unamuno and Ortega y Gasset were as much journalists as they were thinkers or essayists.) Then too, in Madrid (a bureaucratic, administrative, geographically inexplicable city), the theater has often served as an antidote to a bitter social reality. This explains, at least in part, the extraordinary abundance of Spanish theater in the Golden Age, a remarkable literary phenomenon. The existence of a public thirsty for the illusions of the stage helps explain the strange case of Lope de Vega, who wrote more works than there are in the whole of the classical French theater or in the Elizabethan theater.

The audience's role is an important one. It can sometimes stimulate creativity, but during periods of artistic stagnation it can act as a hindrance, serving the interests of the impresario. Even Jacinto Benavente, who began his career at a glorious moment of renewal in all the literary genres, and who lashed his audiences with sarcasm and satire, gradually became the audience's servant. It is against this theatrical background, and in the light of his own previous artistic experiences, that we can best understand the words which Federico speaks at the beginning of *The Shoemaker's Prodigious Wife*: "Esteemed audience . . . (*Pause*) No, 'esteemed' no. Just audience." As in previous plays, the author begins with a prologue. We have already examined the role of the prologue in *Mariana Pineda*, and have said that it emanates from the work itself: it is a *depersonalized* prologue. But here, as in *The Butterfly's Evil Spell*, the prologue is spoken by the Author, and was sometimes read by Federico himself. Its function has become more complex: not only does it announce that the work will center around a "poetic creature," it also announces the theme—the struggle of that creature with "the reality that besieges her, and with fantasy, whenever fantasy turns into visible reality."

These words imply that this struggle is not going to take place on some abstract level, and that the problem will not be posed in hopelessly static terms. It is, rather, a process whereby fantasies are turned into realities, and are then rejected and replaced. This dynamic or dramatic process is responsible for the vital impetus of the leading character, and for the secret joy she takes in failure. In the final analysis, this is a positive, optimistic play, so long as the character has new failures which she can turn into new illusions. I hesitate to speak with such gravity, but . . . perhaps the secret of life lies in this very capacity.

The poet said that he "gave fresh coloration to [a play that might have contained] only disillusioned phantasms." And that "coloration" is precisely what distinguishes the poetic vision of *The Shoemaker's Wife* from its most illustrious forerunner, *Don Quijote*. I am not sure whether Federico was fully aware of this. It is interesting that when he refers to Cervantes he does so apropos of the Shoemaker, and not the main character or theme. Emphasizing the essential Andalusian nature of the work he says he has also allowed himself, "for example when the Shoemaker is preaching, to gently caricature Cervantes." Federico is almost surely alluding not to *Don Quixote* but to the *Entremeses* or *Interludes*. The Spanish theater is richer than any other, ancient or modern, in small theatrical works that combine poetic elements and the observation of reality, and this has been so since the times of the great sixteenth-century poets Juan del Encina and Gil Vicente, a bilingual (Spanish Portuguese) writer of genius. It was this theater, which is sometimes written in prose, that produced the delightful little sketches (*pasos*) of Lope de Rueda, from whom Cervantes learned the genre. The short theatrical piece runs through the whole of Spanish literature under different names—*autos, pasos, entremeses, sainetes, pasillos*—and it is even more enduring than major theater. Both in the eighteenth and in the nineteenth centuries, the Spanish national theater seems to survive by taking refuge in this minor theater. It is accompanied by music as far back as the *autos*, and in the nineteenth century it produces the best comic opera (*zarzuela*) in Europe. (I am giving the opinion of Manuel de Falla, who did not make such statements lightly.)

The most precious plays in this tradition of minor theater are the *Interludes* of Cervantes. In them we can detect Cervantes' noble, slightly pained smile, and an irony that understands and pardons all human weakness. The complexity and artistic maturity of those *Interludes*, the richness of their language, the successful development of the characters (depicted with simple, masterful strokes) are exemplified by *The Wonder Show*,* which reveals as much of Cervantes' genius as does *Don Quijote*, of which it is a version in miniature. Both works contrast vivid reality and an almost palpable fantasy: in the *Interludes* fantasy reaches greater heights because of the spell cast by music and dance.

We can understand *The Shoemaker's Prodigious Wife* better if we see it as a projection, in modern terms, of this traditional line of minor theater. Cervantes' influence can be seen (aside from the struggle between fantasy and reality embodied in the character) in the very plot: it is the conflict of a young woman married to an old man, one of Cervantes' favorite themes dealt with in the *Interludes* and fully developed in the *Exemplary Novels*.

In discussing such literary relationships, it is very difficult to know whether the received elements are consciously incorporated or blindly assimilated. This is especially true in the case of an author like Federico, whose immersion in tradition was more temperamental than it was cultural. I have told on another occasion** of having reminded my brother of the popular poem that gave rise to his gypsy ballad of "The

---

*For *El retablo de las maravillas* and *El juez de los divorcios*. I have used the titles employed by Edwin Honig in his excellent translation of the *Interludes* (New York: New American Library, 1964).—*Tr.*

**See the introduction to the *Three Tragedies*, p. 17.—*Ed.*

Unfaithful Wife" and of Federico's denying he had been influenced by it at all, so completely had he taken possession of the theme.

At any rate, the "caricature of Cervantes" is more far-reaching than the poet's words imply. The Shoemaker's Wife is closely related to Cervantes' *The Divorce-Court Judge*. Several of the women who petition the judge for divorce bear the same features as the Shoemaker's Wife, and they even use similar language, especially Mariana, who asks to be divorced from a husband who is very old. When the Judge asks her why, Mariana expresses herself in metaphorical language that resembles that of the Shoemaker's Wife:

JUDGE: Be more specific, Madam, as to why you are asking for a divorce.
MARIANA: The winter of my husband and the springtime of my life.

The Shoemaker's Wife too would complain of being married to an old man, "in the flower of my life." And, like the Wife, Mariana boasts of the exquisite care and attention she has given to her old husband. The husband accuses his Wife neither of disloyalty nor of unfaithfulness: he sums up his case in words that remind us of the Shoemaker's—"I have been living with her for twenty-two martyred years, putting up with her insolence, her shouting, her fantasy."

This is hardly the right moment to examine such similarities in detail, but Doña Guiomar of the *Interludes* has certain features that will reappear in the Shoemaker's Wife. The transition from illusion to reality is expressed before the Judge like this: "They married me to this man, but this man is not the one I married." And she adds:

GUIOMAR: I beg Your Honor, as earnestly as I can, to divorce me from *him*.
JUDGE: What do you mean *him*? Has he no other name?

When the Shoemaker's Wife complains to another authority (the Mayor), she says: "I have flower pots on the roof, in the doorway, even on the walls. But as for *him* . . . as for *him* . . . he doesn't like them."

Besides, Federico sustains the same thesis as does Cervantes in his interlude: "The worst agreement is better than the best divorce." And there is no doubt that the "agreement" is going to be a bad one. "What a life I'm going to give you!" cries the Shoemaker's Wife. "Worse than the

Inquisition! Worse than the Templars of Rome!"* This harshness, which conceals deep tenderness, is her trademark.

As in certain old lithographs, the masculine characters represent the stages of human life: the Child, infancy; the Young Men, youth; the Mayor, maturity; the Shoemaker, old age; Don Mirlo, extreme old age. The Shoemaker's Wife treats all of them with both harshness and tenderness, for it is on the plane of love that fantasy struggles with reality. That is the meaning of those masculine "stages of life." It is the same in *Perlimplín*. When the poet wants to make Belisa the symbol of adulterous love, he mentions that she has been visited by representatives "of the five races of the earth."

But the grotesque old age of Don Mirlo (who foreshadows the figure of Perlimplín) makes the Wife's flirtation with him perfectly innocuous. Nothing demands so much fantasy from the Wife as this relationship. "Even with *Don Mirlo!*" the Shoemaker will say, in a burst of indignation and reproach, without noticing that this is the very relationship which proves his wife's innocence. At the other extreme is her love for the Child, who completes the circle of her love. The two opposing poles come into contact: the Wife's love for Don Mirlo is as innocuous as her love for the Child—a delightful trio of innocents, with the Wife in the center.

The work has the apparent simplicity of any farce, but there are certain subtle indications of how the theme might have been treated dramatically, for example in the ballad in Act II, where the Shoemaker's double, an imaginary character in a blind man's ballad, projects his plight towards a tragic solution:

> Her friend arrived, racing
> a Cordoba pony
> and told her, sighing:
> if you want, my girl,

*The author stated on another occasion that these lines were based on a somewhat enigmatic poem sung as a flamenco lyric:

> Ni los templarios de Roma
> ni el que inventó los tormentos,
> te *puen* querer a ti tanto
> como yo te estoy queriendo.

(Neither the Templars of Rome / nor the man who invented torture / can love you as much / as I love you now.) See Mario Hernández, "Despedida a Francisco García Lorca," *Informaciones,* Madrid, November 20, 1976.—*Tr.*

we could eat dinner tomorrow,
just the two of us, at your table.
And what will you do with my husband?
Your husband will never find out.
What will you do? I'll kill him.
He is fast, maybe you won't be able.
Do you have a pistol? Better!
I have a barber's razor.
Is it sharp? It cuts like the cold,
and the blade is without a nick.
Are you sure? I will stab him
ten times, just like this—
oh what a marvelous idea—
four times in the lumbar region,
one time in the left nipple,
another in a private place,
and two times on each hip.
How soon will you kill him? Tonight.
As soon as he comes home, down
by the bend in the ditch.

. . . Llegó su amigo trotando
una jaca cordobesa
y le dijo entre suspiros:
Niña, si tú lo quisieras,
cenaríamos mañana
los dos solos, en tu mesa.
¿Y qué harás con mi marido?
Tu marido no se entera.
¿Qué piensas hacer? Matarlo.
Es ágil. Quizás no puedas.
¿Tienes revólver? ¡Mejor!
¡Tengo navaja barbera!
¿Corta mucho? Más que el frío.
Y no tiene ni una mella.
¿No has mentido? Le daré
diez puñaladas certeras
en esta disposición,
que me parece estupenda:

cuatro en la región lumbar,
una en la tetilla izquierda,
otra en semejante sitio
y dos en cada cadera.
¿Lo matarás en seguida?
Esta noche cuando vuelva
con el cuero y con las crines
por la curva de la acequia.

The Shoemaker's Prodigious Wife is the most popular of Federico's minor plays, and perhaps this is so (even outside of Spain) because of the confident way he handles a traditional genre, proven over centuries of use.

THE LOVE OF DON PERLIMPLÍN WITH

BELISA IN THEIR GARDEN

In December, 1928, Federico remarked in an interview that he had finished *Don Perlimplín*. It was probably the following year that he tried to stage the play for the first time with a theatrical company made up of friends and other amateurs. This production was banned by the Primo de Rivera dictatorship, which believed the work to be unedifying. Especially galling was the fact that the protagonist, Don Perlimplín, was depicted as a military officer. It seemed an affront to military dignity that an officer should appear on stage "with huge stag's antlers on his head," and should have his conjugal honor betrayed by "the five races of the earth."

On April 5, 1933, the work was finally performed by an excellent amateur group, the Anfistora Club, which put on various works with a faithful dedication unmatched even in the professional theater—thanks to the intelligence and good taste of its director, Pura Maortua de Ucelay. Federico gave the group his advice and encouragement and even helped direct some of its productions.

Perhaps this is the moment to explain how the name "Anfistora" came into existence. Federico often invented words which (as in this case) had no precise meaning. Once, when he was very young, he said to a woman who did part-time work at our house in Fuente Vaqueros, "Juanilla, you are the *anfistora* of this village." She replied instantly, with something like wounded dignity, "No, child, only of your family." When Sra. Ucelay founded her theater group and asked Federico to suggest a name for it, he remembered the incident and answered, "*Club Anfistora!*" It was accepted without hesitation. Many people thought that the fine-sounding name was of Greek origin.

The complete title of the play, *El amor de don Perlimplín con Belisa en su jardín*, contains two lines of octosyllabic verse. It is subtitled *Aleluya erótica*. When we were children (the custom I am about to describe has long since disappeared), one could buy large sheets of cheap, variously colored paper, each with a series of drawings (the oldest were wood engravings) making up a story. Each engraving was explained by two lines of verse. These broadsides, which fulfilled more or less the same role as do modern-day comics, were called *aleluyas*. The word is now applied to the verses themselves. I remember the "*aleluyas* and misfortunes" of the tall man, the fat man, and the "*Aleluya* of the Land of Milk and Honey." The title of my brother's play came from one of those broadsides. I do not remember which one it was that gave rise to Federico's play, and cannot say exactly what elements of these cartoon stories might have been transferred to it.* *Don Perlimplín* contains certain details which are not found in the original but which capture the comical, exaggerated flavor of the *aleluyas* once sold on the streets. I am thinking of certain light-hearted touches like the stag's horns worn, at a certain moment, by the protagonist, and of the "five races of the earth" visiting the bridal bed.

But there is almost nothing else remaining of *Perlimplín's* popular origin. Federico's play is musical, exquisite, and refined. Don Perlimplín has made a tremendous leap from the paper *aleluya* to the stage prepared for him by the author. And this reveals two of the permanent characteristics of Federico's art: his need to begin with a concrete reality (it was sometimes a reality at two removes, as in *Perlimplín* or the ballad in *Mariana Pineda*); and his skill at turning that reality into a story. I remember a series of poems he wrote for the *Suites*. Before entering the world of fantasy, the poet takes the precaution of putting a piece of wood in his pocket. He touches this talisman from time to time, in order not to lose contact with reality and to return to it at the end of the poem.

*For an account of how Lorca's work was influenced by the popular *aleluyas*, see Helen Grant, "Una *aleluya erótica* de Federico García Lorca y las aleluyas populares del siglo XIX" in *Actas del Primer Congreso Internacional de Hispanistas* (Oxford: The Dolphin Book Co., 1964), 307-314.—*Tr.*

Like *The Shoemaker's Prodigious Wife*, *Perlimplín* reflects Federico's preference for plays of small proportions. There are only four characters in *Perlimplín*, and one of them participates only at the beginning of the play. This gives rise to a dialogue written (so to speak) for four instruments. The dialogue begins on one note, repeated several times, each time with a different tonality.

PERLIMPLIN: ¿Sí? [Yes?]
MARCOLFA: Sí. [Yes.]

The note* is reiterated in the lines that follow, with the same pattern of interrogation and affirmation as before.

PERLIMPLIN: Pero ¿por qué sí? [But why *yes?*]
MARCOLFA: Pues porque sí. [Just because.]

The dialogue is then prolonged like this:

PERLIMPLIN: ¿Y si yo te dijera que no? [And if I were to tell you no?]
MARCOLFA: ¿Que no? [No?]
PERLIMPLIN: No. [No.]

Thus, the theme ends on a single note, the opposite to the one heard at the beginning.

If we were to try to show the succession of syllables in these last three lines, and indicate their stress accent, we would find the following:

o o ó o o ó o o ó
o ó
ó

The perfect succession of anapests in the first line spoken by Perlimplín is followed by the single iamb of Marcolfa's reply. This rhythmic play is accompanied, from the very beginning of the play, by changes in tonality. Remember that in Spanish the interrogative sentence usually ends on a high note, and the affirmative or negative sentence on a low one. In the three lines I have just transcribed, Perlimplín's first sentence ends on a

---

*As it happens, *si* is Spanish for the note "ti" on the scale.—*Tr.*

high note. Then there is an even higher one, from Marcolfa. The exchange ends with a single falling note from Perlimplín. Its lowness is made even more noticeable by its being a monosyllable.

But the rhythmic development continues in a very curious way:

MARCOLFA: Dígame, señor mío, las causas de ese no. [Tell me, Master, the reasons for that "no."]
PERLIMPLIN: Dime tú, doméstica perseverante, las causas de ese sí. [You tell me, stubborn maid, the reasons for that "yes."]

The rhythmic transcription of these two lines would be as follows:

MARCOLFA: ó o o o o ó o o ó o ó o ó.
PERLIMPLIN: ó o ó o ó o o o o o o ó o o ó o ó o ó.

Marcolfa's sentence, which is rhythmically descending, begins with a stressed syllable, followed by *four* unstressed ones. Perlimplín's sentence is characterized by *five* consecutive unstressed syllables ("domés*tica per-severe*rante"). The speaker skips over them lightly, producing a sequence of very rapid notes. If the actors place even the slightest emphasis on the tonal and rhythmic qualities, the words turn into a dialogue between musical instruments.

A fragment of this dialogue reappears later, so that the dialogue resembles a repeated musical motif, whether it is spoken by the same two characters or by Belisa and Perlimplín.

BELISA: ¿Sí? [Yes?]
PERLIMPLIN: Sí. [Yes.]
BELISA: Pero . . . ¿por qué sí? [But . . . why yes?]
PERLIMPLIN: Pues porque sí. [Just because.]

This procedure is too obvious to be considered unintentional. In the situation I have just dealt with, it is connected to the musical structure of the Spanish language itself. Perhaps it reflects a certain state of mind which came spontaneously to the surface during the mystery of the creative process.

On another occasion, in the *Tragicomedy of Don Cristóbal*, one of the characters, Tire-Souls the Cobbler, finds that his words are finished by a piccolo.

FIGARO: Today's the day I'm expecting the great visit.

TIRE-SOULS: Who's co ... Who's com ... (*A piccolo, offstage, finishes his words.*)

FIGARO: Don Cristobita is coming. Don Cristobita with his big club.

TIRE-SOULS: Is he rea ...? Is he reall ...? (*The piccolo finishes his words.*)

FIGARO: Yes, yes. Of course. (*He laughs.*)

Although this vocal and instrumental game does not reappear in other works (at least not in the same way), it shows that to Federico words and music were practically the same thing. In the same *Tragicomedy* the Hour, who has been turned into a character, strikes one o'clock—Ding-Dong!—simultaneously with its mouth and with a bell.

After the initial "quartet" I referred to earlier, the play continues to develop around two people at a time. Never do three people participate as a group. Even in the last scene, Marcolfa appears only after Perlimplín is dead. Before she appears, the wounded Perlimplín is attended by Belisa, who is now very much in love. Thus, the dialogue is always in the form of a duo. It may be that this was one way the play was affected by the simplicity of the *aleluya*.

Nevertheless, this work has been considered to be the one that best displays Federico's artistic craftsmanship, and his skill is maneuvering between lyric and dramatic elements. Despite its apparent simplicity, *Perlimplín* is a more ambitious, elaborate, complex work than *The Shoemaker's Prodigious Wife.** The use of more than one sort of language adds to this complexity. A good example, perhaps a rather extreme one, occurs in the last scene when Belisa says arrogantly, "I never thought he [Perlimplín] was so complicated." This is an extremely lyrical scene, and yet it is not lacking in allegory—it only remained for Federico to give plastic expression to the soul of Perlimplín as it rises to heaven.

The theme of *Perlimplín* has never been properly identified, perhaps because it is so obvious. It is the same as that of *The Shoemaker's Wife.*

---

*In Fall, 1935, a Spanish journalist asked Lorca which was his most successful play. "Successful? None of them! Or perhaps I should say, the ones I haven't yet written. If you ask me which one I like best, I can tell you it's a little play whose true lyricism has scared away professional theatre groups. It is called *The Love of Don Perlimplín* ..." See F. G. L., *Alocuciones argentinas*, ed. Mario Hernández and Manuel Fernández-Montesinos (Madrid: Fundación Federico García Lorca, 1985), p. 31.—*Tr.*

Perhaps what has prevented the critics from noticing the similarity between these two works is the radically different way the theme is treated. I believe that without *The Shoemaker's Wife, Perlimplín* would never have been written. And this ought to remind us of another of Federico's most important literary traits: the diversity yet unity of his output, and also its continuity. Each work foreshadows the next, dramatic or poetic. Such continuity is the basis of all true metamorphosis.

The theme of both the "Erotic *Aleluya*" and of the "Violent Farce" is the "old, honorable husband / married to a tender young woman" (I am quoting from the ballad of *The Shoemaker's Wife*). But in *Perlimplín* the plot is treated differently. The structure of *The Shoemaker's Wife* is an open one. It ends the same way, more or less, as it began, and its ending could give rise to an identical plot. This is so true that, with a few small modifications, the play could have begun from the second act. The first act would have followed from it with perfect theatrical logic. The conflict outlives the characters, and continues after they have disappeared from the stage. Even after the curtain has fallen, we feel a sort of dramatic vibration. Perhaps this shows that Federico's vision of the theater is a logical consequence of his conception of life. One of the characters in *The House of Bernarda Alba* will say, "But things repeat themselves. I see that it is all horrible repetition."

Perlimplín is different. Among my brother's theatrical works, this is the one whose plot is most "necessary," the one where nothing possesses merely episodic value. Everything comes together at the close of the action. The plot cannot go on, and in this sense it is a perfect, i.e. finished play. The characters in *The Shoemaker's Wife* do not change at all during the two acts of that farce. Not so with Don Perlimplín, whose death transfigured him, nor with Belisa, who has been "recreated" by her husband's death.

This finished (or "closed") structure, which runs slightly contrary to the episodic action traditionally found in the Spanish minor theater, gives *Perlimplín* a sophisticated foreign air, as opposed to the fresh, natural Andalusian flavor of *The Shoemaker's Wife*. We could say the same thing of the refined "eroticism" of Belisa.

The Shoemaker's Wife's powers of fantasy, which enabled her to create so many imaginary lovers, have been transferred to Perlimplín. I see him as the sum and the transposition of the characters of the Shoemaker and Don Mirlo. The theme—the struggle between fantasy and reality, a struggle without any possible outcome, and therefore ever renewed—is tied even more closely here to the theme of love. But in the "Erotic *Aleluya*" the theme is reduced to its extreme of body and spirit, both of them stripped bare as befits farce, and turned to music in a poignant, exquisite, lyrical way. Old Perlimplín is the most pathetic of my brother's characters.

The poet has abandoned the popular, Cervantic (and Andalusian) source of *The Shoemaker's Wife*, and has moved toward the sonata, giving his work an Italianate, eighteenth-century tonality, a little reminiscent of Goldoni, of *Serva padrona*, and (for the play's eroticism) *The Magnificent Cuckold*, a work by Crommelynck which Federico knew well. I might add that when I was living in Brussels I met Crommelynck, who had learned of *Perlimplín* from mutual friends. He felt that *The Cuckold* might have influenced Federico's play, but he thought the ending of *Perlimplín* was more skillful.

Perhaps it was the erotic element of this lyrical farce which kept Falla from writing music for it. Falla had been kind enough to collaborate with the young poet, and he asked him to write a libretto set (if I remember correctly) in the period around the end of the eighteenth and the beginning of the nineteenth centuries. I imagine that, given such a setting, Falla hoped to use both popular and learned elements. But of course the work would have to be devoid of any sort of sensualism. He wanted a light work, a costume piece, reminiscent of the cartoons of Goya. Federico tried to write this "comic opera" without success. He was not the man to write a commissioned work, though he must have been tempted by the idea of working with someone as famous as Falla. Among Federico's papers is the outline (he only made outlines for the works he was not going to write).* There are even a few scenes from this opera, whose title was *The Coachman*.** The project was abandoned.

Come to think of it, I am not sure which work came first, *The Coachman* or *Perlimplín*. Perhaps the "Erotic *Aleluya*" was Federico's attempt to write an opera libretto† on his own terms, rather than

---

*This is not quite true: Lorca made a preliminary outline before writing *The Shoemaker's Wife*. It has been published in the edition by Mario Hernández cited earlier.—*Tr.*

**Several manuscripts of this work, which was also titled *Lola the Playactress*, have now been published. See Piero Menarini, ed., *Lola la comedianta* (Madrid: Alianza Editorial, 1981). The play seems to have been written in 1923.—*Tr.*

†In 1933 Lorca says of *Don Perlimplín*, "What I try to do . . . is to bring out the contrast between the lyrical and the grotesque, and to blend one element with the other. This work is supported by music, like a little chamber opera. Its brief scenes are tied together with sonatinas of Scarlatti, and the dialogue is continually interrupted by chords and background music." *Obras completas*, Vol. II, p. 993.—*Tr.*

Falla's. And perhaps this is the source (aside from the poet's temperament and personal background) of the musical and rhythmic nature of its language.

Though it was conceived of in lyrical terms, *Perlimplín* has less verse than almost any of Federico's other works. Even the lyrics sung by Belisa in the third scene were taken from *Songs*, with only slight variations. The first scene had originally ended on a monosyllable *("Sí")*, spoken by Belisa, who is feeling exhausted after a wedding night of open balconies. At one of the rehearsals it occurred to Federico that this monosyllable (uttered in reply to Perlimplín when he asks her naively if she is still asleep) was not a very good ending. Federico drew off by himself, propped his foot on a chair, resting the paper on his knee, and wrote the poignant song which now closes the scene:

Amor, amor,	Love, love,
que estoy herido.	I am wounded.
Herido de amor huido,	Wounded from fleeting love,
herido,	wounded,
muerto de amor.	dead of love.
Decid a todos que ha sido	Tell everyone it was
el ruiseñor.	the nightingale.
Bisturí de cuatro filos,	Four-edged scalpel,
garganta rota y olvido.	broken throat, oblivion.
Cógeme la mano, amor,	Take my hand, love,
que vengo muy mal herido,	I have been badly wounded,
herido de amor huido,	wounded from fleeting love
¡herido!	wounded,
¡muerto de amor!	dead of love!

In *Don Perlimplín*, the poet has delicately woven together the lyrical and the grotesque, cruelty and tenderness, the world of the flesh and the world of the spirit. In these shifting lights we see the timid soul of Perlimplín reach the proportions of a dramatic hero.

WHEN FIVE YEARS HAVE PASSED

When Five Years Have Passed is subtitled *Legend of Time*. The author wanted to give the work a feeling of temporal remoteness, but he also wanted to bound off an exact period of time: five years. As it unfolded, the play would make one feel the different emotions provoked by time, and this would involve regression or simultaneity on different temporal levels.

Time as a theme, and sometimes as a silent character, is one of the most important, most poetic, aspects of Federico's works. The theme of time is dramatically developed in another, later play, *Doña Rosita*, but there it is treated very differently. In *Doña Rosita* the plot *is*, essentially, the passage of time—chronological time. *When Five Years Have Passed* dramatizes the *emotion* of time. The perception of time as delay and as imminence is what affects the dramatic action and, in the last analysis, endows it with meaning. The two works called for two different treatments.

In this play, Federico wanted to explore the possibilities of a freer construction, one which would not be totally bound to the rational logic of the theater. One might say that the work is conceived and executed with the freedom of a poem, and that a certain poetic unity, maintained by means of a series of thematic correspondences is what makes it dramatic. It has even been considered a surrealistic work, parallel, in this sense, to a certain kind of poetry—poetry which breaks out of its traditional mold and works through associations on deeper levels. There is some truth in this, but here Federico wished to create a *dramatic* entity, a play whose poetry would make it even more dramatic.

This would be another way García Lorca combined drama and poetry into one organic whole. It is significant that he kept to the structure of the three-act play (as he did in his major works), corresponding to the three classical moments of dramatic action. Apparently, he wanted to contain the free-flowing plot in a traditional framework, one which had been viable since the time when the great Lope de Vega created it for the New Comedy. Given the work's character, perhaps the best way to approach it would be to examine how its theme and plot unfold.

The theme of time is embodied in the protagonist, the Young Man. To him, there is something death-like in the fulfillment and the consummation of actions. One must postpone the final destiny of things in order to keep them from dying. And thus, in the mad rush of daily life, the present turns into a sort of cemetery; realities are extinguished in the present, which is the moment when death triumphs. The attempt to escape from the natural course of time simply makes life into a long death.

The Young Man struggles against the idea of ruin, the presence of broken furniture, the invasion of weeds, the peeling of walls—all of these silent witnesses to time force us to remember death. One must *remember*, to be sure, but remember "living things, things burning in their own blood, with all their profiles intact." This attitude explains apparently obscure sentences like, "One must remember beforehand." Memory does not project itself towards the past, but rather from the past towards the fullness of things: "One must remember towards tomorrow." The usual mechanism of memory, the one forced on us by ruins, is inverted.

Whether oriented towards the future or towards the past, this sort of memory implies an evasion of reality and of the inexorable march of time. Life is replaced by an imaginary act of projection and of delay. Part of the drama is that the imagination has a slippery subsoil, where reality can easily be confused with representation. Reality itself is constantly changing, for "Who could draw a map of the sands of the desert [. . .], or remember the face of one of his friends?"

A vague dream-like atmosphere takes over the stage and reflects the vital anguish of the protagonist. The protagonist is not a passive character. We witness his painful struggle between life and death, and in fact this is the very struggle that is being dramatized.

The initial dialogue between the Young Man and the Old Man states the theme, right from the outset of the work, with insuperable clarity and exactness. In this dialogue, both characters are perfectly delineated, as is the dramatic importance of the theme of time.

Let us turn next to the figure of the Old Man. Together with the protagonist, he is the character most thoroughly involved in the conflict. Symbolically, he is the most important character in the play. He represents time as limited duration, time that dies with things, with the consummation of acts and events. He is, thus, an abstract reply to the figure of the Young Man.

Time has often been represented symbolically as a great survivor. But here the poet portrays time as an old man, afraid of his own footsteps. It is the Old Man who makes the Young Man dream of something that cannot be realized, the tomorrow which never arrives (for all that arrives is death, both that of the Young Man and that of the Old Man). The Old Man may be able to renew himself in an infinite series of unfinished acts, but he is continually wounded. Thus, at the moments when the Young Man tries to come alive in love, the Old Man appears to feel anguish. He carries a handkerchief in his hand and wipes his brow with this handkerchief, which is spotted with blood at the moments of greatest danger. The last time he appears, he wipes his face with it.

He is an instigator of the action, but to the Young Man he is also a sort of Guardian Angel. Neat, suggestive, irritable, he lives on the same plane as the other characters and struggles with them. The other characters bring out his dramatic and original symbolism. By the way, the vision of wounded time belongs to the poet's very earliest imagery.

Let us see how the plot develops. The story revolves around the Young Man and two women, the Betrothed and the Typist. These two represent sensuality and the enjoyment of the present. The Betrothed represents the body and the Typist represents love as hope and as a timid, idealistic dream.

The Betrothed corresponds to Belisa in *Don Perlimplín*: a case of sensual urgency which, ironically, prevents the Young Man from delaying things for the arbitrary period of five years. Time has raised an unbreachable wall of coldness between these two characters. The Betrothed's attitude culminates in a scene in which she allows herself to be caressed by a brutal Football Player,* a silent character who grotesquely shatters the poetic qualities of the plot.

During his long wait, the Young Man's secretary (the Typist) has formed a sentimental attachment to him. After he has been rejected by the Betrothed and has thus received a deadly wound, the Young Man returns to the Typist. He is desperately searching for the present. But in the Typist the Young Man finds only his own image. The Typist has idealized her love so much that she has turned it into a dream. The Young Man is no longer himself; he is the image which he has created in the girl's heart. They cannot coincide in time, and this drama is expressed in the following dialogue, in poignant poetical terms:

> TYPIST: What is that which I hear so far away?
> YOUNG MAN: Love,
> > the blood in my throat,
> > my love.
>
> TYPIST: Always like that, always,
> > whether we are awake or asleep.
>
> YOUNG MAN: Never that way, never, never!
> > let us leave this place.
>
> TYPIST: Wait.
> YOUNG MAN: Love does not wait.
> TYPIST (*pulling away from the Young Man*):
> > Where are you going, my love,
> > with the wind in a glass
> > and the sea in a windowpane.

This lyrical mis-encounter, from which we have reproduced only the final fragment, is summed up in a progressively dramatic prose dialogue:

*The name of Federico's character is *Jugador de Rugby*, Rugby Player. But I have no doubt that he was remembering the football players he had seen while studying at Columbia University. In an unpublished letter to his family from New York (1929), he tells of watching them practice under his window in John Jay Hall: "The Columbia rugby [i.e. football] team has just now come onto the field, dressed in their black and tobacco-colored uniforms. The players have the quality of sandpaper and tree trunks [sic], and they are frighteningly strong and seedy looking. In a couple of minutes they will break each others' heads open, and no one will care. The same thing applies to rugby players as to picadors: secretly we want to see them smashed up against the fence [. . .] Rugby is a game I really like; not only is it typically American, it has so much emotion, such incredible *natural* beauty that one can hardly swallow."—*Tr.*

TYPIST: I have loved you so much.
YOUNG MAN: I love you so much.
TYPIST: I will love you so much.

Each of them has his own temporal profile:

YOUNG MAN: I was waiting and I was dying.
TYPIST: I was dying because I was waiting.

Now she too is unable to live without her dream. She postpones the definitive encounter, relegating it to the future, "when five years have passed." This is a pathetic idyll, in which the Young Man, in search of love, is newly wounded. But now it is a mortal wound, for his life has ceased to have any immediate meaning. His life will be living death or perhaps he will live on another level of reality. This is the reason why the aforementioned idyll (which occurs in the third act) takes place on a small stage within a larger one reproducing the setting of the first act: the Young Man is now seeking what the Typist was seeking earlier. A series of bridges connects the two levels of reality, the two stages, and the different temporal levels. It is here, perhaps, that the poetry and dramatic qualities of the work come to fulfillment. The next scene, the final one, is the portrayal of the protagonist's death, which has now become inevitable.

The passage from one woman to another, from the Betrothed to the Typist, is brought about by a symbolic figure: the Manikin dressed as a bride. On a final level of reality, the Manikin hopes to live in the bridal dress; the Manikin unites its inert life with the very clothing which has made it a Manikin.

This character is closely tied to the meaning of the work and to the poetic vision of the author. In this drama, objects travel towards their destinies just as do humans or animals. (One of the characters is a cat, just as, in *The Shoemaker's Prodigious Wife*, one is a butterfly. There are horses in *Blood Wedding* and *Bernarda Alba*, and a mosquito in *El retablillo de Don Cristóbal*, while *The Butterfly's Evil Spell* is an animal play.) In Federico's theater concrete things and objects possess extraordinary importance, are endowed with a certain independence, and live with rare intensity.

In this world of objects which come to possess their own poetic or dramatic function, clothes, particularly undergarments, are very important. We need only remember how in *Doña Rosita* the character is symbolized by her dresses, wearing a different color (red, pink, white) in each act. Clothes and undergarments—both those that are actually worn and those that are spread about—possess an extremely important role in *The Shoemaker's Wife*, *Blood Wedding*, *Yerma*, and *The House of Bernarda Alba*.

One special characteristic of Federico's theater is the way his themes sometimes acquire lives of their own. It is only natural for the wedding dress (and when I say dress I mean the entire outfit) to reach the same level as the other characters. Undergarments will be a way of expressing sensuality and death. Sometimes this is suggested directly, and at other times it is suggested through deeper, secondary associations.

The empty suit is always reminiscent of a shroud, and the dressed body always seems to be prepared for a final performance. The bridal dress, symbol of the consummation of love, searches for its destiny through the sensual voice of the Manikin. Appealing to the senses (an immediate, radical form of life), the dress incites the Young Man to search for himself. But, blinded by the idea of a new delay, the Young Man goes beyond the woman he is seeking and beyond his desire for offspring (the sub-theme of this play), and he finds, when it is too late, that delay now means death.

This entirely poetic creature, the speaking Manikin, is the counterpart of the grotesque, speechless Football Player. There is here an exchange of human attributes: dramatically spiritualized sensuality as opposed to undiscriminating enjoyment, bridal veil or helmet. A dreamlike quality, on a different scale, will be shared by both characters.

The conventional value of the passage of time—five years—is underscored by the phenomenon of simultaneity. We can suppose, on the one hand, that between the first and second acts five years have elapsed. The second act is separated from the third by the duration of a lunar eclipse. In the first act, however, time does not flow at all. At the beginning of the act the clock strikes six, and, as the curtain is falling, it does so again. Synchrony and duration are thus superimposed. In the first act, a dead child appears on stage. In Act III the same child crosses the stage, and the stage is identical to that of the first act. In the final scene of the work, with the same stage set, someone remarks that the child has just been buried.

Thanks to a delicately, calculated technique, time flows on different, interchangeable levels. This gives expression to the pure emotion of time—time inhabited by dramatically diverse characters. Two episodic characters appear in the first act. Their function is to emphasize the existence of psychological time. The First Friend lives only in the present and is a great consumer of time. Therefore he has no time for anything and is a sort of aimless motion. The Second Friend is less a case of wanting to live in memory than a case of wanting to regress, to return to the original source. He intensifies the purely dilatory movement of the Young Man. These two psychological levels will be bolstered by dramatic situations, some of them occurring only in the mind of the protagonist. The attitude of the Second Friend (i.e. the desire to regress in time) is perfectly expressed in the song which the poet puts in his mouth:

Yo vuelvo por mis alas,	I am returning for my wings,
dejadme volver.	let me return.
Quiero morirme siendo amanecer,	I want to die being dawn,
quiero morirme siendo	I want to die being
ayer.	yesterday.
Yo vuelvo por mis alas,	I am returning for my wings,
dejadme tornar.	let me turn back.
Quiero morirme siendo manantial.	I want to die being a spring.
Quiero morirme fuera de la mar.	I want to die outside the sea.

All of the elements of this play come together in the poetic dramatization of the theme. Nevertheless, the "reality" of each character is more or less noticeable according to whether he embodies the "drama" or merely its "performance." Some characters actually live the drama, others merely perform it. The Football Player only performs it, in a grotesque way. The Manikin lives the drama and is essential to its development. The importance of the characters to the work has nothing to do with their nature: the Second Friend, who lives by "un-living," embodies a blind, human instinct, one which may be biological in origin, and he is no less "poetic" than the Manikin.

In Act I, Scene 3 we find certain characters who epitomize the "derealizing" intentions of the author: the Harlequin, the Clown, and the Girl who, dressed in Greek style, comes leaping onto the stage with a garland of flowers.

The presence of the Clown and the Harlequin is justified by the fact that, scattered about the forest where the action takes place, there is a circus with carriages and cages for animals. As we shall see, there is symbolism in the fact that these objects block paths and exits. The forest is besieged by the circus, demanding the participation of the other characters.

Let us remember that, in the circus as a spectacle, the clown and the harlequin are the only people who "perform." The other people act like what they *are*: trapeze artists, jugglers, lion tamers, etc. Only the clown and the buffoon free themselves, through their performance, from the rigorous discipline and the danger of circus life. They form a little "theater" within the spectacle as a whole.

This double level is shown in the play by the separate little stage that is set up in the forest: a stage within a stage. Not that this relation is very apparent. But here, where the author expresses his dramatic ideas with the greatest freedom, we witness the flowering of what we might call the "subconscious" of his theater. In the elemental pantomime of the circus clown there is something like a germ of pure theater, standing outside time—extemporaneous, like this play—and evoking the Greek idea of theater. It is no coincidence that the Harlequin takes out two masks which, to a certain degree, are opposite: one with "a very joyful expression," and the other with "a sleepy expression." The Girl, a delicate lyrical character, is dressed "in the Greek manner." The characters also make us think of the *commedia dell'arte*.

These exemplary scenes are rooted in perfect, ancient modes of theater, and are free of the restraints of ordinary theatrical techniques. They seem to reveal a longing for "pure theater," parallel to the search for "pure poetry" on the part of so many contemporary poets. Federico never ceased to feel this longing for essential dramatic values.

Once, when the play was being performed in New York, Valery Bettis, an intelligent choreographer, suggested to me that the Harlequin open the curtain on the first act. She believed that it might confuse the audience not to have this character appear until the third act. In the usual logic of the theater, this was a good observation. But I believe it is the very "extemporaneousness" of the Clown and the Harlequin that makes them what they are. Perhaps too, the presence of the circus is enough to justify their appearance.

Interestingly enough, both characters are conscious of their parts. They know they are "performing" a play within a play.

CLOWN (*pointing*): There.
HARLEQUIN: Where? What for?
CLOWN: To play a part.
A little child
who wants to exchange
his piece of bread
for flowers of steel.

It seems logical to suppose that the author himself was conscious of this. We cannot be sure, for these scenes are full of childhood memories and impressions whose function in the play is uncertain. The Clown and the Harlequin enact two children's searching games. In one of them, related to blindman's buff, we hear the following.

Perdí mi corona,   I lost my crown,
perdí mi dedal   I lost my thimble,
y a la media vuelta   and a moment later
los volví a encontrar. I found them again.

These lines are spoken by the Girl. But they are transformed, modified, given lyrical content and action when they are repeated by the other two characters, with the authority (sometimes rather harsh) typical of the clown and his powdered face. Verses like these awaken my memories of other children's games, vaguely alluded to in the text. These scenes grew out of distant impressions that somehow left their poetic mark on Federico. It seems to me that one of these impressions was the image of the clown, the most persistent motif in Federico's drawings.

Given the dramatic freshness of these passages, it seems a shame that the poet did not further explore the possibilities of this type of theater.

The lyrical game to which the Clown and the Harlequin subject the Girl (who timidly opposes them) revolves around the theme of the search, which is entirely pertinent at this moment in the plot. The Harlequin's first verses allude to the major theme of the play:

El sueño va sobre el tiempo   Dream goes over time,
flotando como un velero.   floating like a sailboat.
Nadie puede abrir semillas   No one can make seeds sprout
en el corazón del sueño.   in the heart of dream.

Among the different characters, each of whom possesses its own degree of poetry, the richest in dramatic emotion, the truest and most pathetic in its humanity is the Yellow Mask. This figure (a woman) is also the one with the greatest number of thematic resonances.

To reduce this character to a simple scheme would mean reducing her dramatic value (as happens in all analysis). The Mask is a woman who has known love, luxury, and glory as an artist, but who has ended up as a concierge. She is the mother of the dead child from the first act; his father was Count Arthur, who abandoned her. It is hardly necessary for these things to be true or even almost true. The character seems stronger if we think she has *imagined* part of her past splendor. Part of her soul has its bitter root in the shifting relationship between reality and fiction.

The playwright wisely resists giving us the character's whole life story. We must reconstruct it from her own wild account, her Italian accent, the well-worn feathers of her grotesque attire. And thus, when we are told near the end of Act III, Scene 2 that this extravagant flower is none other than the concierge, the poet gives us a sudden pinprick of love and poetry.

This character is, in many ways, an intimate part of the drama of Time. Turning back time, the Mask lives the past as though it were the present. She is totally out of synchrony with the situations that occur in the play. By turning back time, she also turns back the plot. In the "performed" part of her life, she is a heartless figure who pays no heed to love: she is the cause of misery and loneliness. When she "performs" her former glory and reveals her hardness, we understand her misfortune and her tenderness. Also, at a certain point in the plot, her attitude resembles the Typist's dream of love. Lastly, the asynchronic development of one of the play's themes depends upon her: the theme of the son (which, as I have said, might be thought of as a sub-plot). The theme of the son seems to be projected both toward the past and toward the future. The dead son and the son who has not yet been born are, respectively, sources of pain and of hope. The "presence" registered on stage is that of the dead child, who appears suddenly onstage in Act I, holding hands with a cat, which other children have stoned to death. The dialogue of the child and the cat sets up the unmistakably unreal level where the plot will unfold. A sensation of tenderness and cruelty emerges both from the death of the cat at the hands of the children and from the central cruelty of which the child himself is a victim.

This is the first dialogue in verse in the entire play, and it is written with the sort of poetic realism that is so characteristic of Federico. Poignant, pathetic lyricism mingles with transcendent irony and mischievous humor. Abandoned in death as in life, the lonely child will cross the stage as an example of that death "at dawn," "outside the sea" of which the Second Friend speaks. The Second Friend is lyrically distinguished by his early death. The dead child and his mother the Mask possess a poetical and human symbolism that makes them two of Federico's most unforgettable characters.

The fluent development of the work, its shifting levels of temporality, and the sentiment of time as anguished delay, consummation, or imminence, should not distract us from the dramatic logic, the rigorous design of its poetic architecture. Neither the tiny lyrical detail nor the author's poetic virtuosity can obscure the fact that in this play the eternal themes of love, time, and death are transmuted into real dramatic substance. The play contains a personal vision and personal emotions, objectified by art, for Federico seems to identify himself with his protagonist, the Young Man. After an arbitrary delay of five years (and there is no more arbitrary period than that which death imposes upon us), the Young Man is slain by Time. This (and the fact that the work was written during the summer of 1931) fills the title with disturbing premonitory resonance: *When Five Years Have Passed . . .**

*García Lorca completed the play and dated the manuscript on August 19, 1931. He was slain in Granada on August 19, 1936.—*Tr.*

BLOOD WEDDING

Blood Wedding was one of the few of my brother's premières I was able to attend, for on other occasions I was away due to work or studies. In fact, I was able to follow the work's gestation, and even its composition, in our Huerta de San Vicente.

The plot of the tragedy originated in a brief news item, about twenty lines long, in one of the local Granada papers. At a wedding in a little village in Almería province, the bride was abducted by her former fiancé. In the richly diverse region of Andalusia, dry, arid Almería (where terraces take the place of normal roofs) sounds an almost African note—a note reflected, rather vaguely, in the emotional tone of this play and in its theme of hereditary blood rivalry.

The gestation of *Blood Wedding*—from brief news item to polished literary re-creation—was a long one. Federico never followed a detailed outline. He would tell me or his friends about a play he was going to write. The project would lie fallow for a time, and would then reappear in a different form. This maturing process was a very spontaneous one, entirely alien to any sort of methodical reflection. Later on, he would write the play in a surprisingly short period of time, as though in a fever of creation.

Unamuno used to distinguish "oviparous" authors, who lay an egg and incubate it, from "viviparous" ones, who give live birth to their works.

The analogy is a suggestive one. The first sort of writer creates externally, the second internally. If there was ever a "viviparous" writer it was Federico.

The première of *Blood Wedding* took place in the Beatriz Theater, Madrid, on March 8, 1933, a month or so before the fleeting presentation of *Perlimplín*. I attended the rehearsals, directed by Federico, in which he showed he was already a skilled director. He had to struggle with actors unaccustomed to a style entirely opposed to ordinary theater, for in *Blood Wedding* stage movement and language have a depth of music that is brought out by the verse. The actor who played the Bridegroom seemed an almost insurmountable obstacle. He was an excellent actor, but he had made his name in light comedy, and was hardly able to conquer the image that the public—and he himself—had formed of his talent. There were other problems with the Woodcutters in the forest scene: Federico had to resign himself to letting the actors (mediocre ones, who had probably never spoken a line of verse on stage) play their roles in their own manner. It is the only time I ever saw my brother lose patience as a director. But of course later on, after the première, he congratulated them warmly.

Especially difficult was the Bride's farewell scene, for it involves numerous entrances of characters on different, carefully calculated levels of the stage, with the alternation of feminine and masculine voices, and the use of verse with an extremely rich rhythm. But it was here that the work scored a huge success. At the rehearsals, Federico would often interrupt the scene and shout, "It has to be mathematical!" and this is precisely what he achieved. He had conceived of this scene as taking place inside a cave, with entrances and lights at different levels. Such dwellings are found in the province of Granada, and do not necessarily belong to poor people. The geological configuration of Granada permits spacious, well-lit caves to be carved out of the earth; one can see them in Guadix, on the road to Almería, and in a few neighboring villages. Federico was struck by this rare accommodation of life to the earth. I think he first saw the caves during a trip we took with Falla to Guadix, the birthplace of Pedro Antonio de Alarcón.

Many years later, when we were both in exile, Manuel Collado, who was the director of the company and who also played the part of the Bridegroom, told me proudly that no Spanish work had ever been as thoroughly rehearsed as *Blood Wedding*. And I believe he was right.

Blood Wedding was Federico's first great success as a playwright. It seemed to confirm his potential as a dramatic poet, and it showed that the public was capable of accepting a theater with noble artistic intentions and room for poetry and fantasy. At the end of the second act, on the night of the première, Federico was called onstage by the audience. I would rather narrate this in someone else's words: "The whole theater bursts into a frenzied ovation, calling for the author. . . . Once they have fallen silent, and their enthusiasm has been calmed, the play continues."* It was the success of *Blood Wedding* which led to the poet's triumphal visit to Buenos Aires and Montevideo [1933–1934]. The Argentine actress Lola Membrives hoped that *Blood Wedding* could liven up an otherwise mediocre season.

Blood Wedding entails the greatest orchestration of formal elements in all Federico's theater, and perhaps this is the secret of its popularity. One of those elements, by no means the predominant one, is verse. *Blood Wedding* was preceded by *Perlimplín*, a work with no realistic intentions whatsoever—*Perlimplín* has a musical lyricism, and its characters draw their sustenance from the vague reality of the *aleluya* from which they remotely descend. What characterizes *Blood Wedding* is that prose is combined with verse, and the verse has an essentially dramatic function.

The Butterfly's Evil Spell and *Mariana Pineda* are plays written entirely in verse. This is natural for they are based on a fable and a ballad, respectively. *The Shoemaker's Wife* and *Perlimplín* represent a total displacement towards prose as the medium of expression. Sometimes statistics can be eloquent. *The Shoemaker's Wife* has one hundred and eight lines of verse, and *Perlimplín* only forty.

But the verse in *The Shoemaker's Wife* (most of which occurs in the ballad of the Shoemaker) is totally functional. The same functional element is present in the songs referring to the Wife, sung simultaneously on and off the stage, in a dramatic interaction (inside-outside, fantasy-reality) beginning early in the play and affecting its very structure. One could not do away with those songs, and certainly not the ballad, without destroying the plot. This is why I call the verse "functional"—the ballad and songs are indispensible to the work's development.

Though *Mariana Pineda* is in verse, we could take away the ballad of the bullfight in Ronda and other ballads without really changing the

_____

*Carlos Morla Lynch, *En España con Federico García Lorca: Páginas de un diario íntimo* (Madrid: Aguilar, 1958), p. 332.—Ed.

work. What, then, is the purpose of those ballads? To answer this question, one would have to examine the function of poetry and of lyricism in the dramatic vision of Lope de Vega and in the Spanish theater as a whole.

The diminished presence of verse in *Perlimplín*—the most poetical of all Lorca's works—is significant in more ways than one. It shows that, although Federico possessed a poetic vision of the theater, that vision did not always entail the use of verse. It also makes it untrue to say that in *The Shoemaker's Wife* and *Perlimplín* Federico was merely applying his lyrical gifts to the theater. What gives those two works their special importance is the way Federico has dramatized essential conflicts of the human soul.

Those who have said (mistakenly, I think) that my brother's works slowly evolve from lyricism to dramaticism will be surprised to learn that, compared to the forty lines of verse in *Perlimplín*, there are five hundred and eighty in *Blood Wedding*. Prose predominates, of course. In Spain theater had always been written *either* in prose or in verse. Only the Romantics, for reasons we cannot explore here, had broken with that tradition. Theater in verse had always been perfectly differentiated from theater in prose. In contemporary Spanish literature, only one great attempt had been made to raise the language of drama to a higher literary plane (higher, say, than the everyday language we find in Benavente's "drawing-room" comedies), and that was the theater of Ramón de Valle-Inclán. But the works of Valle-Inclán are written entirely in prose or entirely in verse. It is true that his prose is as well-wrought as his verse, and loving attention is given to the expressiveness of every word and the rhythmic sweep of the sentence. But the great writer had never broken with the traditional, formal differentiation of prose and verse. In Federico's case—and this is shown by *Perlimplín*—form was merely accidental, a means to an end, so that he was able to go from prose to verse (and contrariwise) without any loss of dramaticism. *Blood Wedding* was his first important attempt to integrate the two forms.

It would be interesting to study exactly how he effects the transition from one form to the other. But here, in the poet's own words, is how the two forms are used:

Well-tempered, free prose can soar to expressive heights, freeing us from the confinement and rigidity of meter. Let us welcome verse at the mo-

ments when the excitement and dissipation of the theme demand it. . . .
You can see that, in *Blood Wedding*, verse does not appear with any
intensity or at any length until the wedding scene. Then, with the scene in
the woods and the last scene in the work, it takes complete command of the
stage.

Verse comes forward when it is called for by the "excitement" (as in
the scene in the forest) or the "dissipation" of the theme. A strange
choice of words, "dissipation." Was he thinking of a scattered fragrance?
Or did he mean the voluptuous relaxation of the theme, brought about by
means of verse?

One of the scenes he had in mind was Act II, Scene 2, where (at least to
Spanish audiences) the work's dramatic intensity builds to a peak. Tech-
nically, the whole of that scene is but the orchestration of a character's
leaving the stage. It is what is known in theatrical language as an "exit."
We have already noticed the extraordinary importance of stage movements in Federico's theater. An exit can be—often is—the very denouement of the work, as in *Mariana Pineda* and *Doña Rosita*; or the
dramatic resolution of a basic, if not definitive, movement, for example,
the exit of the Shoemaker in the first act of *The Shoemaker's Wife*, or
this exit in *Blood Wedding*. Federico is exploring the very essence of
stage movement, and this tells us much about him as a playwright. The
scene is given ample poetic development, but it is more than a simple
interlude, not only because the movement is a basic part of the plot, but
also because it has become *the very material being dramatized*. Had some
other technique been employed, the Bride's departure for the church
might have been but another incident in the plot. But in fact it acquires
the dimensions of an entire act, for the Bride is not only leaving the
stage, she is also taking a dramatic stride towards destiny and death. She
will come onstage again only to witness the consummation of the
tragedy.

In this elaboration of a simple dramatic movement, Federico reveals
the heights of his art, or at least of his artistic craftsmanship. He is
making use of traditional poetic forms which originate in the Middle
Ages and forcefully reappear (in a way that scholars have been unable to
explain) in the songbooks of the Spanish Renaissance. Synthesizing both
learned and popular elements, the poetic fragrance of that tradition
impregnates the very beginnings of the Spanish theater, at the court of
Ferdinand and Isabella. Once again we will have to evoke Juan del Encina

and Gil Vicente, and the rustic shepherds of their theater—shepherds removed from immediate reality but with Virgilian echoes, who address Eros and Venus in language that can still be heard in the Spanish countryside. The Spanish Renaissance has often been misunderstood. It is not generally acknowledged how many creative elements it inherited from the Middle Ages. The synthesis of new and traditional, popular and courtly elements has been a characteristic of most of our greatest poets, from the writers of pastoral to the mystics. The greatest assimilator of traditional art was Lope de Vega, who brought popular genres to the New Comedy with instinctive elegance: lullabies, serenades, threshing songs, wedding songs, the songs of reapers and olive pickers.

Perhaps no one since the time of Lope had utilized this current of traditional poetry as successfully and as elegantly as Federico in the wedding scene we are discussing. No anthology of his poetry would be complete without it. Here, as in no other work, the poet identifies himself with an exquisite tradition of Spanish poetry. Federico borrows, or rather creates, a wedding song reminiscent of the popular tradition, and gives it novelty by having it sung by different characters, making it an integral part of the dramatic action.

Much has been written about the way García Lorca uses popular elements in his poetry and theater, and yet he had never developed those elements so completely and so successfully as in *Blood Wedding*. Nor had he ever allowed them to grow to such dramatic proportions. He repeats the experiment in *Yerma*, where the song sung at the brook acquires the dimensions of a dramatic scene. The song in *Yerma* has its origin in the first two verses of a popular song. Federico changes them slightly:

> En el arroyo claro   In the clear spring
> lavo tu cinta . . .   I wash your ribbon

The wedding song and the song at the brook occupy the same place in both works: Act II, Scene I, and this shows what structural corollaries underlie the thematic diversity of Federico's theater. We might add that the source of Act II, Scene I in *Blood Wedding* is the village wedding scene in Lope de Vega's *Fuenteovejuna*. But in Lope's play, the scene occurs in the first act, not the second.

We have pointed out that Federico's dramatic use of lyrical elements does not begin with *Blood Wedding*, but that this play is part of a process of growth. *Blood Wedding* is the play in which he first made *extensive* use of them, more so than had any other writer of tragedy in modern Spain. His purpose in *Blood Wedding* (if a born poet can be said to have a particular purpose) was to create drama, and he did so here with fewer inhibitions than in any of his other works.

I remember a curious rehearsal in a theater in New York where *Blood Wedding* was being performed as a pantomime without any musical accompaniment and without words. There was nothing but choreography. This may have been a mistake, but it shows what possibilities the work has even when reduced to stage movement. On another occasion, in a series of performances by a larger group under the direction of Boris Tumarin, the choreographer Doris Humphrey thought of an interesting way to depict the arrival of the wedding guests. By working "from the outside in," she tried to give plastic expression to the rhythm of their arrival, something which the poet had created "from the inside out." This view from "outside" the scene might also have been erroneous, but it is no less significant, for it shows that Federico's plays can be reduced to the bare schematic essentials of time and space and can survive as theater even when the text has been barbarously stripped away. Few plays would be able to withstand that test.

Blood Wedding is also the work that best illustrates one of the central ideas of Federico's theater: the world as governed by blind forces. The dramatic action is but a way of approaching the mystery of an overpowering, hostile will. It is no accident that none of the characters has his own name, except for Leonardo; no accident that those blind forces (Death, the Moon) take shape on the stage; no accident that the irrational impetus of the horse very nearly becomes a real character. That realm of mystery, of which man himself forms part, is alluded to by Leonardo:

que yo no tengo la culpa,	. . . for I am not to blame;
que la culpa es de la tierra	the earth is,
y de ese olor que te sale	and the odor that comes
de los pechos y las trenzas.	from your breasts and your hair.

This mode of existence means that man is at the mercy of inexplicable forces. This is where part of the drama lies. Man moves towards a destiny beyond his individual consciousness, and thus his slightest voluntary actions acquire true meaning on another plane of reality:

. . . pero montaba a caballo	. . . but I was riding a horse.
y el caballo iba a tu puerta.	and the horse went to your door.

The moon will shine down on that horse and make it glow with "a fever of diamond." The horse will grow so large that the Bridegroom will say, "There is only one horse in the world and it is this one."

Things and even forms are *more*. Or else they cease to *be*, in order to *be* on another plane. The Bridegroom will say:

> Do you see this arm? Well, it is not my arm. It is the arm of my brother and that of my father and that of my entire family. And it has so much strength that it can rip this tree out by the roots if it wants to.

But it it typical of the poet, not only in his theater, but also in his poetry, not to let the innumerable details of immediate reality dissolve away into abstraction. The poet attends to tiny details (the color of some ceremonial shoes, which are red when they ought to be black) and to important ones (the personification of death and the moonlight as agents of the tragedy).

More than other works, *Blood Wedding* strives to give form to a certain attitude of man towards the realities that surround him. Death and the Moon are tangible characters, rather than symbols or abstract universal values: they exist in connection with one specific, concrete death. Death will say to the Moon, in a line of verse:

> Shine on the vest, and draw the buttons apart.

> Ilumina el chaleco y aparta los botones.

Death is given remote echoes of individual vengeance. The poet individualizes the motives of these two characters, and puts them on the same level as the other creatures. When Death (portrayed as a Beggarwoman) appears in the final act, her dramatic texture seems neither more nor less real than that of the other characters.

The strange individualization of Death, which ceases to be a universal abstract symbol, is full of human feeling, and pulses with an ancient idea—the accidentality of death. Death is not the end of a vital cycle, but rather its frustration. All death is violent, and all death is a little like assassination. Man does not perish like a flower, he perishes like the vase holding it.

The way the poet handles his dramatic material grows out of a certain view of how man relates to his surroundings. Man's surroundings begin with the solid reality of shoes, vests, buttons, passions, and emotions, and climb to the very threshold of mystery. At the same time, destiny, death, the light and its physical contours descend to the level of daily reality. This play of poetry and reality will always attract and disconcert readers and directors.

This is also how one should understand the play's Andalusian character. Perhaps Andalusia was an inevitable setting for this work. *Blood Wedding* is the play most closely tied to its Andalusian background, both real and imagined. It would be difficult to say why this is so. The answer lies in the poet's personal experiences and observations, the fact that he was born in Andalusia (which is a way of being universal), the way in which he associates human attitudes with a landscape and other external circumstances, and even in his rich sense of color. Chromatically, *Blood Wedding* is the richest and most refined of the three rural tragedies. Colors, especially red, are ubiquitous, both on the actual stage and on an ideal level, both mentioned and alluded to by the text. As in *Yerma*, white will be emphasized. In *The House of Bernarda Alba* black will predominate over white, and other colors will be virtually absent. But in *Blood Wedding* there is explicit mention of both the dominant and secondary colors, and in the third act Federico goes so far as to indicate the color of the ground—radiant white. No doubt such an indication was very unusual in his time, at least in Spain.

Perhaps the Andalusian note is also present in the tender relationship between man and the earth, and in man's submission to dark forces, especially Destiny. The horse in *Blood Wedding* is also dramatized, and the poet gives bodily form to the rider that gallops across his poetry towards death.

I would like to add, in closing, that part of the final passage (the one beginning "Neighbors, with a knife . . .") was originally assigned (if I remember correctly) to the Bridegroom, and that the work ended on the following words, spoken by the Mother: "May the cross protect the living and the dead." Because this ending did not seem very intense (although in my judgment it was better), Federico decided to lengthen it into a poem in dialogue (not a very successful one, in my opinion). That is the way the work now ends, and it ought to be printed that way. But if I were directing *Blood Wedding*, I would omit it.

YERMA

The première of *Yerma* took place in Madrid on December 29, 1934, with Margarita Xirgu in the leading role. By then Federico was an established author, mostly because of the success of *Blood Wedding*. The theater served as a sounding board for his poetry and helped make his name better known. But his prestige as a poet allowed him to impose an artistic vision designed to enrich the national theater. Who would have suspected that, beneath his happy, carefree exterior, and his inability to accept any sort of academic discipline, was a desire to set an example, a deep concern for the artistic education of the people, and a yearning to give new dignity to the theater in even its humblest manifestations? Addressing the "theater family of Madrid" after a performance of *Yerma* given especially for them, Federico would affirm:

> I speak tonight neither as playwright nor poet, nor even as a simple student of the rich panorama of human life, but as an enthusiastic, devoted friend of the theater of social action. The theater is an extremely useful instrument for the edification of a country, and the barometer that measures its greatness or decline. A sensitive theater, well oriented in all its branches, from tragedy to vaudeville, can alter a people's sensibility in just a few years, while a decadent theater, where hoofs have taken the place of wings, can cheapen and lull to sleep an entire nation.

The "social action" which the poet speaks of in his "Talk About Theater,"* from which I have just quoted, also formed part of Federico's work as director of La Barraca.

The première of *Yerma* was ruffled by winds that presaged the outbreak of civil war. Previous political incidents had made trouble all but inevitable. It seems that there were plans for a protest inside the theater, not so much against Federico, perhaps, as against the leading lady, who was a personal friend of eminent politicians of the Republic and, especially, of Manuel Azaña, one of the best prose writers of the day. One of Don Manuel's works, *La corona*, had been performed by Xirgu herself, and no Spanish politician at the time aroused more polemic. Perhaps, also, some wished to punish Xirgu for Azaña's having stayed, as a guest and friend, at her house during an unhappy period of persecution.

The performance began amid protest and muffled noises, mostly from the upper seats, but the noise began to die away as the performance went on. When the curtain fell at the end of the first act, and again at the end of the play, Federico received the biggest ovation that the Madrid public had ever given him. All of literary Madrid was at the Teatro Español that night—Benavente, Unamuno, Valle-Inclán, as well as representatives of younger generations. Unamuno, whose stature as a writer of genius grows constantly with respect to the rest of the Generation of 1898, generously told Federico (and my brother repeated this to me) that *Yerma* was the work which he himself would like to have written. In fact, Unamuno had already dealt with the theme of frustrated motherhood in a theatrical work to which *Yerma* is not entirely unrelated (*Raquel in Bondage*).

Among Federico's works, I think that *Yerma* is the most difficult for an audience to assimilate. It would be difficult to say why. Perhaps it is because the play has an unsatisfactory denouement. But perhaps the opposite is true: the denouement which the author proposes, the only one possible, is what makes *Yerma* the most quintessentially dramatic (one could also say poetic) vision in all my brother's theater.

This work reveals, better than do others, a certain aspect of Federico's theatrical production, an aspect rooted in the very best tradition of tragedy: its dramatism derives entirely from the intensity with which a character lives out an inner struggle. As the drama develops, we witness emotion growing more and more tense, until it reaches the breaking

*See *Deep Song*, pp. 123-126.—*Tr.*

point. The reality surrounding the character serves only to intensify her emotion. And, because the struggle goes on inside her, that reality is purely episodic. Strictly speaking, *Yerma* has no plot, and is just the opposite of *Blood Wedding* (remember that the latter play originated in an "event") or *The House of Bernarda Alba*, which attempts to cast light on objective reality. In *Yerma*, nothing really happens. Everything happens *to* the protagonist, around whom the tragedy revolves.

The characters in *Blood Wedding* are, for the most part, the dramatic victims of external forces; and the author tries to make these forces concrete, raising them to the category of characters. But, as I have said, in *Yerma* the conflict has been purified and made completely internal. Yerma's situation is dramatic or tragic because she feels it to be so: the same situation would seem different, could even be advantageous, to another woman. The author points this out repeatedly in the play itself. Lorca felt no contradiction whatsoever between the poetry and the tragedy of his creation. He affirmed repeatedly—more often than he did of any other work—that *Yerma* was intended as tragedy. And he said that one element of that tragedy was the subordination of plot to passion, in a process of increasing tension. The following excerpt, from an interview given during the rehearsals of *Yerma* for its première in Barcelona, is revealing:

"*Yerma* is a tragedy. A tragedy based on honor. From the very outset, the audience supposes that something awful is going to happen."
"And what happens?"
"What happens? *Yerma* has no plot. Yerma is a character who develops in the six scenes that make up the work. As befits a tragedy, I have supplied a chorus which comments on the action, or the theme of the tragedy, which is always the same. Notice that I said 'theme.' I repeat, *Yerma* has no plot."

This dramatic vision would thus be totally contrary to those works which revolve around external action, the theater in which there is only "plot." Much of the classical Spanish theater was written in the latter mode, especially the comedy of intrigue which probably gave rise to a joyful, light-hearted, ingenious vision of the theater, and which has never ceased to produce exquisite works. In some of these comedies plot is turned to poetry and music. Others depend on a more or less risqué brand of humor, as in modern vaudeville.

Yerma is but another of the theatrical experiments in which Federico explored the possibilities of pushing one kind of drama to its extreme limits. This artistic attitude polarizes his entire theater into tragedy and farce, the two purest—most extreme—forms of theater. I would not hesitate to call the comedy of intrigue "pure theater"; at the other extreme lies *Yerma*.

Some say that in the three rural tragedies Federico progressively purified his theater. This is not entirely true. Certain errors in perspective have led to a distorted vision of my brother's dramatic output. The existence of a *trilogy*, and the tragically accidental fact that *Bernarda Alba* was his last work, have helped confuse the idea of his *evolution* as a playwright (although evolution is a dangerous term to apply to Federico's poetry and theater). It is true that *Yerma* reflects a purification of elements with respect to *Blood Wedding*. Its theatrical design is much simpler. But *Yerma* is also simpler than *Bernarda Alba*. *Yerma* is unique among the three tragedies because of the accidental nature of its plot, which envelops and surrounds the intimacy of the only major character. *Bernarda Alba* does not intensify the dramatic vision of *Yerma*; on the contrary, it rectifies it. For *Bernarda* carries plot further than *Blood Wedding* by including a large number of external elements. Those elements came close to turning *Bernarda* into a tragedy of social character, and they permit the author to classify the play as a "photographic documentary" on the villages of Spain. When one looks back on *Yerma* from the perspective of *Bernarda Alba*, *Yerma* seems an extreme of poetic stylization, and *Bernarda* an extreme of realistic stylization.

Nor should we be distracted by the elements of fantasy which appear in *Blood Wedding* (as compared with *Yerma*). It is true that such elements are an integral part of the play. (We might say, in fact, that as a dramatic creation the play culminates in the last act, set in the forest, where characters and personified natural forces are joined in total harmony.) And yet the reduction and simplification of *Yerma* reflect a stylization in the direction of poetry, the inevitable effect of Yerma's inner conflict.

The stylization and schematic nature of *Yerma* will be better understood if we remember the technique Unamuno used in his novels, particularly *Abel Sánchez*. Unamuno believed that the progress of a living passion, stripped bare of its external elements, allows the novel to "de-realize" itself and draw close to drama and poetry. He identified poetry with the novel: novelistic action lean enough to reveal the work's pathos and drama. What happens in *Yerma* is that Federico prunes away the elements of fantasy found in *Blood Wedding*, in order to give the play dramatic intensity. That dramatism is heightened, in poetic terms, inside the protagonist. I would like to imagine that when Unamuno said that *Yerma* was the play he himself would like to have written he meant something more than that he and Federico had used the same theme: he meant that he felt *Yerma* to be his. Without Unamuno, I do not believe that *Yerma* could have been written. Or it would have been a very different play.

But without a doubt Federico knew what he was doing better than we do as critics. So as not to confuse its character, one need only notice the title and subtitle which the author gave his work: *Yerma. Tragic Poem.* It is the only one of his plays which Federico specifically designated as a poem. The title alone is significant because it announces the radically poetic nature of the leading character. Yerma is a name invented by the poet. In Spanish the noun "yermo" is fairly common, but the feminine adjective is rare, and here it is turned into a proper name.* This is noteworthy because, among the important characters in his tragedies, it is Yerma who reveals the very least inspiration in reality.

The poetic nature of *Yerma* is confirmed also by its dramatic language. Obviously, there is much less verse in *Yerma* than in *Blood Wedding*. But this should not confuse us about the nature of the work. The function of the verse in *Yerma* is more "poetic" than in the first tragedy. In *Blood Wedding*, the great novelty, as far as language is concerned, is the way in which prose and verse are combined, and the gradual transition from one form to another. Verse is used in what are probably the most dramatic scenes. There is dialogue in verse, and, in the poetic-realistic texture of the work, verse is as normal a means of expression as prose. Yerma does not dialogue in verse, but she is the only important character who *speaks* in verse. Much of the verse in the work is, in fact, spoken by her. And yet she only uses this form of expression when she is alone. It is not a form of communication, but of desolation. When she can no longer restrain her passion she bursts into poetry:

> Ah, what a meadow of pain!
> Ah, what a door closed on beauty!

Yermo (from Latin *eremus*: wilderness, desert) is barren land that cannot be cultivated. In older Spanish it was often used to mean a deserted, solitary place: the Desert Fathers were referred to as "los Padres del Yermo."—*Tr.*

For I ask to suffer a son, and the air
offers me dahlias of sleeping moon. [. . .]

But you must come, love, my child,
for the water gives salt and the earth fruit,
and our womb holds tender children
just as the cloud carries sweet rain.

¡Ay, qué prado de pena!
¡Ay qué puerta cerrada a la hermosura!
que pido un hijo que sufrir, y el aire
me ofrece dalias de dormida luna. [. . .]

Pero tú has de venir, amor, mi niño,
porque el agua da sal, la tierra fruta,
y nuestro vientre guarda tiernos hijos,
como la nube lleva dulce lluvia.

Because verse is not a normal means of expression in this play, Yerma's verse monologues are markedly poetical. With respect to *Blood Wedding*, *Yerma* reflects, both in conception and in technique, a certain poetic vision of the theater rather than (as has been affirmed) a setting aside or a rejection of poetry. Federico was perfectly justified in subtitling the play "Tragic Poem."

The critics have thought of *Bernarda Alba* as the "definitive" culmination of the author's dramatic language: some have said that Federico reached this point after pruning away all expressive elements and cultivating with true virtuosity a laconic, almost artificial sobriety. But all this is far from the truth. After carefully examining the prose in the first act of all three tragedies, I have reached the conclusion that the most sober, spare, synthetic language is that of *Blood Wedding*. The briefest, most rapid exposition (both in the total number of words and in the average number of words spoken by each character) is found in *Blood Wedding*. And the slowest, and most elaborate, exposition is that of *Bernarda Alba*. Dramatic language and schematic simplicity of plot had already been exploited in *Blood Wedding*, and it is in this first tragedy that they are carried to their furthest extreme.

These purely formal considerations prove that the theater of García Lorca is, at least in its technique, not so much a matter of evolution or "progress" (though these might be detectable on other levels) as of adapting the means of expression to the artistic purpose. From this angle, what surprises one is Federico's variety of purpose. In this his theater resembles his verse.

In the course of his development as a poet, *Poet in New York* is no more "definitive" than the *Gypsy Ballads*, nor is *Bernarda Alba* more "definitive" than *Blood Wedding*. Had Federico lived longer, he would probably have "returned" from the daring surrealistic technique of *Poet in New York* to a greater intimacy, in the Granadan style, and in fact this really happened. In the same way, one could expect his theater might have returned from the supremely stylized ultra-realism of his last tragedy to the poetic fantasy of his earlier ones. The following statement, from a 1935 interview, is relevant here:

"Tell me, García Lorca, do you have the impression that your present literary form is, in fact, your definitive one?"

"No. That is nonsense. Every morning I forget what I have written. It is the secret of being modest and working courageously. . . . In fact, I am planning to write several plays of the human, social type.* One of these plays will be against war. These works have a material that is very different from that of *Yerma* or *Blood Wedding*, for example, so that one must treat them with a different technique."

I have said that the denouement of *Yerma* is not entirely satisfactory, but that the ending seems the inevitable psychological climax of a state of unbearable inner tension. The work ends in a state of frenzy and there is no doubt that what the final scene does is to orchestrate that frenzy. The author is no longer satisfied with poetic exposition, and he turns to music and to dance.

The death of Juan (the husband) at Yerma's hands is a frenetic act that borders on madness in an atmosphere of dark, unleashed forces. The protagonist's final words are, "I have killed my son. I myself have killed my son." She has closed off the last and only source of her hope: the author preferred this ending, which is as tragic as it is illogical, because it represents, in stubborn contradiction, the triumph of Yerma as *yerma* (barren). And thus the denouement implies that the protagonist, in great agony, has finally accepted her destiny. By destroying the source of her

---

*One was the unfinished *Play Without a Title*. See Carlos Bauer's translation (New York: New Directions, 1983).—*Tr.*

hope, she has also destroyed the source of her despair. Perhaps it is this that made the poet say that *Yerma* was truly a tragedy.

Let us turn from the characters to the conflict. In *Blood Wedding*, events happen to the characters. But Yerma bears her conflict alone. If there is in *Yerma* (as there is in *Blood Wedding*) a blind, outer force, a normative, central, mysterious will directing mortals towards their destiny, it would lie in this—that Yerma's sterile body is filled with the burning desire to feel fecund and fecundated—like a piece of land—and that in the end, she feels she is breaking into painful cracks, like the dry earth in the ballad of Tamar and Amnon:

La tierra se ofrece llena	The earth shows itself
de heridas cicatrizadas,	full of scarred wounds,
o estremecida de agudos	or shudders with sharp
cauterios de luces blancas.	cauteries of white lights.

Yerma feels increasingly alienated from Juan, not so much because of the sterility of her union with him, as because of the indifference with which Juan accepts that sterility. Sharing the drama with him would have given Yerma some possible solution. We can assume that had Juan burned with the same desire for paternity, had he shared Yerma's pain, she would have lavished upon him all her frustrated maternal instinct. I think the play itself hints at this possible solution, and perhaps this is what Yerma's final words ultimately mean: "I myself have killed my son."

Whether or not anyone has noticed, the psychological conflict is developed progressively throughout the work. In the last scene, when the tragedy is ending, the author finally shows explicitly what sort of relation has been uniting (better said, separating) the couple. Yerma's passion has been exacerbated by the incessant fertility of nature, and a wall of hostility and incomprehension has arisen between her and Juan, till she is surrounded by agony and solitude.

This psychological situation conditions the couple's sexual relations. Juan has reduced Yerma (the victim of her own blind passion) to a mere instrument of pleasure, in the most primary, elemental sense: the cold possession of an ardent body. And thus, in the eyes of the protagonist the relationship is devoid of any biological impulse, even of the living appetite of the flesh, and of any emotional and even *moral* basis. I add this final adjective in view of one of the most intelligent commentaries I have ever read about *Yerma*. Referring to Yerma's attitude, the critic in question demonstrates the coincidence of a deep biological urge, governed by natural forces, with the traditional religious criterion governing marital life: the final justification of the act of love lies in procreation.* Yerma's motives (motives contradicted by the violence with which the play ends) would make her a synthesis of instinct and culture: a particular passion in a particular social milieu. It would be unthinkable for Yerma's drama *not* to revolve around her husband, and equally unthinkable for her to renounce the passion for which she lives and dies. This was the way Federico conceived the play, and one must judge a work on the author's own terms. Otherwise, we would be helpless against the ingenious argument that a timely marriage might have thwarted the greatest work of the European Renaissance (I mean *La Celestina*) and the hypothetical possibility of a *ménage à trois* might have done away with *Othello*. It cannot be.

It is at this meeting point of instinct and society that the work is born, and perhaps I can say something of its genesis. Frankly, the only real-life incident that I can distinguish in *Yerma* is the pilgrimage, which, strangely enough, seems the one least real and most surely invented.

In Moclín, a little village in Granada, located in the foothills of the Sierra Nevada, there is a pilgrimage attended by childless women who pray for the blessing of fertility. We ourselves never went to craggy Moclín, but it was not far from our lands in the Vega and the name of the village was fairly well known because of the pilgrimage. And furthermore, I don't know why, the children's stories told in the Vega used to begin with the following words:

Esto era lo que era.	Once upon a time
Colomera en una era	Colomera on the threshing floor
y Moclín en un cerro.	and Moclín on a hill . . .

And in fact it is on a hill that we find the chapel where one venerates the image that bestows fertility. But this religious side of the ceremony, with its idea of miraculous grace, is tarnished by the rumor that the women get pregnant for somewhat more natural reasons, amid festive, bawdy dances in the open air. So powerful is this rumor that on the day of the

---

*Guillermo Díaz-Plaja, *Federico García Lorca. Estudio crítico* (Buenos Aires: Kraft, 1948), pp. 221-22. [Author's note.]

novena, the pilgrims, on horseback or in carts, are received by youths and little children shouting "Cuckolds! Cuckolds!" As they pass through villages and wend their way down country roads, one hears the jangling of strings of goats' and sheep's horns. The whole Vega seems to resound with that shout, and there are always serious incidents even before the pilgrims arrive in Moclín.

Perhaps in rare cases the malicious version of the "miracle" did actually occur. But on the whole it is quite unthinkable, given the conjugal morality prevalent in the region and the attitude of the average Granadan toward adultery. This being so, perhaps the so-called "natural" explanation has deeper and more ancient roots. It is well known that, from earliest times, the Catholic Church has superimposed religious celebrations on the old pagan customs it was trying to uproot. And it is no less true that in archaic backward regions the old pagan customs somehow filter through. For example, most people do not know that when they buy presents at Christmas time or send Christmas cards they are following a Roman tradition.

I have never seen the miraculous image at Moclín, but to judge from the lithograph we had in our house in the Vega, it was a crudely painted picture, just as appears in *Yerma*. In the bedroom of our country house there was also a picture entitled "True Effigy of the Most Holy Christ of the Cloth."* Federico would often contemplate the crude lithograph and hold forth on the pagan character of the image, and Federico's imagination stretched much farther than mine did.

As for the final dance in the pilgrimage scene of *Yerma*, it comes from a dance of northern Spain, from Asturias I think, and perhaps it is bacchic in origin. It is danced by a man and a woman. He carries a horn and she, I seem to recall, a wreath of flowers. I do remember very clearly the dialect names of the two objects carried by the dancers: the *pilueta* and the *tronaor*. Federico has brought out the erotic character of the dance and has given masks to the couple.

From this pagan feeling, placed in a poetic social setting (where religious ceremony acquires the character of an ancient rite); from the mixture of instinct and tradition; from blind, individual passion, punctu-

---

*A much venerated image in Andalusia, especially in the neighboring province of Jaén. The "cloth" is the sudarium, the handkerchief of St. Veronica, on which Christ impressed his face on the way to the crucifixion.—*Tr.*

ated by cries of collective encouragement—from all this is woven the central character—a poetic, tragically solitary creature, born amid the almost miraculous fertility of our lands in the Vega of Granada.

HONOR IN *YERMA*

Some interpretations of *Yerma* insist that the sense of honor is what brings on the tragedy. They speak of a conflict between honor and the desire for maternity. This is true. And yet to me it does not seem sufficient to explain the tragedy or, better said, to explain the character of Yerma herself.

The *duty* to remain faithful to her husband is not felt by Yerma as a *social* duty, or at least not as an *essentially* social one. We might say that matrimony is a sacrament here not in the ecclesiastical, but rather in the natural sense. If offers access to the fullness of being, which to Yerma means maternity, the realization of her essence as a woman. And this consecration cannot be betrayed; otherwise, it would endanger not a social relationship or mere conjugal duty, but a natural relationship and, in a way, a sacred one: the almost magical union that gives human meaning, or simply meaning, to the act of procreation. Clearly Yerma realizes that the act of giving birth would carry with it duties toward her son. But the act itself is felt as a right, and its negation as an offense or as a punishment.

She does not want a son, she wants *her* son. Yerma is not a sheep, but a woman. It would not be right to reduce the problem to biological terms. What she wants is precisely the son which is denied to her. This also means that the character belongs to a social circle, of which she is the unknowing center. But it is also a natural and magical order, and perhaps this is much more important than the religious order which gives meaning to the final dance of the male and female. It is a circle of erotic character, one from which she is absent. Yerma is the only entirely "clean" character in the play, with the exception of María, whose name may be symbolical. What the character signifies is the complete sublimation of erotic feeling: she is the counterpart of Belisa in *Perlimplín*.

Yerma, then, incarnates humanity, face to face with the fertility of nature. She symbolizes unity: the unity of man and woman, legitimized by the difference, or the individualization of the two parts, which is, after all, what separates man from animal. Strictly speaking, what Yerma is defending is her right to be a woman, in the double and (for her) unique meaning of woman/wife.* And thus, the sense of honor, the merely social or institutional aspect of matrimony, would be a purely mechanical explanation of the play, although that level, too, is implicit in the work.

The problem would be much clearer if the poetical plane had predominated, and if the play had been set in a world outside history, and the primitive ritual of the final dance had been present from the very outset. The magical and ritualistic elements of the pilgrimage (which refer to Yerma's inner conflict) merely point to its ultimate roots. The causes of Yerma's sterility are not important. No matter what they are, they are felt as a tragic fate or a curse. Yerma is denied a son, her son, against all human justice and order. And it is only by killing Juan that she can break out of the circle into which she has been placed. That act also signifies the acceptance of a tragic destiny: the triumph of Yerma as Yerma. This solution links the character with the Mother in *Blood Wedding*, who, like Yerma, will no longer have anything, no longer hope for anything, all hope having been blinded after the death of her son.

Mujer means both "woman" and "wife."—*Tr.*

DOÑA ROSITA THE SPINSTER

This play was performed for the first time in Barcelona on December 13, 1935, by the company of Margarita Xirgu. No one could have supposed it would be the last time Federico would ever see a performance of one of his works.

The very title announces the richness of its verbal world: *Doña Rosita the Spinster, or The Language of the Flowers.* It is Federico's only work with a double title, of the sort sometimes found in the classical and Romantic theater. Since that period, double titles had sometimes been given to light works or to the Spanish genre of operetta known as *zarzuela.* The title hints ironically at a certain type of atmosphere. It is instructive to compare this title with that of *Yerma.*

Doña Rosita breaks the sequence of the three rural tragedies, remarkable for their concentration and compactness. Federico's language now becomes more slow-moving, with greater attention to detail. Let us remember that in Act I, Scene 3 of *Blood Wedding*, we pointed out that each character speaks an average of only six words. We now find Doña Rosita with a speech that contains five hundred twenty words and is interrupted only once, by the words "Daughter! Rosita!," which come from the Aunt. If Federico had applied the same technique he used in the third scene of the first act of *Blood Wedding*, this passage from *Doña*

Rosita might have been broken into eighty-six interventions! We must bear in mind that the entire scene in *Blood Wedding* contains only seven hundred seventy-eight words, a third more than Doña Rosita's speech alone. All this goes to show that when studying the development of the author's technique, we must be attentive to how he adapts the means to the artistic purpose he has in mind and to the material with which he is working.

The subtitle—*Poem of Granada, at the Turn of the Century, Divided into Various Gardens, with Scenes of Song and Dance*—hints at the diversity and abundance of the elements involved. Particularly rare for Federico's theater is the mention of a specific time (1900) and a place (Granada).

The poet had already written a play connected with Granada, but this was before he had much experience as a playwright. I am referring, of course, to *Mariana Pineda* In *Doña Rosita* he wanted to dramatize the atmosphere and the spirit of the city without any "historical" intentions, and, because the theme was an invented one, he had a bit more freedom. In order, perhaps, to reflect the soul of the city (the most poetic and melancholy of the great Andalusian cities), it seemed best to look at it from a distance, as though it were an old photograph. There are none of the immediate, violent details and harsh close-ups that we sometimes find in *The House of Bernarda Alba*. I remember Federico speaking enthusiastically of old hairstyles and leg-of-mutton sleeves. I believe he had already thought, long before, of Doña Rosita as a name for the leading character. But the play took a long while to jell.

During one of Federico's stays in Madrid, José Moreno Villa, who was the librarian of the Royal Palace, read him a passage from an eighteenth-century botany book, a fragment describing the *rosa mutabilis* (not *mutabile*, as Federico apparently wrote), a variety of rose which is red when it opens, turns a deeper shade of red when it blossoms fully, and then grows more and more pale, until it turns white and withers away. Federico has told of this in an interview. After stating that he conceived of the play in 1924, he adds:

> When Moreno Villa finished the marvelous story of the rose, I knew my play was finished. It seemed unique and unalterable. And yet I did not write it down until 193[5]. The years themselves have embroidered its scenes, composing verse for the story of the flower.

Other roses mentioned in the play were probably culled from other books: the eglantine rose, the *muscosa,* the *hispida,* the *pomponiana,* the damascene rose. But the rarest roses, those named in Latin, are probably from the same book as the *mutabilis*: for example the *declinata,* the *inermis,* the *sulfurata,* and the *mirtifolia.* Given Federico's delight in language, we can safely suppose that he shared the enthusiasm with which his characters mention these roses and describe them.

The work was written at our country house in Granada, with all the passion and fervor my brother always put into the act of creation. To get a sense of atmosphere, Federico (who was ordinarily very careless in these matters) collected some magazines (perhaps the *Ilustración Española e Iberoamericana*) and a few little books and almanacs from the turn of the century. I do not know where he found them, but their pages, torn from the bindings, were all over the house. In one of them he found the "language of the flowers," the "language of the fans," and also, perhaps, "the language of postage stamps," all of which are mentioned in the play.

There are a few allusions in *Doña Rosita* to historical incidents: the automobile race from Paris to Madrid with the death of Count Zborinsky; the purchase, by the Shah of Persia, of a Panhard Levasseur with a twenty-four-horsepower engine, etc. The author evokes the atmosphere somewhat ironically by alluding to kinds of cloth, musical compositions, customs, and fashions. He mentions objects like Mr. X's gift to Rosita: a broach which is "a mother-of-pearl Eiffel Tower borne by two doves carrying the wheel of industry in their beaks," or "a belt buckle showing a serpent and four dragonflies." By mentioning all this, Federico evokes a time that is too recent to be historic and too distant to be present. It all seems faintly ironic, as when one looks at an album of old photographs—what strikes one immediately are the extremes of fashion, before fashion has turned into style.

Upon all this the poet embroiders his own memories, which help give his characters their special profile. Perhaps in no other work by Federico are there so many childhood memories. Among them is an old teacher from a private school: a failed life, like so many other ones in the drama. He has the same name—Don Martín—that he had in the school we attended as children, the one I told about earlier. Don Martín taught literary theory, literature, and also logic and ethics. His was a noble life, dedicated to things of the spirit, in the face of a harsh, adverse reality. He was a dreamer, and a little quixotic. The play mentions the title of the only book that he ever published, *Matilde's Birthday*. There are other references to school life—the poet suddenly remembers the definition of "idea" which he had learned in Don Martín's class: "the intellectual representation of a thing or object."

There is an extremely important element of social criticism in *Doña Rosita*, and this explains the appearance of certain characters, for example, a professor of political economy, Sr. X, who was modelled on another real-life person.* Sr. X makes excessive, almost comical use of polite formulas: in him, Federico wanted to satirize a sort of vacuous professorial pedantry.

UNCLE: You will never convince me. (*He sits down.*)

SEÑOR X: (*resting his foot on a chair and playing with his cane*): No doubt, no doubt. A full professor of political economy can hardly argue with a rose grower. But today, please believe me, quietism and *obscurantist* ideas have fallen quite out of style. Nowadays people follow figures like Jean Baptist *Seye*, or *Say*—both pronunciations are correct—or Count Leon *Tol-STWAH*—pronounced *Tol-STOY* in the vernacular—who is as elegant in form as he is profound in thought. I feel myself to be part of the living Polis, and I am no friend of *Natura Naturata*.

Federico amused himself by making this character say things really said by other well-known professors. It was José Ortega y Gasset who uttered the following dictum: "The earth is a mediocre planet." Another illustrious professor was the source of this reply to a banal question: "My dear sir, I cannot say; I lack a sufficient fund of experience."

There is also a real-life basis for the unmarried sisters, who are supposed to project, in a grotesque and pathetic way, the drama of the protagonist. The family name of the Escarpini sisters is a take-off on another Italianate name from the social world of Granada: the Ayolas, the daughters of a photographer from a rising social class, girls who were already well-dressed but not yet well-educated. As I remember them, I think of the gold lettering at the bottom of many of our family photographs: "Ayola, Photographer." The author also mentions the most aristocratic families of Granada: Ponce de León, Herrasti, the Baroness of

*See p. 69.—*Tr.*

St. Matilde of the Papal Blessing. The last name is meant to imitate the local titles of the papal pseudo-aristocracy. Other local characters are less real than they are poetic. In Granada, they sing a *fandanguillo* with the following words:

Granada, calle de Elvira	Granada, on Elvira Street,
donde viven las manolas,	where the *manolas* live,
las que se van a la Alhambra,	the ones that go to the Alhambra
las tres y las cuatro solas.	in groups of three and four.

These *manolas** are among the innumerable characters that come from the proverbs and songs of Spanish folklore. There is a well-known Andalusian song that says

La Lola se va a los puertos.	Lola goes off to the ports,
La Isla se queda sola.	the Island is all alone.

Manuel Machado, in one of his Andalusian poems, perhaps the prettiest of them all, has asked

Y esta Lola ¿quién será,	And just who is this Lola,
que así se marcha, dejando	who goes away like that,
la Isla de San Fernando	leaving the Isle of San Fernando
tan sola	so lonely when she goes?
cuando se va?	

Federico takes it a step further, and brings the *manolas* onstage. They are episodic characters, but in the pretty ballad to which they give rise we can hear the questions the poet must have asked himself.

... ¿Adónde irán las Manolas	Where are the Manolas going,
mientras sufren en la umbría	as the water jet and the rose
el surtidor y la rosa?	suffer in the shade?
¿Qué galanes las esperan?	What lovers await them?
¿Bajo qué mirto reposan?	Under what myrtle do they rest?

*The *manolo* and *manola* were types made popular in the eighteenth-century one-act play (e.g. those of Ramón de la Cruz) and the nineteenth-century sketch of manners (e.g. Ramón de Mesonero Romanos). The *manola* is a woman from the working classes wearing a mantilla and fancy popular dress. Her joy is to promenade and be seen.—*Tr.*

¿Qué manos roban perfumes	What hands steal perfume
a sus dos flores redondas? [...]	from their two round flowers? [...]
¿Quién serán aquellas tres	Who are those three,
de alto pecho y largas colas?	with high breasts and long trains?
¿Por qué agitan los pañuelos?	Why are they waving their handkerchiefs?
¿Adónde irán a estas horas?	Why are thcy out so late?

And thus, although they are personified on the stage, their poetic existence is just as mysterious as ever.

The type of woman symbolized by Doña Rosita, the woman who consumes herself and withers away as she awaits a love that never comes, is an oft-repeated theme in Federico's work. As far back as his *Book of Poems*, there is a passionate elegy inspired by such a woman. Her name, Maravilla (Wonder), fit her perfectly. She was the most splendid dark beauty I have ever set eyes on. We heard about other such women closer to our own family: my mother told us about a spinster we were too young to know, but whose story is faintly echoed in *Doña Rosita* in the lover's flight to America.

In the play, Doña Rosita becomes a symbol of Granada, a city Federico identified with collective frustration. It is a city lyrically forgotten, in the backwaters of time. In the elegy I have just mentioned, he tells Maravilla:

> You are the mirror of an Andalusia
> which suffers huge passions and remains silent.

> Eres el espejo de una Andalucía
> que sufre pasiones gigantes y calla.

And he concludes

> But your great sadness will rise to the stars,
> like another star, worthy to wound and eclipse them.

> Pero tu gran tristeza se irá con las estrellas,
> como otra estrella digna de herirlas y eclipsarlas.

In a somewhat later poem, where the dramatic tone has been replaced by lyrical, intentionally child-like irony, the poet will say:

Las estrellas	The stars have no
no tienen novio.	boyfriend.
¡Tan bonitas	As pretty
como son las estrellas! [. . .]	as they are! [. . .]
Pero aguardad, muchachas,	But wait, girls,
que cuando yo me muera	for when I die
os raptaré una a una	I will carry you off one by one
en mi jaca de niebla.	on my pony of mist.

We might say that the poet felt this frustration as a form of injustice tied to a specific social phenomenon: the way in which an inert society prevents women from realizing their possibilities. The author wanted to heighten the conflict by having it occur in provincial surroundings, even more confining because of the historical period in which the play takes place. But he also wanted to protest against the cruel laughter—sometimes silent laughter—which the drama of the spinster provokes even in more advanced societies, and the lack of charity these societies show towards the bitterness and sting of frustration in love. This idea appears in *Doña Rosita*, as though the thorns of the *rosa hispida* were now growing on the stem of the *mutabilis*.

In an interview given in 1935, the poet made these comments about the play:

> It concerns the tragic history of our social life: the Spanish women who did not marry. The play begins in 1890, continues in 1900, and ends in 1910. It takes in the whole tragedy of Spanish and provincial pretentiousness [*cursilería*]. This is something younger generations will smile at, but which possesses deep social drama, for it shows what the middle class was like.

Federico suggests that the conflict was slightly removed from him in time. It probably seemed a little faded. The poet was quite sensitive to changes in historical reality, and all of his poetry is created *in vivo*. The distancing here is a form of stylization. So, in a different way, is the ultrarealism of *The House of Bernarda Alba*, a play whose social theme has faded over the years more than that of *Doña Rosita*. This distancing or stylization which makes the poet turn many of his characters into symbols also makes them representative of Spanish life. But there is a profound, human level where the Spanish element ceases to be Spanish and becomes universal. The struggle between fantasy and reality in *The Shoemaker's Prodigious Wife* does not depend upon any sort of Andalusian background, nor does the maternal tyranny, blent with sexual or social prejudice, of *Bernarda Alba*. The "photographic" element Federico speaks of in the latter play lies in the creation of atmosphere and in a certain artistic technique, a stylized ultra-realism which is less a matter of content than of form.

Consequently, although *Doña Rosita* takes the Granada of 1900 for its background, what really matters is the theme, frustrated love, and that theme cannot be tied to any one time or place. It is true, however, that in no other work except *Bernarda* did Federico make the conflict so dependent on social elements. He says in the interview from which I have just quoted that, besides the drama of the unmarried woman, he wanted to portray "that of Spanish pretentiousness [*cursilería*]."

The noun *cursilería* and the adjective *cursi* are difficult to translate into other languages. *Cursilería* is a desire for things beyond one's means. It is pretending to belong to a higher social level, and not being able to reach it. Essentially, it is poverty ashamed of itself. It is forced—and sometimes complacent—concern for the outer things that can conceal poverty: more feathers in one's hat, more curios and trinkets, more affectation in the voice. The word can be applied to suffering, to a gesture, to an expression, to a melody. *Cursilería* can coexist with abundance. But true *cursilería* is born from indigence and necessity, and is almost always tinged with social aspirations which, because they are both legitimate and impossible to fulfill, make it pathetic and comical. When *cursilería* is met with the laughter and mockery of society, real drama can occur.

It is true that the protagonist and the rest of the household are free of *cursilería*, but not the other characters. Some show it in comic ways, some in pathetic. Or perhaps we should say that the whole stage is bathed in the doubtful light of *cursilería*, and that all of the characters are affected by it.

The theme of *cursilería* has been ably dealt with in the contemporary Spanish theater. Benavente wrote a play entitled *Lo cursi* (What is *cursi*), and the great writer of *sainetes* Carlos Arniches, whom the best critics consider superior to Benavente in the liveliness of his dialogue, once built a whole grotesque tragedy around the theme: *The Young Lady from Trevélez*. (Trevélez, as it happens, is a village in Granada, and perhaps

Doña Rosita is not entirely unrelated to this work.) Because it involves trying to be more than one is, and an attempt to replace things with their mere appearances, there is a deeper element in Spanish *cursilería*. Here too we find fantasy and reality in opposition. We might say that the theme has its remote, literary roots in the poor, fanciful squire in *Lazarrillo de Tormes*, perhaps the first character of the European novel, and in the miracle of the *Quijote*.

Doña Rosita's lyrical subconscious is the spirit of Granada. But there is another silent character, a more important one: Time. In reality nothing happens in this play. Time passes destructively over suits and dresses, objects and colors, over the bodies and souls of the characters, destroying both reality and appearance. Truth emerges through disillusionment. García Lorca's theater often gives bodily form to the major themes of his vision of the world. The feeling of time, which runs through all his poetry (time as eternity, time as imminence—"I will never get to Córdoba" . . . "at five o'clock in the afternoon.")* Time becomes a character in more than one of his plays, for example in *When Five Years Have Passed*, where time mingles, as in the best Spanish tradition, with the feeling of death.

THE LANGUAGE OF THE FLOWERS

Among Federico's papers I have found a list, in a woman's handwriting, enumerating the symbolic meaning of thirty-one flowers. It is curious to see how closely the poet follows the meanings given in the list. From it he takes fourteen flowers, and adds five more: dahlia, iris, passionflower, hyacinth, and everlasting. Only in a few instances does he change the meaning. For example, the honeysuckle is associated on the list with "maternal love." The poet says:

> La madreselva te mece,   Honeysuckle rocks you,
> la siempreviva te mata.   the everlasting brings death.

But even here, the action of rocking can suggest the idea of maternity and of cradle songs. The list continues:

*Refrains from "Rider's Song" and "Lament for the Death of Ignacio Sánchez Mejías," respectively.—*Tr.*

Rose: Beauty.
Narcissus: Vanity.
Daisy: I think of you.
Carnation: Coquetry.
Sponge-tree*: Jealousy.
Bindweed: Frivolity.
Pansy: "I will never forget you."
Red Rose: "I do not trust you."

Notice that sometimes the flower itself tells its symbolism, as though it were speaking. Federico uses this double means of expression in his ballad. At one moment he says:

Son celos el carambuco;   The spongetree is jealousy,
desdén esquivo, la dalia.   the dahlia, cold disdain.

But at another moment he says

"Sólo en ti pongo mis ojos",   "I have eyes only for you,"
el heliotropo expresaba.   said the heliotrope.
"No te querré mientras viva",   "I will never love you,"
dice la flor de la albahaca.   says the flower of the basil.

The heliotrope appears on the list saying "My eyes look only at you," while beside the word basil the list simply says "hate."

Federico had to invent symbolic values for the flowers he himself added. The dahlia is "cold disdain," the hyacinth "bitterness." As for less known flowers, he preferred to keep to the meaning on the list: the sponge-tree is "jealousy," the hedge-mustard is "scorn." Flowers common in Granada keep the meaning assigned to them on the list: the jasmine is "faithfulness," and the spikenard, "friendship."

On the other side of the page is another list, in the same hand, giving the abstract symbolism of the colors. What Federico does is relate the colors to the flowers themselves. Of the ten colors appearing on the list, he uses only four, changing the meaning of two of them. The list says:

*Acacia farnesiana, also known as huisache, cassie, and popinac: a tropical and subtropical shrub with deep-yellow flowers.—Tr.

> Yellow: Hate.
> Red: Rage.
> White: Purity.
> Blue: Heavenly Love.

The ballad reads as follows:

> Las amarillas son odio;   Yellow flowers mean hate,
> el furor, las encarnadas;   and red flowers mean rage.
> las blancas son casamiento   White ones are marriage,
> y las azules, mortaja.   and blue ones, the shroud.

Thus, white and blue acquire a more tangible meaning, with social or death-like overtones.

A poet creates both when he deals with "given" elements and when he modifies them. These are small acts of creation, to be sure, but they become meaningful in the context of the work. Even in tiny details like these, one can observe the creative mechanism of an artist. The contrast between the lifeless list and its use in the play—the ironic way those meanings are turned into poetry—shows the efficacy of this particular creative act. As I look at the list I feel a certain melancholy. The handwriting is almost surely that of a certain "spinster" who was a close friend of ours, one of the most refined and intelligent women in Granada.*

---

*The author was thinking of Emilia Llanos Medina. Two of Federico's letters to her are found in *Selected Letters*, pp. 11-12. The list is not, however, written in her hand.—*Tr.*

THE HOUSE OF BERNARDA ALBA

The manuscript of this work, the last complete play that my brother wrote, is dated June 19, 1936, two months before his death. In posthumous performances in diverse languages on every continent, *The House of Bernarda Alba* has contributed as much to its author's fame as *Blood Wedding* did during his life. These circumstances, together with the very tonality of the work, and its peculiar dramatic texture, have produced a certain lack of focus in the criticism of all of García Lorca's theater, about which I must now make some general observations. These will help explain the special nature of *The House of Bernarda Alba*.

Bernarda Alba has been judged to be the poet's most mature work, something like a starting point for what his dramatic production might have been had he lived longer. This assumption is both widely held and (unless duly qualified) erroneous. No doubt a process of maturation is visible in the work of all artists. Between Federico's first plays and *Bernarda Alba* there occurred nothing less than the creation of a dramatic style. And yet the chronology of that creation does not reveal a continuous evolution nor a process of continual perfecting in any one direction—no clear line of evolution that would allow us to foresee what his theater might have become. As a poet and as a playwright, what Federico undergoes is a continuous metamorphosis (though this too is a sort of vital process). And therefore, upon careful consideration of his plays, we reach a conclusion diametrically opposed to that of previous critics. That is, the work which might have followed *The House of Bernarda Alba* would not have borne any apparent relation to it. Even when Federico writes two pieces in the same genre, for example the *Tragicomedy of Don Cristóbal* and the *Retablillo*, they go off in different directions—extreme lyricism as opposed to mordant realism—and possess entirely different structures. And even when two works have the same theme, the theme is treated differently and the plays are scarcely related to one another: *The Shoemaker's Wife* and *Perlimplín*. Those who study Federico's theater with the false idea of evolution will have to explain exactly how *Doña Rosita* can be the work that comes immediately before *The House of Bernarda Alba* and how the latter work could conceivably have announced the form of the theater that was to have followed.

The continuous change and unified style of Federico's theater can only be explained by carefully studying his language, the technique of his dialogues, and the way he manipulates time, space, and other basic elements of theater. Leaping to our conclusion, we might say that what characterizes the dramaturgy of García Lorca is the way he adapts technical procedures to artistic intentions that vary with every work. When we consider what Federico created before he wrote *Bernarda Alba*, we can assume later works would have been entirely unrelated to it in their intentions. There is, in fact, some proof for this statement, though until now only I have known of it. After *Bernarda Alba*, Federico wrote the first act of *The Dreams of my Cousin Aurelia*. The very title of this piece is symptomatic of a radical change. This work turns out to be the very antidote to *Bernarda Alba*. One goes from the harsh objectivization of the world of *Bernarda* to an intimate, tender evocation: the leading character is Federico himself as a child, and verse acquires capital importance. This change in direction is similar to the one that occurs in his poetry: he moves from the desolate, negative vision of *Poet in New York*, to the lyricism, so typical of Granada in its tonality, of *Diván del Tamarit*.

And yet, the overvaluation of *Bernarda Alba* in relation to the poet's other works is easy to explain. For one thing, it is a final point of reference. People have always seen in it something like the rectification of a poetical vision of the theater, and a step toward the type of realism that has come to be considered appropriate to "normal" theater, theater *par excellence*, as opposed to "poetic theater." *Bernarda Alba* would be the final triumph of the playwright over the poet. To me this means that neither *Bernarda* nor the rest of García Lorca's theater has been properly understood.

The currents of the modern theater show to what extent the roots of traditional artistic realism have withered, and have been triumphantly supplanted by fantasy or by a neo-realism grounded upon other artistic assumptions. No doubt the theater took longer than other genres to break away from habitual procedures of narrative development, and it broke with them less completely and abruptly. But today, when even the so-called "theater of the absurd" finds easy access to the stage, it is less difficult to understand what Federico meant, more than thirty years ago, when the protagonist of *The Shoemaker's Prodigious Wife* asked for a theater "where people are not afraid to see a tree, for example, change into a ball of smoke, or three fishes (for the love of a hand and a word) turn into three million fishes to calm the hunger of a crowd." He was calling for a theater that could accept the artistic truth of the incredible, whether invented or real, and the struggle between these two elements which goes on inside the human soul. That struggle is the very theme of the work from which I have just quoted; it finds expression there in the form of a light-hearted farce.

Much has changed in the theater since García Lorca wrote (with the apparent freedom of poetry and the rigorous logic of drama) of the vital anguish caused by the passage of time. The simultaneity of temporal planes and the tense poetic language that bring home that idea create a plot in which drama and poetry fuse with rare intensity. I am referring to *When Five Years Have Passed*. The work is inaccessible to "the many," but this hardly justifies the ineptitude of journalistic critics who have entirely overlooked its far-reaching implications and have found its connection with later authors to be a mere coincidence, both amusing and inexplicable. Were we to consider these aspects of García Lorca's art to be inessential, we could never hope to understand the type of realism which appears in *The House of Bernarda Alba*. García Lorca himself contributed to this misunderstanding when he declared, pointedly, at the end of the cast of characters: "The poet states that these three acts have the intention of a photographic documentary." Many have taken the words at their face value, without asking what the poet's "intention" really was. Those words can be interpreted correctly only in the context of Federico's own particular vision of drama. The following words, from the critic Francis Fergusson, are illuminating:

But it would be a mistake to take its realism too straight. The label "photograph," like the label "alleluya" on *Don Perlimplín*, indicates the very self-conscious style, which alludes to a whole context of meaning. *Bernarda Alba* is a period play like the others; it utilizes the conventions of nineteenth-century realism with the same kind of sophisticated intention as that with which *Don Perlimplín* utilizes its more ancient conventions.*

Perhaps we should qualify Fergusson's statement that all of Federico's works are "period plays." Strictly speaking, the only period plays are *Perlimplín, Mariana Pineda,* and *Doña Rosita.* It might help us to understand the author's intentions if we consider how he himself titles his works. *Mariana Pineda* is a "Ballad Divided into Three Engravings"; *Perlimplín* an *"Aleluya"; Yerma* a "Tragic Poem"; *When Five Years Have Passed* a "Legend of Time"; *Doña Rosita* a "Poem of Granada," arbitrarily subdivided into "Various Gardens." The label "photograph," applied to *Bernarda* is thus easier to understand. It is not essentially different from the "engravings" of *Mariana Pineda.* The poet's intention is to stylize in the manner of a photograph.

The photographic lens does indeed produce a sort of stylization: it can capture a fleeting expression and give it permanence, or enhance a non-essential detail. Upon assuming the intention of photography, the author also accepts its limitations, beginning with color: there will be a debate between black and white (color photographs were still unknown). If I am not mistaken, my brother once told me of a plan for a work that would start from the enormous enlargement of a wedding portrait hanging over the mantelpiece in a sordidly furnished room.** In different ways— photograph, engraving, garden, ballad, legend, or poem—García Lorca attempted to dramatize material with a previous artistic existence. What he does is to modulate a literary reality of the second degree. The realism of *Bernarda* is, so to speak, reality in the second degree.

*Francis Fergusson, *"Don Perlimplín,* Lorca's Theatre-Poetry," in *The Human Image in Dramatic Literature* (Garden City: Doubleday and Company, 1957), p. 95.—*Ed.*

**This would have been in 1926. In late February or early March, Lorca wrote to his friend Melchor Fernández Almagro: "There is no doubt at all that I really *feel* the theater. A few days ago it occurred to me to write a play whose characters would be photographic enlargements: the people we see in the doorways of houses, newly-wed couples, sergeants, dead young people [sic!], the anonymous masses with their mustaches and wrinkles. It will be something awful. If I can get it all *in focus,* it will be deeply moving. In the midst of all these people, I will place an authentic fairy." See C. Maurer, ed., F.G.L., *Epistolario,* Vol. I (Madrid: Alianza Editorial, 1983), p. 147.—*Tr.*

I would not hesitate to say that imaginary elements play as important a role here as they do in any of my brother's works. He begins with a village atmosphere, one he remembers from his childhood. This atmosphere has already been subjected to the sort of de-realization where details, whether accidental or meaningful, become more precise or concrete, larger or smaller, as in a vividly remembered dream. Onto this he projects a plot that has been invented in its entirety. Most of the characters' names are real, as are certain minor circumstances and events. All this helps the poet carry out his artistic intentions, even though in the reality to which these details originally belonged they meant something else or were nearly meaningless.

The poet's powers of inventiveness are working with concrete facts, and, creatively, he heightens their reality. He does so with what we might call an "ultra-realistic" sense. None of the created characters is faithful to its distant model, except, as I said, when it comes to details. The characters who do not form part of the family, both those who appear onstage (Prudencia, Poncia) and those who are simply mentioned, are taken from reality, as are the references we might call "environmental." There are so many such references that one is tempted to admit that *Bernarda* has a genuine realism. Of course, the poet exercised his artistic criteria merely by *selecting* a certain type of occurrences, for example, his mention of Prudencia's husband, who was so resentful of the village that he never used the door of his house and jumped over the fence of the corral to get to the fields. This was a real fact. The character and mutual relationships of Bernarda's daughters do not follow reality; they merely respond to the demands of the plot the author has invented. The character of Adela, the mainspring of the tragedy, is entirely a creation of the poet, except for the name. As I said earlier, all of the names are real except for that of the leading character. The name Bernarda *sounds* like the character Federico portrays. An energetic village matron whose authority is confined to her own family circle, she will become the gigantic protagonist of the *House*. Her possible madness, her erotic deviance are reflected in her Mother, María Josefa, who does not come from a rural milieu. This María Josefa, for that was her real name, was the grandmother of some friends of ours, extremely distant relatives. We used to visit them when we were children. The old woman's erotic madness flowered in her speech: incongruent, continuous, very rapid, full of reiterations, and enunciated in a small and beautiful voice. I remember vividly her extremely delicate head and her hair, half white and half blonde. Federico has captured and poeticized her "automatic" conversation, and we can suppose that she really uttered some of the things she says in the play. The snatches of poetry that come from the mouth of this character, and which might easily be attributed to the surrealistic technique of the stream of semiconscious or unconscious associations, are really Federico's attempt to reproduce the incongruent automatism of the speech of that poetic and real being. The poet's master stroke was not simply to remember all this, but also to inject it into the atmosphere of the play. He managed to convert María Josefa into a "pole" of poetry and madness for all the other characters. To be more specific, María Josefa becomes, through repression and contrast, the unleashed image of her daughter, Bernarda herself. The dramatic function of this poetic symbolism, which causes the character of the mad old woman to become larger and larger, has not always been properly understood.

We have seen that Federico's theater possesses extraordinary diversity, and this diversity might be defined as a successful adaptation of the means to the special artistic end that the author had in mind in each of his plays. The technique of the dialogue could not have been the same in *Bernarda Alba*, an ultra-realistic work, as in the farces with lyrical and musical intonations.

And yet, within this diversity there is a personal vision of the theater, one which gives surprising unity to Federico's entire dramatical output. *Bernarda Alba* is as unmistakably *his* as *Perlimplín* or *The Shoemaker's Wife* or, in the last analysis, any of his brief dramatic *Dialogues*.

A study of the way Federico treats dramatic space in his theater shows that there is an important relationship between that which happens invisibly offstage, and that which happens before the eyes of the audience. It is true that this relationship forms part of the theater as a genre, but Federico was keenly aware of its dramatic possibilities. He also saw it as a limit of the genre itself. The only way to transcend that limit is to recreate it on its own terms. This is the solution of all creative artists: to use artistic forms as the raw material of art. The value and theatrical function of visible dramatic space depend on the way the artist sees the relationship between "inside" and "outside." There are modes of theater in which the visible space *receives* all the action, or all the essential action, and thus space conditions the action and, in a way, determines it. There are dramatic actions which *create* or (what is the same thing) *seem* to create their own dramatic space. The essentiality of the action (not of the place of action) determines the accidentality of the place. Naturally, things must occur some place, and that place must be the one which the spectator sees: if not there would be no theater. But what I mean by "accidentality" is that in the work of Federico the visual space is so closely bound to the virtual one, the unseen one, that neither can exist without the other. It is as though the stage lay open not only towards the spectator but towards the world beyond the stage, the world surrounding it. This, I repeat, is true in all theater, but it is not always deliberately turned to good dramatic use. In *Blood Wedding*, for example, Federico sets up a certain action in the clearing of the forest. Potentially, what the spectator sees could occur any place else in the forest. And in fact one of the figures which appears, the light of the Moon, is also virtually present throughout the entire invisible space. Both the place of the action and the Moon, who appears before the spectator, are necessarily "accidental" in nature. This is due to the very nature of the space (forest) and the nature of the character (light). And thus, strictly speaking, this technique cannot be said to have had many antecedents (one of them would be Greek theater), for it derives, above all, from a special vision of dramatic space. The forest in *Blood Wedding* is a place of passage. What is being dramatized is a search, preliminary to the tragic moment.

Often the space created by Federico is a place of passage: the character comes from a place which is dramatically alive, and is on his way to another place which is invisible but is also made dramatic by the action. In *Doña Rosita*, for example, the curtain rises at the very moment when the Uncle of the protagonist is coming through the door. What he will do is to carry on, before the eyes of the audience, an action (a very small one) which he has begun previously some place else in the house. This linkage of spaces by means of action is typical of García Lorca's theater. In the same work, a little while later, Rosita *enters* the stage searching for a hat which she has already looked for some place else; and this search makes another important character, her Aunt, *leave* the stage with the same purpose. Rosita comes onstage and crosses it hurriedly on her way to another space, which is situated outside of the house itself and has already been dramatized by the dialogue. The stage does not receive the action passively; rather, within the limits imposed by the genre, it becomes a focus which irradiates space.

The Shoemaker's Prodigious Wife begins with a prologue in which the author speaks with his character before she comes onstage. The Author says to the Wife: "Let's begin; you are coming from the street," and he places her at the door. But when the character begins to speak she is not facing the public. Her shoulders are turned to the audience, and she is carrying on a dialogue with another invisible audience, situated in a region beyond the stage, a region which will come to life as the play goes on. The visible or invisible presence of that region will influence the very plot. And this invisible presence reflects, in turn, another typical feature of García Lorca's theater: the importance of the collective or social element—a determining factor not only in *The Shoemaker's Wife* but also in *Blood Wedding*, *Yerma*, and *The House of Bernarda Alba*.

When we spoke of the beginning of *Doña Rosita* and of *The Shoemaker's Wife*, we happened to mention the door. The door is clearly the limit that separates or, better, unites the two dramatic spaces to which I have been referring, and it is not surprising that it assumes extraordinary importance in the theater of García Lorca. This is no place for a detailed analysis of the theme, which would perhaps be the single most revealing way to study the poet's theatrical technique. If that study could be separated (and it cannot) from the overall study of his vision of dramatic space, we might title it "The Function of the Door in the Theater of García Lorca."

I say that it is not separable because the theme of the door is merely one aspect of the whole visible zone embodied in the stage settings. The inside/outside relationship is expressed, in all Lorca's theater, by the dialogue itself. This is quite logical; what is, in fact, special about the poet is the importance he assigns to this type of dramatic dialogue. It is through dialogue that he gives special vividness to the "outside" elements—the atmosphere, the weather, the season, the temperature, the light, the exact time.

The poet uses many different procedures (besides plot and dialogue) to create, or enhance, the relationship between one space and another: the butterfly that comes onto the stage, the whistle, the melody of a flute, the wind which suddenly opens a door, the kick of a horse on the outside wall, songs, shouting, odors, bells, etc. One might say that at times in García Lorca the stage is the zone that lies between the space occupied by the audience and the regions beyond the stage. And I believe that Federico himself was perfectly conscious of this interplay.

I said before that almost all, perhaps *all*, of Federico's works vividly exemplify this feature of his theater, and that in this play it simply comes to the foreground. In *The House of Bernarda Alba* the inside/outside relationship turns into the very material being dramatized. It is this, perhaps, that stamps the work as Federico's own. Here the author has chosen a totally *closed* stage, which seems to contradict his preference for open, communicating ones, like the house in *The Shoemaker's Prodigious Wife*, which turns into a tavern, a theater, and even a public square. At bottom the same interplay is occurring. And thus, the general observations which I have been making about García Lorca's theater hold true for his third and last tragedy.

THEATRICAL SPACE

The vigorous dramatism of the central character, Bernarda, makes it easy to overlook the author's intentions in the title: *The House of Bernarda Alba*. The "subject" is house, and the word (*casa*) is underscored by the assonance of the words Bern<u>a</u>rd<u>a</u> and <u>A</u>lb<u>a</u>, where the letter "a" predominates.

I am going to deal first with mere physical space. In keeping with the poet's custom in other plays, both the dialogue and the plot help to construct the house. The characters allude to it as a totality on several occasions, and help to objectify its physical reality. More than once Bernarda says "my house," and she says "this house" six times in the course of the play. As the tragedy develops there is also repeated mention of the parts of the house: living room, bedrooms, patio, corral, upstairs rooms, generic reference to "the rooms," walls, outside walls, partitions, roofs, floors, closets, and cupboards. One can tell from the plot, and because it is explicitly stated, that the house is on a corner, with one side on the street and the other on an alley. The door of the corral seems to open onto the fields. There are so many references to the house that it becomes a sort of silent character.

And naturally the liminal spaces (I mean the windows and doors) assume major importance, as they do in the rest of the plays. The singing of the reapers in the second act seems to symbolize the participation of those architectural elements:

Abrir puertas y ventanas,	Open the doors and windows,
las que vivís en el pueblo.	you who live in the village.
El segador pide rosas	The reaper asks for roses
para adornar su sombrero.	to adorn his hat.

For the sake of brevity, I invite the reader himself to examine the tragedy: any attentive reader will see that the window is an extraordinarily important element. But perhaps it would also be helpful to mention, at least in passing, the role of the door. First, the arched doorway at the entrance to the house, through which Bernarda enters, with innumerable women ("two hundred," the author writes; we may suppose that the figure was not intended to be *realistic*). Also, the back door, outside the visible zone, through which the men go out to the patio. The front door will not open again, except outside the play, when the story is over, when it is time to mourn the dead daughter. So that the door becomes a symbol of death. I remember an early poem of Federico, part of which has been lost, alluding to this symbolic relationship:

Una puerta	A door
no es puerta	is not a door
hasta que un muerto	until a dead man
sale por ella.	goes out through it.
Rosa de dos pétalos	Rose with two petals
que el aire abre y cierra.	that the air opens and closes.

And I remember another door, banging dramatically in the wind and revealing a deathly emptiness—the one which puts an end to *Doña Rosita*, after the most perfect "exit" in my brother's theater.

But to return to *The House of Bernarda Alba*, I hardly need insist on how the dialogue underscores the definitive importance of the door used by the village women. Remember how the sisters listen from behind the doors of their respective rooms in the second act. Remember also the end of that act, where Bernarda defends, as though it were a military redoubt, the door through which her daughters want to leave the house. Perhaps the most dramatically effective scene in the third act is the struggle between Martirio and Adela in front of the door that opens onto the corral. And, finally, there is the door which they have to break down to reach the body of Adela, the character who has paid for rebellion with her life.

The entire play moves inwards, towards the inside of the house. The first act occurs in the room just inside the door; the second in an inner room which opens onto the bedrooms; the third, in the patio. The visible action ends at the door of the patio, which opens onto the corral. That door marks a limit, and the scene I have just mentioned occurs directly in front of it. Beyond it is the natural world, the stallion that looms larger and larger in the night, the unrestrained howling of the dogs, the stars that shine like fists. An inciting world of instincts which has been made more and more dramatic in the course of the play. Pepe el Romano belongs to that ambit, and into it he flees, out the last door of the house, towards life. He does so in perfect counterpoint to Adela, as she enters her room, in a flight towards death. Both movements occur outside the visible zone.

Within the closed space of the *House* there is an even narrower prison, that of the old woman, María Josefa, who escapes out of her room *towards* the house itself. This movement intensifies the symbolic value of the character. She resembles the seed in the fruit. It is hardly necessary to add that the theme of the door takes on an obsessive quality in the incongruent speech of the old woman, who escapes into the lyrical sublimation of primal instincts:

Neither you nor I want to sleep.
The door will open by itself
and on the beach
we will snuggle in our coral hut.

Bernarda,
leopard-face.
Magdalena,
hyena-face.
Little lamb!
Bah, bah . . .
Let us go to the boughs of the manger in Bethlehem.

Ni tú ni yo queremos dormir;
la puerta sola se abrirá
y en la playa nos meteremos
en una choza de coral.

Bernarda,
cara de leoparda.
Magdalena,
cara de hiena.
¡Ovejita!

Meee, meee.
Vamos a los ramos del portal de Belén.

Despite such physical and psychological imprisonment, the whole play is riddled with echoes, murmurs, and sounds from the outside world: the singing of the reapers, the lynching, the wild howling of the dogs, Bernarda's dialogue with the stable hands (invisible masculine characters, like the men involved in the mourning in Act I), the whistle of Pepe el Romano (his only presence on stage), the stallion kicking the outside wall. Many things come through the walls: sensations of light, temperature, the state of mind of the village (sometimes calm and sometimes violent), looks, gossip. But all this only reinforces the solidity of the house, so carefully constructed by its creator. I believe that very rarely in the theater has anyone constructed a spatial atmosphere with such skill and such awareness of its dramatic function. For convenience and economy, this work is usually performed with only one stage setting. This is a mistake.

The movement towards the inside of the house is accompanied by changes in the weather, the light, and the colors (within the dominant white/black tonality dictated by the work's "photographic" intention). In Act I, the room is "extremely white," while Act II occurs in a "white room" and Act III within "white, slightly bluish walls." Against this background we see the black dresses of the characters, and the least dash of color acquires unusual expressive violence; for example, the red fan, after the mourning of Act I, or the green dress in Act II. Color and light gradually decrease as the action moves inwards, towards its ultimate location. In the darkness of the third act, the women are wearing white petticoats. Color and clothing symbolize the erotic note now nearing its tragic denouement.

These sensations of light and contrast are part of the treatment of dramatic time. Time as slowness, as simultaneity, as imminence, as rapidity, is portioned out in a masterly way, with an almost musical rhythm. Sometimes a tiny detail acquires major importance and meaning. Here is the way the play begins, for example. After describing the setting, the author notes: "When the curtain rises, the stage is empty. The pealing of bells is heard. The Maid comes onstage."

MAID: By now the sound of those bells is hitting me right between the eyes.

The materialization of the sound—"right between the eyes"—so typical of Federico's dramatic language, creates a physical link between the character and the church tower. What is interesting to note is how the dramatic action begins with the very entrance of the Maid. We may suppose she speaks the first word on coming through the door. And that first word is *ya* ("by now"), which alludes to an external action, the ringing of the bells. It might seem like a minor, isolated detail, but in fact the simultaneity of the action, and the immediate link with external space are typical of the author's theater. The proof of this significance follows immediately. Hardly has the Maid spoken that sentence, the work continues:

> PONCIA (enters eating *chorizo* and bread): They have been at their chanting for more than two hours now. Priests have come from all the villages. The church looks beautiful. Magdalena fainted when they began the first prayer for the dead.

Poncia is coming from the external space she is describing, and she is doing the same thing the Maid did at the door when the action began. For a moment, both actions and both spaces are prolonged, joined by the sound of the bells. Notice Poncia's repetition of the temporal adverb, "now" (*ya*). "They have been at that chanting for more than two hours *now*." The sound of the bells is not simply what is known in theater language as "special effects" or "sound effects": it has a dramatic function. If I had more time I would discuss in greater detail the role of these bells, which mark the time of the play, from the moment they are first heard, pealing for the dead man, Bernarda's husband, until, outside the play, they ring for the death of Adela. Bernarda will command her daughters, "Arrange for a double death knell at dawn."

One problem entailed by dramatic time in the theater is that the continuous flow of the action can only be shown in a fragmentary and discontinuous fashion. The treatment of time and of dramatic space helps to define the style of a playwright. In discussing Federico's theater, I have already referred to time, rhythm, musical development, and we have even mentioned time as a dramatic theme in itself. When I spoke about the beginning of *The House of Bernarda Alba*, I pointed out how the entry of the first character is tied to an external action that is already taking place. Here, as elsewhere in the tragedy, this is probably a way of creating a feeling of temporal and spatial continuity. That continuity is expressed by the word *ya*, the first one in the work. Examining this technique, I went to the beginning of Act II, and I find that it begins like this:

ANGUSTIAS: I have already [*ya*] cut the cloth for the third sheet.

Act III begins like this:

PRUDENCIA: I must go now [*ya*]. I have already paid you a nice long visit.

Both at the beginning of the play and between one act and another, an action has previously taken place. This re-establishes the vital continuity of the plot, which, as we said, often transcends the limits of the visible stage.

I do not know exactly how this interplay of time and space is absorbed by the spectator. Nor am I sure that such tiny details were the result of a conscious effort. I think not. I believe that they simply arise from a certain idea of dramatic time and space. If that interplay is expressed in similar, sometimes identical formulae, it is because it grows out of a personal vision with an astounding unity of style. If I had told my brother that all three acts of *Bernarda* begin with the word *ya*, he probably would have been extremely surprised. And yet, let us remember the entrance of Rosita, which we discussed in connection with the "spatial linkage" in that comedy. Her first words, when she bursts onto the stage, and the play has hardly begun, are:

ROSITA (*entering rapidly*): And my hat? Where is my hat? They have already [*ya*] rung the bells thirty times in San Luis.

This is the same sort of dramatic interplay that I have pointed out in *Bernarda Alba*.

The action in *Yerma* begins like this:

YERMA: Juan? Do you hear me, Juan?
JUAN: I'm coming.
YERMA: It's already [*ya*] time.
JUAN: Did the oxen go by?
YERMA: They already [*ya*] did.

Here again, we have a dialogue that begins when one of the interlocutors is still absent. An action, a very minimal one, is surrounded by previous temporal circumstances.

Mariana Pineda begins with a prologue which purports to create a poetic, legendary time for the drama. The existence of a prologue linking the world of the spectator to the fiction being represented is another typical device of Federico's theater. The prologue can be an almost imperceptible part of the action, and it usually prepares the audience for the entrance of the leading character and for the genuine start of the action. This is what happens in *Mariana Pineda*, *Doña Rosita*, and even *The House of Bernarda Alba*, where the entrance of the character is strongly dramatized. When the prologue of *Mariana Pineda* comes to an end (and bear in mind that this work was written nine years before *Yerma*), we hear the following fleeting dialogue:

> WOMAN: Girl! Don't you hear me?
>
> GIRL (*from far away*): I'm coming right away [*ya*].

We need not go into greater detail about the interplay of time and space. Let us simply say that the expression "Don't you hear me?" implies that this is not the first time that the woman has called the girl.

When I spoke of *The Billy-Club Puppets* (written before *Mariana Pineda*, the work in which I said Federico had already created his dramatic language), I analyzed the beginning of the piece, revealing the subtle interplay of time and space. That whole discussion would be relevant here. All I want to do now is to call attention to one word in the first paragraph of the play:

> ROSITA: I have *already* [*ya*] pricked myself four times on the final "r" in "To My Beloved Father."

I have no doubt that the reiteration and placement of that modest temporal adverb (*ya*) is of deep significance. What becomes very clear, now that we have gone into the matter in detail, is the unity of technique and of style which characterizes Federico's work, both dramatic and poetic. This despite the fact that no poet of his day produced an *oeuvre* that was more diverse and varied. It is certain that the technique I am examining is used to great perfection in *Bernarda Alba*, but I am not trying to explain it or judge it as a stylistic feature. In fact, it can only be appreciated in conjunction with other habits equally typical of Federico. Besides, this preoccupation with dramatic time and its personal expression is present as early as Federico's first play, *The Butterfly's Evil Spell*. After the prologue we hear these words:

> LADY COCKROACH (coming to the pasture):
> A clear, calm morning!
> Already [*ya*] the dawn is breaking.

Perhaps in a first play by another author those first words would not have been significant. But they are in the case of Federico. Placing the action at a specific time, and showing it in a light that begins at exactly the same moment as the dramatic action itself, are features that become an essential part of his theater. The dialogue that immediately follows links up with a tiny previous action and with a space that is invisible to the spectator. It is interesting that the poet says, in the stage directions immediately preceding the start of the action, "Lady Cockroach comes out of her house." He then adds, in the first words of the dialogue, "[she comes] to the meadow." Notice that the character's first words are spoken at the door of the cave, so that when the curtain rises the stage is still empty and the second character does not speak until reaching the visible space. The interplay is the same that occurs in *Bernarda Alba*. Who would have thought this possible?

One of the different ways in which time is represented in Federico's theater is to bring it on stage in person. It is as though the time of day were one of the characters. Sometimes, in fact, it is. In the *Tragicomedy of Don Cristóbal* we saw how the Hour pops out of the clock on the wall; it rings a bell and says, "Ding-dong! One o'clock!" The temporal circumstances, the exact moment when the action comes to perfection is usually carefully indicated. I have already commented on García Lorca's feeling for time. Readers of *Bernarda Alba* will remember how the plot revolves around the time of day, indicated with great precision in the dialogue. At the end of the first act, we hear the following dialogue:

ANGUSTIAS: What time is it?
MAGDALENA: Probably twelve o'clock by now [*ya*].
ANGUSTIAS: So late?
AMELIA: Just about.

That is, the bells are about to ring. In the second act, there is another important exchange, preceded by the stage direction: "Little bells are heard in the distance, as though coming through several walls."

MAGDALENA: It's the men who are going back to work.

PONCIA: A minute ago it rang three o'clock.

MARTIRIO: What sun!

These words are spoken at exactly 3:01. From the coolness of the house, the poet evokes the blinding sun outside. He is also alluding to a rural custom. In summer in Andalusia they ring the church bell at noon and work is suspended. At three o'clock another bell signals that it is time to go back to work. The distant little bells show that the work animals are going by. From noon to three, it is time for the siesta, in the drowsy silence of Andalusian villages. The time which separates the first act from the second is totally inert. And perhaps this too has its significance.

At the beginning of Act III, Prudencia is visiting Bernarda's house and we hear the following dialogue:

PRUDENCIA: I am going now. I have paid you a nice long visit.

BERNARDA: But wait. We hardly ever see each other.

PRUDENCIA: Have they sounded the last call to rosary?

PONCIA: Not yet. (*Prudencia sits down.*)

At the end of the visit, the author writes: "Bells are heard in the distance" (remember that we are inside the house), and Prudencia says, "The last call."

As we said earlier, the bells give rhythm to the development of the action. They are perceived more and more faintly—like the hour, the colors, the light—as the play moves inward, and violently bursts in the middle of the night. This is not peculiar to *The House of Bernarda Alba*. With the exception of *Mariana Pineda*, which ends with a "marvelous, delirious" sunset, night coincides with death, from *The Butterfly's Evil Spell* to the present work. The poet himself, who appears as a character in the *Retablillo*, will say, with a shade of irony, "I am a poet of the night." Of the night? He was also a poet of light, who could see that mortal wounds burn "like suns." "Ask for lights and for bells," he exhorts one of his characters, who has been condemned to death. Contrasting light and shadow are the two sides of a "living coin that will never / be minted again."*

Perhaps it is the struggle between instinct and society, and between liberation and repression which, as we were saying earlier, makes *Bernarda Alba* so characteristic of García Lorca. The hardness of Bernarda—she is flint to her daughters—reveals Federico's tenderness and understanding for those frustrated in love. On a different emotional scale, and with a different treatment, this theme appears in the rest of his plays as well.

The ultra-realistic focus also determines the way in which Federico will treat the role of the maid. The importance of this character, who has been a vital part of theater since the Roman comedy and who was revived by the comedy of Lope, is treated by Federico in his own peculiar way. Federico may have been following a long literary tradition, but the maid, more than other characters, will express a world of personal experiences, based on a specifically Spanish social reality. The maid acquires more and more importance, and in *Doña Rosita*, the play immediately preceding this one, she plays a major role. In *Doña Rosita* the maid forms part of a very human relationship, where loyalty borders on the pathetic without ever going outside the bounds of reality. I would not hesitate to say that the Housekeeper of *Doña Rosita* was Federico's ideal, most typical maid, the one closest to reality, and one of the best conceived maids in his theater.

In *Bernarda Alba*, Poncia will develop parallel to Bernarda, until she begins to function as a sort of antagonist. The master/servant relationship has been intensified, but the warm affection of the previous work has disappeared, and has been replaced by personal and social (class) antagonisms. This relationship, which is far richer than that which exists between Bernarda and her own daughters, becomes an essential part of the drama and is one of its most successful aspects. Poncia from *Bernarda Alba* and the Housekeeper from *Doña Rosita* are two diametrically opposed types of maids. They show the author's capacity to create opposite types from the same reality. I have known both of the maids: I knew Poncia, for that was her real name, only distantly. The maid in *Doña Rosita* worked in our house. She was Dolores. May God bless her!

*The author is quoting from two of the *Gypsy Ballads*. See "The Death of Antoñito el Camborio" and "Ballad of One Doomed to Die" in *Selected Poems*, pp. 76-84.—*Tr*.

THE STRUCTURE OF THE TRAGEDY

The slow, realistic pace of *The House of Bernarda Alba* differs from the kind of fluent action that Federico preferred in his theater. It would be difficult to say just what temporally "fluent action" is, when the theater, almost by definition, is fragmentary in character, except for the rare cases in which the represented action takes exactly the same time that it would take in reality. This does not usually happen without violence, except in the minor actions proper to short plays and skits. Action on a larger scale must ignore the so-called unity of time. In a closed theater, the solution would be to adopt the structure of one continuous act, but this is almost impossible. In an open theater the solution would be the infinite fragmentation of time (this too is impossible) and the adaptation of space to the essential movements of the action. Infinite fragmentation and complete temporal unity (insofar as either is possible) are the extremes of two theatrical visions, and neither one has ever been realized.

Immersed, in this as in other things, in the traditional Spanish theater, García Lorca tends to fragment his works into scenes, even though most of them are written in three acts. The best examples of fragmentation would be the *Tragicomedy of Don Cristóbal, Blood Wedding*, and *Yerma*, where there are six, seven, and six changes of set, respectively. *The Shoemaker's Prodigious Wife*, on the other hand, takes its cue from minor theater, from the *sainete* or interlude, and it constitutes an exception: it is the only work with a single stage set. Here again we can see how Federico adapts his techniques to suit the purpose and genre of each work. What actually happens in that play is that the set evolves from a closed place into a public one: the action comes to a close when the Wife closes her door, and it ends inside the house, with a visible space riddled, like the one in *Bernarda*, by shouts, songs, and bells. In contrast, *Don Perlimplín*, a much shorter work, has four changes in the set. *The House of Bernarda Alba* follows the traditional scheme of three well-delineated acts. Besides the parallel circumstances I have already mentioned—the identical beginnings, the indication of the time of day—notice that each act has three parts. Each act begins with something like an introit. The one in the first act is very obvious, for the author sketches out a sort of prologue to prepare for the sensational entrance of Bernarda. The act ends when all of Bernarda's daughters, with the help of the maid, drag María Josefa into the seclusion of her room. The shouts and imprecations of the old woman heighten the violence of this scene.

The second act begins with a domestic scene: the daughters are gathered around Poncia sewing the sheets for Angustias' bridal trousseau. It is a moment of repose, the most conspicuous moment of *détente* in the play. For once there is even a hint of merriment. The author opens up certain planes of human coexistence that the plot will immediately pull shut. The repose is made even more *noticeable* by the violent ending of the preceding act. This act ends with the exterior scene of the lynching. Only the crowd noises make it present onstage.

Act III begins with another restful scene, the visit. This kind of lull in the action is a procedure Federico often used in his theater. Among other things, he was trying to bring onstage characters who were not essential parts of the main plot. It would tell us much about Federico's personal vision of the theater if we were to study how he justifies the presence of his characters.

The action will start again from this new *détente* and progress towards the final suicide. As minor units, the acts decrease the amount of dramatic tension and slow down the intensificatory process that functions throughout the play. In the mathematical center of the tragedy—the middle of the second act—is the invisible scene of the reapers, the only time song is used. It is a fleeting moment of lyrical distension, typical of Federico's theater.

In other, more fluent theatrical schemes, the author allows the audience to *see* the action as it unfolds, and perhaps this is the best way to produce a sensation of discursiveness. But in *Bernarda Alba*, the action which causes the tragedy is not shown to the public, it is hidden. I am referring to the secret erotic relationship between the male character, Pepe el Romano, and Adela, the youngest of the daughters. Perhaps this contributes to the sensation of restraint, or sustained tension. The dramatic event—which is exposed in a calculated way at the end of the third act, triggering the tragic denouement—has been consummated as early as the second act. In reality, it happens in the time which elapses between the first and second acts, a time which is not represented. There is, then, a hidden action and a visible one, and the work derives its psychological tension from the relationship between them. There are characters who operate from the hidden action, the one that is invisible to the audience, and others who work from the visible action, among them Bernarda herself, blinded by her desire to dominate others.

The element of hidden action that passes into the represented action in the form of suspicion, caution, antagonism, and innuendo is carefully administered, so that Bernarda's confidence in her own vigilance (which continues until the final outburst) will be plausible to the audience.

This type of underlying action, which revolves around an invisible character, is typical of Lorca's technique, even though *Bernarda Alba* occupies a very special place within his theater. With certain very noticeable variants (the ones demanded by a different genre), we find it also in *Perlimplín*, where the "young man in the red cape" triggers two parallel actions: the love which Belisa feels for him (and this is represented) and the hidden intentions of Perlimplín. If we wanted to adduce other examples of this double action, we might mention *The Shoemaker's Prodigious Wife*, where it takes on the character of farce. The Wife reveals to the audience her own intimate feelings in the presence of an adventitious character who turns out to be her husband. The twofold action is underscored, in dramatic counterpoint, by the fact that she sees her own drama represented in the ballad of the Shoemaker.

It might be argued that in the case of *The Shoemaker's Wife*, the author is simply utilizing a well-known prop: the disguise. And this is true. But this technique, which is traditionally a merely accidental one (as it is in the case of Perlimplín) is the very raw material of the action in *The Shoemaker's Wife*. In a less conscious way (or so it seems) but a more functional one (if that is possible), the exterior action of the *Tragicomedy of Don Cristóbal* revolves around the concealed truth that the protagonist is not what he seems: the secret of his conduct lies in the fact that he is a puppet, a fact which is not revealed until the end of the piece, where it sets up the denouement.

Bernarda reigns proudly over a world of external, social appearances, which do not conquer but merely hide another world of collective instincts. Pepe Romano is a myth. Blind, vital force is resolved in death and in emptiness, and this is the very nub of the tragedy. That death and that emptiness were first revealed at the very beginning of the play, when the bells peal and the curtain rises on an empty stage.

My analysis has brought out the impressive technical rigor of the development of *The House of Bernarda Alba*, and its own particular quality within the poet's theater. It has also revealed, in passing, certain features that unify Federico's style and reflect his will or his instinct (perhaps both: conscious effort and dramatic temperament) as he sought to re-elaborate, on his own terms, the basic elements of the theater as a genre.

In *Bernarda Alba*, as in the rest of Federico's work, the concepts of space, time, action, and dramatic language are tightly woven into an artistic object. And yet the dramatic structure into which they combine can indeed be analyzed by the critic. The author himself provides us with many unifying threads. I believe that the only way to study a creative work comprehensively is to see how the artist uses the basic assumptions of a given art form, and how those assumptions are modified by such use. In the preceding pages, we have observed some of García Lorca's particular habits, and have opened some paths towards the study of his theater. We have seen that the poet does not follow any one formula, repeated with minor variations in all his works (as is the case of Lope de Vega and other playwrights whose unity of style is a mere result of the repetition of one basic formula). Instead, Federico takes pleasure in varying that scheme and in varying the tone of his expression—tragedy, comedy, farce. Such diversity emerges from a personal vision of the basic assumptions of theater. Had we not revealed analytically, although superficially, the inner bonds uniting his different works, it would have been unthinkable to discover in his first plays the same features that appear in his mature ones. It would have seemed totally senseless to compare *The Butterfly's Evil Spell* and *Bernarda Alba*. Well, it is not. If these comparisons reveal anything, and without a doubt they do, it is probably the extraordinary depth of his dramatic production and of his creativity. Perhaps it is not too early to consider García Lorca a classic of the contemporary theater.

INDEX